The Philosophy of Value

The Philosophy of Value

by
DEWITT H. PARKER

with a Preface by
WILLIAM K. FRANKENA

Ann Arbor
The University of Michigan Press

Printed in the United States of America
by The Lord Baltimore Press, Inc.

PREFACE

When Dewitt Henry Parker died in 1949 he left behind a manuscript on the philosophy of value. It was not complete, and even the chapters which were written had not all been put into final form. It seemed to me, however, that it constituted a sufficiently rounded work to make a book and that it was important enough to deserve publication. It appears here with some editing on my part, but, with the exceptions noted below, essentially in the shape in which it was found.

Parker here expounds his last thinking on the subject of value and morality. He is not simply restating the content of his earlier work, *Human Values*. That book was mainly concerned with a study of the central values of life, such as health, knowledge, and love, and relatively little with more theoretical questions about the nature of value and of value-judgments. In this book, the discussion of human values in the earlier work is summarized in a few pages, and theoretical questions are dealt with at length, although with many concrete illustrations and in terms which any educated reader can understand. Moreover, Parker's point of view is somewhat different in this book. He still identifies value (intrinsic) with the satisfaction of desire, but

v

he adds that it is expressed in volitional statements. In other words, he contends here that value-judgments are not assertions which are cognitive and capable of truth or falsity, but ways of expressing the wishes, satisfactions, or attitudes of the speaker and of arousing similar wishes, satisfactions, or attitudes in the hearer. In this respect, he espouses a position which is now at once very popular and widely discussed.

This gives the present work a contemporary relevance which the earlier no longer has. At the same time, as in that work, we have here a perceptive, sensitive, and warm discussion of value and its expression which will seem like a rich garden to many who find the fields of recent analytical philosophy somewhat sere. This quality will give Parker's last book a unique place in the literature of value-theory today.

The philosophy of value expressed here is more or less complete as far as it goes, but Parker meant to supply it with a metaphysical context which seemed to him essential. Already in *Human Values* he announced his intention to write a metaphysics of value. This, as far as I know, he never did, although some of what he would have included may be found in his *Experience and Substance*. In the present work, however, he intended to put his revised theory of value in a larger context, by providing opening and concluding chapters of a metaphysical character, and by making reference to these in the other chapters. But the concluding chapter was never written, and the introductory one could hardly be kept without making the book seem obviously truncated; it has, therefore, been omitted, and the passing references to the metaphysical setting of value have for the most part been taken out also. The result is not a shortcoming which other recent books on ethics and value lack, but it would be a defect in the eyes of the author.

WILLIAM K. FRANKENA

CONTENTS

The Philosophy of Value

CHAPTER I

THE DEFINITION OF VALUE

To ANYONE thinking about experience in a casual way, it would seem that value, or the good, must, of all things, be easily discerned and its nature easily formulated. What else should push itself so assertively into clearness as the objective of desire, planning, and effort and the reward of all our struggles? That it should be puzzling in any given case to determine which of two alternatives is better and, more perplexing still, to determine the highest good for oneself or for all men (the *summum bonum*) would be expected, but that this or that is good seems obvious. Who is in doubt as to the goodness of food, of song, of love? If no one, should not the nature of the goodness of such things be obvious? Yet the history of man's thought about value shows that its nature is not obvious, but hidden as by a veil.

However strange it may be, we can find reasons why this is so. One reason is the endless variety of values, as numerous as the tonal colors of orchestral music: sensuous, ambition-satisfying, aesthetic, moral, recreational, dream-fulfilling, religious—and in each of these kinds countless instances—a richness overwhelming

3

to thought seeking some common essence. In surveying this variety, we may become skeptical as to whether there is any common denominator of all values—anything in common, say, to the enjoyable pungent taste of a lemon and to the heroism of a soldier defending with his life some point which he knows he cannot hold. Perhaps the quest for the common nature of all values is as vain as the effort to find a common nature, not to all colors or to all sounds, but to all colors and sounds. And—again from a superficial point of view—one's skepticism of a common denominator might readily be confirmed by a survey of primitive cultures, which would reveal what weird things and weird practices have been felt to be valuable. Might it not be that the terms "value" and "the good" have no fixed meaning, but are ambiguous, applied now to one kind and now to another, so that the essence of the good which philosophers so pathetically seek is merely nominal and unreal?—no more real than the essence corresponding to the term "essence" itself, which may mean now an extract, like the perfume of roses, now an Aristotelian form, and now again the important common qualities of a class of things? Is there any common meaning to "good" when we speak of a good road, a good woman, a good God?

Another reason, closely allied to the last, why it appears difficult to define value is its well-known relativity, expressed in the trite saying, "One man's meat is another man's poison." Because of this relativity, there appears in the world not a mere difference, not a mere multiplicity of values, but an opposition. The good of one man is not merely different from that of another, but it is evil to him, therefore not good at all. If it were only *another* value, there might still be something in common, some point of resemblance or overlapping, between the good of one and the good of the other, but how can there be a common nature between a particular man's good and what, from his point of view, is no good? The question is a strong statement of this type of objection—we shall see how cogent it is presently.

Even when universal validity is admitted with reference to certain standards—for example, the moral—if any relativity at all is granted, on no matter how trivial a plane, the difficulty persists. Although you and I may agree about the morally excellent, if the perfume of the lily is delightful to me but is sweetish and sickening to you, a challenge is posed to any generic definition of the good.

A last obstacle confronting any fresh attempt at a philosophy of value is the multiplicity, not of facts, but of theories already existing. Many, yes, most, of these seem to me ill-considered, confused, treacherous, and superficial. If one could simply ignore them, certainly one could save time. But a scholar has his conscience, forbidding him to ignore anything that makes sufficient noise or exerts enough influence to force itself upon his attention. It requires stamina to continue to be able to think and to speak one's own language in the midst of this babel of voices, for it is extremely easy to adopt some flattering manner of thought and speech about theories alien to one's own. If, however, the scholar does maintain his intellectual self-possession and integrity, and if he listens intently, the confusion of tongues takes on a certain pattern; a few dominant families of languages begin to be discernible, in which a few types of thought come to expression, each seen to be based upon some real, if narrowly isolated or carelessly analyzed value fact; so that he can, if he will, learn something from each.

In the face of all these difficulties, the best procedure, I believe, is to offer a basic theory which, it is hoped, will circumvent them and which will embody what is judged to be true in the views of the past, constructing it with a prayer that it be not just another voice added to the existing babel. Such a theory, presenting a *generic* concept, will cover, if successful, all species of value, but will not express what is distinctive of any one species. If, therefore, the reader is looking for a definition of moral value, or of aesthetic value, he will not, he could not, properly find it in this discussion. Yet he should find a concept that is common to these and to all other values, a basis, therefore, upon which a theory about each species might be constructed.

It is important to understand, moreover, that the theory I have in mind is concerned with intrinsic value, not with value as a means or an instrument. The absoluteness of the distinction has been denied, and with a measure of truth in some cases, but prima facie at least we can distinguish between the value of a good garment as a "confection" of materials and the value that resides in making, looking at, or wearing it, and between the value attributed to a flute as a physical thing or instrument and the value of playing the flute or listening to its music. I shall show that the latter is the primary sense of value and that the other can be deduced from it, although, perhaps paradoxically, intrinsic value depends causally upon those things to which value in the derived, extrinsic sense is attached. A satisfactory theory will resolve this paradox.

Now the primary insight into intrinsic values is that they belong to activities or experiences. These alone are, properly speaking, values. *Things* may be called "good," but only because they contribute something to experiences. They are valuables, not values. They may be good, or even goods, but they are not the good. Thus a well-made musical instrument is good; it is also a good, a valuable; but its goodness consists in the fact that it makes possible a musical experience to be enjoyed, which is the value or the good to which it contributes. Similarly, a diamond may be called good or beautiful and may be said to *have* great value, but it possesses its value only in the seeing and enjoying of it; when it is not seen and enjoyed, its beauty or value is, in Aristotelian language, merely potential, not actual. Only if we should suppose that the diamond somehow sees and enjoys its brilliance, that the flute hears and enjoys the sounds that emanate from it, and that the violet thrills to its own freshness and color, as a girl might, would they have value in themselves. Linguistic usage differs in these matters both among people at large and among philosophers, and some confusion may result, but there is little excuse for it. In this book I shall try to be consistent and to use the term "value" or "the good" only when referring to experiences having actual or intrinsic value; I shall speak of mere things as being valuable or as having attributed value.

Value, however, could not be defined simply as activity or experience. Habitual acts have minimal intrinsic value, although, of course, as background or as means they may have great extrinsic value. Moreover, some activities are evils, not values, in the positive sense. Therefore, although experience is, I shall claim, essentially value, positive or negative, good or evil, there must be some factor, still to seek, which determines whether it is good or evil, and how great a good or evil. This would be the value factor. Prima facie, this factor would seem to be some thing of many names: satisfaction, pleasure, joy. An activity that is an enjoyment appears to be exactly what we mean by a value. Whether it be sensuous, the smelling of a hyacinth; aesthetic, the hearing of a Mozart melody; ambition-satisfying, the winning of a long-worked-for place of eminence; moral, the triumph of a "cause"—all these are satisfactions. And if this factor is eliminated from these experiences, they appear to lose their value. A scent or a melody unenjoyed, a prize that turns to ashes in the mouth, would not be good as ends, although they could conceivably be good as means.

One might have some doubt about moral acts, whether they can properly be called enjoyments. When the maquis submits to torture rather than betray his comrades, is his act a pleasure? Yet does it not possess intrinsic moral value? In order to answer this question, we shall ask another: Does not the maquis want to hold firm, and when he does so, *must* he not feel satisfaction? And if he did not want to, would his act be his? And if he felt no satisfaction in it, would he not be repudiating it? If the good man does not do the right willingly and take satisfaction in doing it, is he not a slave or an automaton? The use of the term "pleasure" is, I believe, the prime cause of the difficulty here, because we usually associate it with pleasures of the senses, as when we describe someone as a "man of pleasure." There are, we shall maintain, different kinds of value, and for each, one term is more appropriate than another—"pleasure" for the sensual, "beauty" for the aesthetic, "blessedness" for the religious, "quiet satisfaction" for the moral. As we have suggested, one might, to be sure, infer from this diversity of terms a skepticism of any universal definition of value at all; yet a careful examination reveals that there is something common to them. And if the moralist finds it inept (to put his emotion in this matter mildly) to give one name to such diverse experiences as dining, self-sacrifice, and the hearing of the *Eroïca,* nonetheless, if they do have a common nature, some appropriate term must be found for it, and the most neutral term in use is "satisfaction," the most colorful is "joy."

But is this factor that appears to constitute the intrinsic value of an experience attached to it in some external fashion, as one might wear a charm about one's neck to bring one luck? Some discussions by philosophers who are hedonists, as well as some by psychologists, might appear to bear out this supposition. Yet when we look into experience, it ceases to be plausible that value has no relation to any other factor in experience, and that it merely descends—heaven-sent, as it were—to grace certain activities rather than others.

One factor to which value is intimately related is desire, if we use this term in a broad sense to include what may be designated wish, purpose, drive, instinct, conation, and the like. Many satisfactions, perhaps all, as we shall see, occur as assuagements of desire or as realizations of goals or plans set up by desire. The satisfaction of eating when hungry, of making love when one is in love, of winning a prize long coveted and worked for, of securing the victory anxiously planned for—these are a few illustrations of how closely satisfaction and desire are related. Here satisfaction is not a mere by-product of desire, it is hardly distinguishable from it. Moreover, enjoyments are objectives of desire. The pleasurable smelling of a rose sets up in me the desire to have the experience again and impels me to the sniffing that leads to the renewal of the enjoyment. This is true of all passive enjoyments. I hear a melody, then desire to hear the rest of the composition, so I stop and listen. It is true also of more active enjoyments. A young scholar writes an article embodying the results of his research and enjoys doing so; he then desires to write another article. Or a young businessman runs for local office, perhaps reluctantly; then he discovers that he is enjoying himself immensely, whereupon no one can dissuade him from running again. Every enjoyment is at least potentially the objective of a desire to retain it or to institute its like; and if competing desires or external circumstances did not interfere, this potentiality would always become an actuality. We might, perhaps, therefore define value as the objective of desire,[1] as that which would satisfy desire.

But at this point in our argument there is at least one good objection to such a definition that we must consider; it is a relational definition, and while such definitions are sometimes the only ones we can frame, they are not entirely satisfactory because they may not tell us much about the intrinsic nature of whatever it is that stands in the relation involved. If, for example, we define blue as the color resulting from the stimulation of the retina by a wave of light of such and such a length, do we know the intrinsic nature of blue? The blind man would understand us, but would he know what blue was like? Moreover, is it not conceivable that some other hue might be caused by the same wave length of light? We cannot deduce the hue from the wave length. Similarly, although we do know from our study thus far that enjoyable activities or satisfactions are

[1] Not the *object* of desire, if by object be meant a thing. If I want a book, the book is the object of my wanting; but the objective is the activity of reading the book. See the discussion following and my criticism of R. B. Perry, pp. 34 ff.

objectives of desire, we do not yet know that they are the only objectives, and we have not yet produced any argument to show that we could deduce that they are from the mere concept of their being an objective of desire.

Perhaps, as we have hinted, the relation between value and desire is so close that we could use the definition which makes value the objective of desire, after all. In the first place, a careful scrutiny may show that the objective of desire is always a satisfying activity or passivity. It certainly is not, as we have already indicated, a thing. A man may say that he wants a house, but what as a fact he wants is to live in the house or to sell it, and not merely this, but to live happily in the house or to get a pleasurable profit out of it. He would not want the house if he were to live unhappily in it, or if the house were to be sold at a loss or were to become a burden to him. If by "object," then, we mean either a thing which is a mere means to the assuagement of desire, or even a thing so intimately related to desire that it participates in its assuagement, as a house does when we live in it, then an object is neither the goal or objective of desire nor value itself. Moreover, we must distinguish between the objective of desire as what we have in mind as its goal, and the realization of the goal so conceived. Not the goal itself but the realization is value (with qualifications to be given in due time). For if the goal is not realized, there surely is not value in the positive sense. To repeat: we must carefully distinguish (which, unfortunately for value theory, is not always done) between the object of desire, a thing, the objective of desire, and the realization of the objective, which is usually some satisfying activity or passivity. The confusions that exist are partly due to the ambiguity in the meanings of "object" and "objective"—the first now signifying a thing, now a goal, the latter, now a goal idea in the mind, now the realization of that idea (an activity or event). When value is defined as the objective of desire, we should mean the satisfying activity that realizes the goal idea or objective.

In the second place, the relation between the satisfying activity that realizes the goal of desire and desire itself is still closer. For often the satisfyingness, the joy of the activity, stems from desire itself; it is because the activity is what we want that we enjoy it. Or, to express the same meaning differently, we enjoy the activity because we are having our way in it. Satisfaction is then the assuagement of desire. Thus, if I do not want a certain honor—say membership in an honorary society—election will not bring me pleasure; but if I do want it, I shall be pleased. Or if a certain career is not what I desired, I shall not enjoy pursuing it as I should if it were the one I chose. And we can notice, as we gradually come nearer and nearer to the goal of desire, how satisfaction increases, reaching its high point when the goal is attained; for example, in writing a book, halfway I am pleased; three quarters to the end, I am more pleased; at the completion of my task, most pleased of all. In all such cases, desire is seen to be the cause of value.

Against this line of argument the old observation may be urged that we often find we do not enjoy what we wanted when we get it, and that, on the contrary, we often enjoy what we did not want. This may be true; I may not want to live in the city, yet living there I discover that I am enjoying myself; or having wished to live in the country, I am bored. In the old days, many a girl found herself happy in marrying the rich young man whom her parents picked out for her, and many others found themselves miserable, wedded to the men whom their hearts desired.

A careful examination of such cases reveals, however, that they do not tell against the supposition that satisfaction is the assuagement of desire. For in any one of the cases mentioned, or in any similar case, realizing the objective will bring joy and failing to realize it will bring sorrow, at first. If you want to live in the country, you will be pleased when you get there just because your wish has been fulfilled; and, on the other hand, if you go to the city, you will feel an initial frustration. So the unwilling bride will at first be sorrowful and the willing one will be joyful, whatever be their eventual feelings, because the longing of the one has been balked and that of the other fulfilled. And if the unwilling bride becomes happy, that will be because her desires for comfort and security, and perhaps certain sexual impulses unknown to herself, are satisfied, whereas all these desires may be frustrated in the life of the willing bride. Yet in the heart of each there may remain a feeling never confessed, of sorrow to discolor eventual happiness or of joy to relieve eventual distress, because for the one her partner was not quite what she dreamed, and for the other, he was her dream, however blighted. Even so, the man who did not wish to live in the city finds that the delights offered by theaters, museums, art exhibitions, night clubs, or the like, overwhelm his aversion to noise, dirt, and cramped quarters; while the man in the country, who has all that he wished of fresh air and vistas, finds no opportunities there for the things the city would have offered him.

The crucial test, however, as to whether all satisfaction comes from the assuagement of desire, or whether some of it comes from another source, depends upon the examination of the activities through which, generally, desire is fulfilled. We can, sometimes, distinguish the joy that stems from the one from the satisfactions yielded by the other. That this is true can be most readily seen in those circumstances where desire is, as it were, blind, never having experienced the activities through which it is appeased. Granted that, in such cases, part of the satisfaction is derived from the fulfilling of the desire, may not some of it flow from the activities themselves apart from desire? The best examples are found in hunger and sex. Undoubtedly, part of the satisfaction derived from coming together with the young woman a youth desired to possess is derived from the fulfillment of that desire, but if he is "innocent" he could not have foreknown all the pleasures he will experience from the activities and passivities involved. How then do these pleasures come from his desire? Or the newborn child may be hungry, but it cannot foretell and cannot precisely desire those pleasures it will receive when it finds its mother's breast. Whence come they? Or consider another case: the child will want the candy offered him because it is candy; but will the novel pleasure he receives from its taste have its source in the fact that he wanted the candy even though he could not have wanted just that taste since he had never experienced it? And some pleasures seem to be entirely unwished for and unsought, as those connected with the scent of flowers when we walk in the woods of a May morning, or of music which we chance to hear in passing by the window of some musician's house. Is not the joy in such activities, and especially in such passivities, a bloom upon them, as Aristotle conceived it to be, a natural flowering of them, independent of the self with its desires, its plans, and its purposes? And even when all these joys have been had and we long to renew them, can we claim that our longing for them creates and explains them? We are thus confronted with the old problem as to whether (a) we find ourselves active or passive in certain pleasurable ways, independent of desire, and then afterward desire them; or (b) these activities and passivities are wanted in the first place, and then, because so wanted, they give pleasure.

In the crucial examples mentioned, it is clear that if the satisfactions issue from desire, the desire cannot be the desire *for* them, after they have once been experienced, but must, somehow, be a desire *within* them, when they are first experienced. When the desire for them is fulfilled in them, the total satisfaction must represent the confluence of two streams of desire. And what could be the desires preceding the organic pleasures of taste, smell, sound, and touch when they surprise us unsought? Furthermore, have we any reason for supposing that such desires exist?

There is one good argument, I think, for supposing that they do exist, an argument essentially analogical, based on our knowledge that some satisfactions do come from the assuagement of desire. As we have seen, the man who wants a certain honor is pleased if he gets it because he wanted it. If he does not want it he is not pleased. And unless you are hungry your food does not, as we say, taste so good. Or if you do not desire your mate, the pleasures she gives you will not be so great. Now, I am asking, may not such facts be clues to the understanding of all the organic pleasures that surprise us when they come, or even a clue to the passive pleasures of sense? May there not be—must there not be—desires of the organism of which we are not aware, desires of the ear, the eye, the tongue, and especially of the erogenous zones, the assuagement of which are the uninvited pleasures we have been discussing? In these circumstances, it is as if our minds coalesced with satisfactions of the body, not with the desires of the body. The relation of mind and body is so close, however, that perhaps these very desires are subconsciously present to us and account for the prescience of joys to come which instinct seems to provide. This argument seems to be in line with the doctrine of contemporary physiological psychology according to which all satisfactions arise from the release of "tissue tensions or needs" (quaint phrase!). The hypothesis is, then, that every activity or passivity is really an *impulse* and that its joy is the assuagement of that impulse. Even the senses—of touch, of taste, of vision, and the like—have their needs, which are assuaged by the appropriate sensations. If this is correct, we have a unitary theory of joy. Yet the complexity of joy would survive, coming partly from organic impulses appeased and partly from the fulfillment of conscious desires for these or other types of joy. We may, therefore, define value as either a joy-giving activity or passivity or else as the assuagement of desire; the two definitions come to the same thing.

Yet even now, although we have found a broad generic definition that will hold, we have not yet discovered an adequate description of value, at least not one that covers human value, with which we are specifically concerned in this essay. For an important aspect is omitted, the social. And apart from this factor, certain critical types of value, those, for example, connected with remorse and duty, obviously cannot be understood. Yet not only values such as these, but all human values are social. Moreover, they are social not accidentally but essentially. Even the most animal and organic impulses, such as those involved in sensing, in food, and in sex, yes, and in elimination, are social in men.

What, however, do we mean by calling them social? Let us first consider certain meanings which we might entertain, but which I am sure are not the right ones, although they are all true enough, in their way.

We might suppose that desires are social because many persons belonging to the same group have similar objectives. I want to drink tea and so do you; so we both do so. Many of our enjoyments have a class or national character. The French take chocolate and rolls for breakfast; urban Americans have coffee, toast, orange juice, and a prepared cereal; some farmers add eggs and bacon. And, in general, it is true that we want and enjoy the same kinds of things that people in our set want and enjoy; it is hard, perhaps impossible, to desire and enjoy what some others do not. Psychopathic individuals make the surprising discovery that a sizable percentage of the population have tastes like theirs. But the mere similarity of the wishes and pleasures of people does not make them social, although it does, as we shall see, provide an important base for the social. All the cows in a meadow eat grass side by side, but do we know that they are social?

We might think that values are social because men co-operate or compete with each other in action. Several men will pull together on a rope in order to drag a boat ashore, and hundreds will act together on an assembly line in building an automobile. On the other hand, many men will compete for nomination to a political post, and armies will fight armies. This fact is also important for the social character of values, but does not make man a social animal. Bees co-operate in building a hive; but are they social? Human beings are objects of sexual and parental interest to one another, and co-operate or contend against each other in the actions involved; so do animals, the sexes copulating with each other and rearing or suckling their young, but does this make them social?

Finally, men live within an institutional network, economic, political, legal, religious, and linguistic. They employ a common currency; transact business, buying and selling according to custom; they marry or get divorced within or beyond the limits of the law, determined by assemblies of the people and codified in public documents; they worship together in temples and in accordance with a tradition perpetuated by holy books—their behavior in all these varied modes being mediated by a special kind of behavior, language. This fact, or group of facts is, to be sure, of the utmost importance for the social character of language, but if it means merely that a man's behavior is determined by that of other men, by whom he is stimulated and to whom he responds in certain routinelike and predictable ways; or if it means merely that his behavior is determined by things which he himself has fashioned, such as books and tools, which have a longevity greater than his own, it does not by itself make him social. He lives also within a lawful and predictable physical nexus, and his life is determined by trees, rivers, mines, rainfall, the sea, the stars, and the seasons, things from which the stimuli continue to carry on from generation to generation. Well, if the social nexus is essentially the same sort of web, no matter how much more finely meshed, why should it rather than the physical be decisive, granted that the physical nexus is not?

The answer is that not any one of the facts described above, important as it is, constitutes values social, but rather the following: first, our awareness of the desires and satisfactions of other persons and their awareness of ours; not how we behave in relation to each other, but our knowledge of the feelings that accompany and determine behavior. All of our feelings are either known to others or, when they are not known, the very fact of their being unknown affects their character. Each person is a mirror to the others, and whatever is not reflected in it is warped or deflected. The unknown becomes the hidden, the secret. Hence our very privacy and solitude are paradoxically social. Either we want to make our thoughts and feelings known or, if we do not, that is part of their significance. And for many, what is not under the eye of the neighbor is under the eye of God. Hence it is not that we both drink tea, or even that we do so side by side that makes tea-drinking social, but that each knows what the other feels when he is drinking. This knowledge is, to be sure, mediated by the fact that we are performing similar acts, but the social significance is not in this mere manner of performance, but in the knowledge itself. Likewise, it is not the bare fact that men co-operate and compete that causes them to be social, but that they know that others are co-operating or competing, adding their wills to mine or opposing mine, and so eliciting love or hate. It is not that the woman's body is being wooed by me and finally is at my disposal that makes sexual congress social, but that she knows that she is being sought and consents, this knowledge and consent animating her body and creating my pride and happiness in possession. Again, it is not by itself important for values that the parent fosters and protects the child, but that the parent knows and the child knows that this is so, together with the love and counterlove accompanying this knowledge.

What is significant in the routine of institutional life is not that, to the observer, a man's behavior is determined within this "field," but that the desires and satisfactions of the participants as they are experienced partly control and are partly controlled by it. The mere fact that I am writing English words, words of a certain shape, and that you will read similar words when a copy of the book of which they are part is finally printed and published, is important for the social character of values only because you will experience their meaning and be moved to approval or disapproval of me, the author; and because, as I write them, I know (or hope) that some reader will give or withhold his assent to what I assert and will feel accordingly. Just so, that which gives to the law its social value is the fact that I the plaintiff know that you the judge and you the defendant know what the law is, and each knows that the rest of us know what it is, and that the feelings of all of us are colored by this knowledge. Or if I buy a house from you, what makes the transaction social is again the fact of knowledge: that I know that now you are willing to sell and that you know that I am willing to buy for cash on the line, and, because of this knowledge, I rejoice in possessing what I have wanted to possess, and you rejoice in receiving the money you wished to receive by this purchase.

Yet merely to live our values under the eyes of others is not all that we mean by their social character; there is a further factor that must be brought into view, namely, that these values are partly created by the demands that we know others are making upon us. They expect me to do certain things in certain ways, and I expect them to do rather much as I wish. And we take account of the demands of others not, as we take account of wind and weather, because we have to do so, but because we want to do so. What we want of each other becomes a standard for our values, a pattern or mold for them. Sometimes I may want you to act in one way and you may want me to act in another way, in which case how each shall want himself to act will be a compromise or integration of both our desires.

We can give at least two reasons why we want to meet the demands of others, reasons so obvious that we should hardly be justified in mentioning them were not at least one of them oftentimes neglected and did not both of them have important implications. One reason is our dependence on others for the co-operation necessary for the fulfillment of our own desires. This is especially true in a culture such as ours in which each person can himself do so little in order to satisfy his own complex wants. I can do for myself little more than make a cup of tea or boil an egg; and for either of these purposes I have had to depend on the people who gathered the tea, raised the hens, made the pot and the stove. Now then, if we are useful to them, they will at least keep us in being and, out of gratitude, do us favors. Most especially do we need the favor of those who have power over us and have the means to be good to us, such as parents and superiors. Moreover, in the end, they need us even as we need them, and when the organization of the group to which we belong is democratic, power and authority will be spread among its members, and the striving for favor will be mutual. The second reason is this: the mind, like the body, has a sexual component, a desire for union, for what we call mutual understanding and agreement, whereby our sense of isolation is overcome. This is love, which seeks favor not as a means, but as an end. The same reasons that impel one to meet the demands of others impel one to make demands upon them. I wish to meet their demands because by so doing I help myself to realize my own desires and make demands upon them such as will further my own ends. A good deal of morality can be explained in this way. I praise kindness and courage because I want the help of other men and they in their turn want my help. But that is not a sufficient explanation, for love enters here also. I make demands upon other persons for their good, as when I require courtesy and good manners of my children, in order that they may be enabled to win the good will of members of their group and profit accordingly.

I wish to emphasize, however, what in passing has already been asserted, that the standard is not determined merely by the demands of other persons upon me, but also by my demands upon myself. Into this, I shall enter at length when we come to the general subject of standards; here it will suffice to remind ourselves that we set a standard for each kind of activity determined, intrinsically, by what we think will provide maximum satisfaction for it, and, extrinsically, by what we believe will make the maximum contribution to the realization of our life plan. But the life plan itself, for the reasons cited in the foregoing paragraph, has to take account of the wishes of our fellow men. The standard is, therefore, an anticipation of satisfaction, put into relation with the demands of others as they affect our own demands. It is a compromise and integration of these factors.

Both the character and the intensity of the satisfaction or value are affected by whether or not standards are met. If I fail to meet specifically moral standards, then whatever satisfaction I may obtain through an activity that runs its course nevertheless is qualified by a feeling of guilt or insecurity, which cannot be entirely overcome by a compensating attitude of defiance. If, on the contrary, an activity conforms to the standard, its own native satisfaction will be re-enforced by the peculiar satisfaction that is derived from union with the desires of one's fellow men.

We may therefore distinguish three levels in a value: (1) satisfactions in relatively spontaneous activities or passivities; (2) satisfactions arising from meeting the objectives of conscious desires; (3) satisfactions arising from the meeting of the personal-social standards set for these satisfactions. In general, however, these are not separate satisfactions, but rather ingredients or layers of single complex satisfactions.

But is there not perhaps a fourth layer? Phenomenologically, yes; but for our time, and for most philosophers in our time, it is problematical. The experiences of sin, guilt, and sanctification appear to point to demands upon us by whatever we may mean by "God" or "the Divine." The feeling of a peace and blessedness not of this world and passing all understanding is a satisfaction difficult to explain in terms of activities relating merely to oneself or to other persons belonging to an ordinary group. The uniqueness *as feelings* of the horrendous and the holy seems certain, whatever one may decide about their origin or their objects. Nevertheless, since there appear to be people in whose experience they are lacking, and since we are now seeking a definition of the universally human good, we may, for the time being, and for the purposes of this chapter, omit them. In a measure, moreover, as many have maintained, they are included in the social, in its broadest interpretation. For God denotes, as we shall argue, a center of experience, possessed of desire and satisfaction, only not subject to the limitations of time, space, and knowledge that restrict us. The religious experience is a unique form of social experience. God's demands upon us, although irreducible to my own demands upon myself, or the demands of members of my group, are still standards, generically the same as other standards.

Do the three, perhaps four layers of satisfaction have any common factor? I think we have shown that they have. The common factor is the assuagement of desire. For if activities and passivities are impulses running a course to appeasement; and if, as we have shown, the objectives of desire are always activities or passivities which fulfill it; and if, as we have hinted and shall prove in detail, demands and standards, whether set up by oneself, by other persons, or by God, are themselves desires seeking realization (desires regarding desires and satisfactions), and their realization is itself a kind of satisfaction, then our thesis is demonstrated. More evidence for the sufficiency of this thesis will be given when we examine the objections to it. But while believing that the minimum definition, the common factor in all value, may be given as satisfaction of desire (using this term in the most inclusive sense), no study of values can be adequate which does not recognize the complexity at once of every human desire, and therefore of every human satisfaction, a complexity at least threefold, perhaps fourfold.

Having undertaken to give a general definition of value, I wish next to consider certain objections to it. These may be listed summarily as follows: (1) The definition has been given in terms of desire, but perhaps it should be given in terms of aversions; as freedom or escape from isolation or loneliness, from pain, danger, annihilation, or not-being. (2) Some joys and assuagements of desire are not good but evil; perhaps, as certain religious leaders have claimed, all are evil. (3) The good should be defined, not in terms of single desires but in terms of the whole self, even of the whole situation or "field" in which the self functions. (4) The good is relative to different unique individual centers of experience; hence there is no common nature of value. (5) Closely allied to this last is the contention that, since any statement "this is good" is volitional (appraisive), every definition of the good must be normative, an expression of what ought to be, not, as the definition seems to propose, of what is (satisfaction). (6) Our definition is psychological, naturalistic, but value is definable only in nonnaturalistic terms, such as "ought" or "fittingness." (7) Values are not experiences (as are satisfactions of desire), not subjective but objective realities. (8) The good is not definable at all, since it is a simple, nonnaturalistic predicate. (9) The good is not the satisfaction of desire, but the *object* of a desire or motor-affective attitude. This last definition admits of various interpretations depending, as we shall see, upon whether the object is taken to be a *thing* or an emergent relational predicate of a thing.

Since the following chapter will be devoted to the study of alternative theories, we shall not now consider objections (6), (7), (8), and (9), which make use of definite, rival constructive definitions, but only the first five, which are either difficulties besetting all theories of value or else objections which can, I believe, readily be met by a clarification of our own definition. Of the first set of objections, (1), (2), and (3) can be met by clarification, and (4) and (5) are difficulties of all theories of value. The study of all of these objections will lead to a further elucidation and enrichment of the definition.

The first objection, that we should have defined value in terms of aversion rather than of desire, is one unlikely to be made by anyone in sympathy with the main current of Western philosophy, with its almost uniformly affirmative attitude. Yet under the influence of Eastern thought, and recently among the various types of existentialism, from Schopenhauer through

Heidegger and Sartre, we find what we may call the value heresy that the good is essentially an avoidance, an escape, be it from pain, from danger, from limitation, from conventionality, from loneliness, or from death. With all the diverse implications of this theory we cannot at present be concerned. We must confine ourselves to their bearing upon our general definition. It will, in fact, suffice to make two points: first, that aversion itself is a desire; and second, that not all desires are aversions. The child (and sometimes the man) who rests happily only when there is someone else in the house at night and who, on the contrary, is wakeful and anxious when alone is *desiring* something (company) quite as much as does the child who desires a stick of candy; and the satisfaction that is the feeling of safety or union in the former situation is as much a satisfaction as the pleasure in tasting and sucking the sweetmeat. The desires have different occasions, and the satisfactions a different quality, but generically, as satisfactions, they are the same. And that not all desires are aversions is clear from such simple desires as those for sensuous pleasures like sweet tastes and odors and such positive satisfactions as triumph and intellectual understanding. There is, as we shall see, a particle of truth in saying of the latter that they are desires to escape from defeat and confusion, but the quality of the satisfaction is richer than that; it is something more than mere relief. How in fact desire and aversion are related we shall study in our chapter on the analysis of value; we shall find that, although the positive cannot be reduced to the negative, they are closely intertwined.

The second objection, that some satisfactions, even perhaps all, are evil, has a close relation to the preceding point. Let us consider the more conservative part of the statement first. It has been held, specifically, that the satisfactions which we call cruelty and lasciviousness are evil. If we can show that this is a mistake, we shall, I think, have gone a long way toward proving our case to the effect that, on the contrary, all satisfactions are good, that the good is satisfaction. But before we go further let us be sure that we are not being trapped by words. The very words used to designate certain acts—such as the words "cruelty" and "lasciviousness"—have a connotation of evil. In using these words we have almost committed ourselves to viewing them as evils. We are arguing in the manner for which Socrates berated Callicles in the *Gorgias*. So let us try to consider the acts rather than the words for them. And we can, I believe, concentrate our attention on cruelty.

We can see without much difficulty that it makes a difference whether we have in mind a cruel act of ourselves or of another person. For a cruel act of another person, if practiced on ourselves, is, from our standpoint, unquestionably evil, extrinsically. When practiced on one of our own group, it is also evil extrinsically, partly because we put ourselves in the place of the victim, making his attitude ours, and partly because, as revealing a habit or tendency in the perpetrator of the act, it is a standing menace to ourselves. When practiced on an enemy we are not sure (the dropping of the atom bomb on Hiroshima). But so far we have not considered the cruel act for itself. (When I write "we," I mean myself and whoever may be the reader of these lines. Since I am doing the writing, I shall have to consider it for both, leaving to the reader the privilege of correcting me if I am wrong in interpreting him.) And we see at once that we cannot consider the cruel deed strictly for itself, for as a deed it is always someone's. Whosoever it is, if it be his free act and deed, we know that, if unopposed by any prohibition or counterimpulse of charity, it will bring satisfaction to its author, since it springs from an impulse which has run its course to fulfillment; it would not be cruelty if it did not. And we also see that, if our definition is correct, such an act done by the "red Indian" is an intrinsic good, for it both assuages an impulse and meets an expectation or standard. On the other hand, if done by me, and I suspect by the reader, it is not a value; because, when you or I do it, it is opposed by our moral standard of conduct, which, being frustrated, overwhelms the satisfaction it would otherwise give, with dissatisfaction. Therefore, for me to do it, or for you to do it, is not value, but evil. For Mr. G. E. Moore also, it is evil. But from this analysis it is clear, I think, that cruelty is not evil intrinsically, not evil *an sich* (in itself).

Hence our conception of value is in nowise put in jeopardy by the case of cruelty; on the contrary, it is confirmed. For when cruelty is evil, it is evil because it frustrates the impulse to love, the imaginative putting of oneself in the place of another. When we accomplish this imaginative act, then cruelty to another becomes like cruelty practiced on oneself, an evil. Similarly, an intemperate act that endangers my security or any long range plan of myself is evil, for as soon as I realize its implications, it ceases to give the satisfaction it would bring apart from reflection. That there is a still unsolved problem here, I do not deny; but it is a problem for the theory I am defending, not an argument against the theory.

The most extreme form that the foregoing objection might take, namely, that all satisfactions are evil, is, I believe, a view that, strictly interpreted, has never been held. It has been held that all *desire* is evil, for the alleged reason that none can be fulfilled. This ancient attitude toward desire, more widely held in the East than in the West, we shall examine in its proper place. At this moment the remark is sufficient that, far from being an objection, this is really a confirmation of our view, for the implication is that if desires could be fulfilled in satisfaction, they would be good. A less extreme form of this objection, one often maintained by certain types of mystics, would be that not all, but certain kinds of desires and satisfactions called "earthly" or "bodily," are evil. This is obviously a theory closely similar in general character to the doctrine of G. E. Moore and others, the difference being in the kind of desire and satisfaction thought to be evil. But here again there is confirmation rather than refutation of our basic philosophy of value, for such desires and satisfactions are condemned not because of their intrinsic nature but because of their actual or possible competition or interference with those of a heavenly or spiritual kind, which are themselves identified with the good.

The third objection is directed against the definition of value in terms of the satisfaction of *single* desires. Instead, it is urged that the good must be defined in terms of the whole self, or even of the whole situation or *field* in which any desire, or even any self, is but a factor.

Our answer to this objection will be partly to meet, but also partly to postpone, the issue it raises. Insofar as we meet it, we shall, I believe, nullify its force as an objection to our definition. For any intelligible view of the self must describe it as either itself a desire, of which what are *called* desires would be only modes, thus implying that the self would be the sole desire; or else as a desire which I shall call of "highest order," with reference to which ordinary desires would be of "lower order." If now there is only one desire that can be identified with the self ("care," *cura, Sorge,* or what else), then its assuagement would be value; if, on the other hand, the self is the highest integration of all lower desires, then their satisfaction as so integrated would be the good. In either case, our definition of value would remain essentially correct. We shall, however, as suggested, postpone the decision as to which theory of the self is correct and how what are usually denominated desires are related to it.

That value is a function of a situation must be conceded. Desire itself has its causes in the organism and in the environment; hunger, for example, is awakened in the organism and directed toward food lying in the environment. Since, as I should hold, there is no way absolutely to isolate a situation from the world of which it is a part, it becomes true to say that value is a function of the universe. But the recognition of this truth should not be made to obscure the problem of a definition of value. The problem is where in the situation or where exactly in the world does value most definitely reside? I am in the United States, in Michigan, in Ann Arbor; but to say these truths is not to say where most intimately I am. I must proceed to specify: in my house, in my room, in my bed, and finally in my body. In parallel fashion, I am claiming that value is satisfaction and that satisfaction resides in the self, even though it be connected as an effect with the organism and the environmental situation. The fact that value resides most intimately in the self is the same fact that some desire in the self is the *sine qua non* of value; value is satisfaction, but a satisfaction of desire.

Now I admit that there is evidence that seems to belie these assertions. Beauty seems to reside in the sunlit leaves, in the tones of the chorale; pleasantness in the taste and smell of the lemon. We say the chorale and the leaves *are* beautiful, the lemon *is* pleasant, as if we were attributing the value to them rather than to our own desires and satisfactions. Since this evidence, however, is basic to the rival theses (7) and (8) and will be studied in the following chapter, we may leave it with the tentative assertion, there to be proved, that value is, to be sure, out there, but only because the self, with its desires and satisfactions, is also out there, on the boundary of the inner and outer worlds.

Our next, and penultimate, objection is to the effect that, since the good is always relative to unique individual centers of experience, there is no common nature of value. The good is always for you, or for me, or for someone else; it is as individual as individual centers themselves. Moreover, since the good of various individuals may be in conflict, the good of one may render impossible what might be the good of another.

This objection is so closely allied with that following that its full force and the full effect of our answer can be appreciated only through a consideration of the latter. But it will be well to go as far with it as we can, in order to settle certain points.

The relativity of values, as we have stated it, is really no barrier to the definition of value as satisfaction, for even though there be a certain individuality belonging to the values of each person as compared with those of another, they have the same generic substance as being satisfactions. A generic definition is all that we are seeking. We are, moreover, able to recognize in the satisfactions of another the same generic structure that we observe in our own. There, too, we find the strata we have noted: the primary satisfactions accompanying primary impulses and the satisfactions arising from meeting the standards and expectations set up with reference to them. Even when there is such a conflict of desires that the satisfactions of another person spell doom to my hopes, as when my rival wins the prize for which we are both contending, I am able to take cognizance of his satisfactions as being generically the same as the satisfactions I would have had if I had won; the same also as those that may be left to me. I can place myself imaginatively in his situation and see that this is so.

The last objection is the most troublesome of all, not because it nullifies our definition but because it raises questions which we shall be able to answer fully only in the course of later chapters. The objection may be restated briefly as follows: the good is not a fact but an ideal; hence no descriptive definition of the good is possible. The expression "this is good" is the expression of a wish, not of a fact; of what ought to be, not of what is. So, for example, a definition of beauty could not be obtained by examining works of art and then setting down their common characteristics; for beauty is an ideal to which actual works of art or other so-called beautiful things may never attain to. Hence, only a volitional definition of art is possible; a statement not of what art is, but of what I want of art. In fact, any set of works of art to be examined for common characteristics is determined by my decision that this or that claimant is the kind of thing I want a work of art to be. The definition is therefore prejudiced at the outset; and as ideals for art differ, so will definitions of art and the classes of things called "art."

There is, however, one fact overlooked in this argument, which otherwise is not without cogency, namely, that what I want of art is not independent of, or utterly different from, what art is. As will be argued at length later, any standard I may set up, whether for art or for other things, is, in a measure, a reflection of my satisfactory experiences of such things. I can have no idea, still less no ideal, of art, before I have enjoyed an actual work of art. I do not mean that there is no creative element in the formation of ideals, but that no ideal can depart very far from some experience of satisfaction had. Moreover, what I want is not unrelated to what *you* want, and since my own nature develops out of the past of my culture, it is not unrelated to an actual tradition. I may, of course, want something different from what you want, but not anything utterly different *in kind;* and however revolutionary my desires may be, they are always desires for some new experience of satisfaction. There are differences and oppositions among the currents of desire; yet even when I stand in one and you stand in another, fighting against me, I can imaginatively place myself where you are and perceive that what you seek is, generically, what I seek—a joy-bringing activity. It is true, as Aristotle said so long ago, that no definition covers the whole individual nature of any fact; but it can cover the generic nature, and that is all that is claimed for any definition of value; no more is certainly claimed for ours.

CHAPTER II

SOME RIVAL THEORIES

THE ONLY satisfactory reason for accepting a philosophical theory is the same as that for accepting a scientific theory—that it appears to cover the facts. It would seem, therefore, that if one has constructed such a theory one's task is done. Yet in philosophical literature this has rarely been felt to be the case. It has uniformly been demanded that the thinker confront his own theory with rival, alternative theories. Why has this been so? In a measure, I am inclined to think, out of professional courtesy. Philosophers do not like to be neglected by their colleagues and take it amiss if their names and views are not mentioned in a discussion.

But this explanation is hardly sufficient. A more pertinent and important ground is the fact that a thinker can hardly be sure of his own view unless he has confronted it with others. For unless he has, there lurks in his mind the uneasy suspicion that perhaps some facts have been neglected by him which other theories have covered better. To be sure, if philosophical theories were pure inventions of the imagination, as cynics aver, that would not be so. On the contrary, however, every serious philosophy is based on facts, however misinterpreted. One can be more sure, therefore, that one has really embraced all the facts if one studies the views of other thinkers.

It is not mere courtesy, but humility which impels me to add this chapter to the last, although I must confess that some of the views now to be examined seem to me naïve or confused. It will not be possible to review all the extant theories of value, but an effort will be made to give consideration to those that have been most influential in the recent past. Sometimes, as will transpire, their insufficiency is due to a lack of technical accuracy (I would say "metaphysical" acumen, if the adjective were not now in such disrepute); hence it will be impossible, I warn the reader, not to enter into technicalities in discussing them. But a technical discussion does not have to be unclear or inaccessible to the general reader; and I shall try to make this one as forthright and lucid as possible. I shall also hope to make it the occasion for bringing certain aspects of our own theory into prominence.

The first contrasting theory that I wish to discuss is the theory that value is resident in objects; that it is a quality of them on an equal footing with any other. The beauty of a Bach chorale, it is claimed, is no less its own than its harmonic and melodic structure; the beauty of a human body belongs to it no less than its arms, legs, hands, feet, and face. The utility of a chair is in it as its back, seat, and legs are in it. The martyr's death and the crucifix *are* holy things. If one asks why, if values are thus objective, they should be neglected by scientific investigation, the answer is that what is ordinarily called "science" is a specialized branch of investigation and that it is the task rather of poetry and philosophy to study values. Consistently with this view, values have been called "tertiary" qualities of objects, a third layer, so to speak, on top of the "primary" and "secondary" layers of qualities. Some values, on this view, would presumably be permanent, as, for example, the aesthetic value of the chorale, the moral value of the martyr's death, while others, like the value of a chair or of a human body, would disappear with the breaking of the chair or the aging of the body.

There is an intriguing simplicity about this theory; one's will to believe it is strong. And in certain elementary instances it appears to be true. These are where the value belongs to structures given within experience. When we appreciate the Bach chorale, at least what everyone would call its apparent value is in the chorale itself—that is to say in the experience of the chorale; and when the believer looks at the cross its apparent value is in the visual configuration. This is true because the sensuous shapes are immersed in satisfactions, and both are factors in a single experience. Similarly, the beauty of the beloved belongs to her form as I intuit it. There is no difference between the value and the satisfactions; and the *esse* (the "being") of both is *percipi* (their "being perceived"). But difficulties arise as soon as we forsake this elementary level. The proponents of the theory claim that the music, the human body, and the rest possess their values even when we do not appreciate them. The chorale and the beloved body, they would say, are possessed of value independent of my joy in the former or of the sweetness of my love for the latter. Beauty is not in the lover's eye, but in the thing itself. The satisfactions are not the values, rather they are avenues by means of which we acquire knowledge of them. Like any other organ of knowledge, feeling may be absent or it may be perverted and mistaken. The feelings of the Nazis regarding war and cruelty were perverse; those who have no positive feelings for Bach's music are as blind as the bat.

The difficulties inherent in this extension of the theory are two: first, there is no evidence that feelings *as such* are cognitive; and second, there is no evidence that values exist in such structures as animal bodies and musical compositions independent of the experience of an appreciator. That values are there when they are not found to be there is pure assumption; and the fact, so often cited in discussions of this matter, that people seem to find *opposed* values in similar structures speaks against independently existing values being there. One cannot explain the distaste of some people for certain types of music or certain phenomenal bodies on the basis of *blindness,* because something in the way of value is felt; and to attribute the difference to perversity is to invent a new theory to bolster up what is to be proved. Who, pray, is perverse—those who praise or those who condemn the symphonies of Brahms? And is my taste or the Hottentot's wrong with regard to feminine beauty? It is evident that the problem of standard value is being raised and that unless some more plausible theory can be found to answer it, we may have to fall back on this one, with all its defects.

In my eyes, one of these defects, not yet mentioned, is dogmatism. The good, the right, and the beautiful are somehow there and whoever feels them as being there knows what they are. When there is disagreement there is no argument—except to call your opponent perverse or blind. But to my thinking the greatest difficulty which the theory has to confront is to inform us what these "absolute" values are. For me, at any rate, they have no standing in reality and no intelligibility, except as rooted in desires culminating in satisfactions. I have so far never found any communicable essence of value corresponding to what is alleged to exist by the proponents of this theory; yet there is a challenge here which we shall try to meet in our discussion of the theory of value as the expression of an imperative.

Nevertheless, the theory is not without its modicum of truth. Although feelings are not as such cognitive, they are usually combined with activities that are. The drive for food and sexual expression leads to activities of exploration ending in the discovery of objects that bring satisfaction. Love is "blind" in not realizing eventual defects and difficulties but also very canny as to what promises immediate satisfaction. Moreover, our desires and satisfactions have correlates in the external world, and while not themselves forms of knowledge may nevertheless be-

come evidence of realities. The desire for food and our satisfaction in it exist in a context of organic processes and in relation to parts of the physical world that may serve as nutriment.
Our sexual impulses are intimately related to bodily organs and
functions—our own and other persons. That the food is "good"
or the woman "beautiful" is evidence of a profound harmony
between ourselves and nature, as Kant knew. I would not oppose Schopenhauer's thesis of the metaphysical significance of
music as providing hints of the character of reality. Musicians
also have believed this; they may very well be right. But while
as metaphysician, I would admit this to be true, I cannot see that
it solves any problem in the theory of values. Music may be a
symbol of the world order and of the values of the Supreme
Being, not because these values are in the music when no one
hears it, but because they are an analogue of them when one
does hear it. And no matter how far the values excel ours in
magnificence it seems clear that they must be generically the
same as our own—made of the stuff of desires and satisfactions.
This insight is confirmed by music itself, which, as Schopenhauer says, is an image of the will. The mere multiplication of
values in the world does not, by itself, reveal anything new concerning the essence of value itself, even though they be divine
and give us comfort and support.

The second view that I wish to discuss is like the preceding
in placing value in the object, but differs radically in regarding
value as a variable aspect of the object dependent upon desire
or interest. This view has been given prominence in our own
country by D. W. Prall and R. B. Perry.

Unfortunately, these writers give different and not entirely
consistent statements of their theories. For example, Perry defines value as "any object of any interest," which seems to make
of value an *object* or *thing,* and yet in an explanatory sentence
he says "that which is the object of 'interest' is *eo ipso* invested
with value, where value seems to be a relational attribute."
Again he says, "Value is but a specific relation into which things

possessing any ontological status whatsoever, whether real or imaginary, may enter with interested subjects"; here value seems to be a relation, and later value is defined as *both* relation and character as follows: "We have then been led to define value as the peculiar relation between any interest and its object; or that special character of an object which consists . . . in the fact that interest is taken in it." [1] In similar ambiguous fashion, D. W. Prall writes, "the being liked or disliked of the object is its value" and "value is the existence of an interest relation between a subject and an object." [2] We then seem to have value defined under three categories: thing, attribute or character, and relation. The general context, however, of all these definitions enables us, with good will, to reduce them to two, combining the first two with the second, as follows: value is the object of interest qualified by its relation to interest, and value is "an interest relation" between a subject and an object.

Interpreted in either way the theory is, from our point of view, sound insofar as it makes interest the necessary ground of value, instead of a mere avenue for the apprehension of value, as in the first theory. Yet there are insuperable difficulties attaching to the definition of value as a specially qualified object or as a relation. Let us consider the former alternative first.

Now we do, of course, speak of objects as values or as having value. In commercial advertisements we hear of bargain sales as offering unusual values, as if the goods were themselves values. We speak of a precious stone as having great value; and more specifically we ascribe beauty to the sonata and goodness to the deed. But, although language is always a useful clue in philosophy, it cannot be taken as decisive for the solution of problems. How misleading it can be is illustrated when we ask ourselves just what attribute attaches to an object when interest is taken

[1] *General Theory of Value* (Cambridge, 1926), pp. 115, 116, 124.

[2] "A Study in the Theory of Value," *Univ. of Calif. Publications in Philosophy*, III, No. 2, pp. 215, 227, 254.

in it? Two cases must be considered, one when the "object" lies within the experience of the subject and one when it is outside of (transcendent to) this experience. For example, suppose I am interested in the contour of one of the trees in my yard as I look at it in the summertime, finding it beautiful. Then that aspect of the tree lies within my experience, and one may well say that the object of my interest (the visual form of the tree) is qualified by my interest, for the two interpenetrate; we could say that the contour was beautiful or that here was a case of beauty of contour, making either the value an adjective of the object or the object an adjective of the value. In this type of case, therefore, it would appear to be true that interest qualifies its object. But suppose, a long way from home, I begin to ponder the problems of having the tree trimmed and how the trimming would affect the contour. Obviously, I am still interested in the tree, but obviously also my interest and the tree are not parts of my one experience; the tree is a *transcendent object*.

To be sure there is a concept of the tree and probably also an image of the tree in my mind, but these are not *objects* of my interest; they are instruments of my interest: I am interested *through* them, not *in* them. Now in this case, I ask, is the value of the tree an adjective or quality of the tree? Literally, the answer must be an unqualified no. It is doubtful whether the tree in Ann Arbor is altered in *any* way by the interest I am taking in it far away in New York—all its chemicophysical and living qualities remain the same. If while I am pondering the trimming of the tree, a botanist were to examine the tree, he would not discover any alteration in it as a result of my pondering. Of course, since thought and interest are real processes they probably have some effect, or would have some effect if they were not counteracted, on the tree; but they would also have effects on all the things in the universe; and none of these effects would be, so far as we know, specifically of the nature of value; they would be physical and chemical in character. Or, if we accept an "idealistic" view of reality and are prepared to maintain that all events are of the nature of desire, satisfaction, or frustration, the effects of my thought on the tree could not be necessarily *that value* which I ascribe to it. Let me illustrate: suppose that an elderly man is indiscreetly attentive to a young woman; then his interest in her will undoubtedly have an effect on her, and an effect of a special value character, but not necessarily the value which she has for him; it may even be contrary in character, for she may hate or despise him. Such values engendered in another subject by the values of a given subject I have called reciprocal values.

The result of this discussion can be summarized in the statement that value cannot properly be defined as a character supervening upon an object because interest is taken in it, for the reason that in all cases where the object is transcendent to the subject no such value can be found in it. This, however, is just one reason. There are others, as we shall see.

But before investigating these, let us examine another possibility: that having value is not being an actual object of interest, but being a potential one. The "gem of purest ray serene" buried in the earth has value as a potentiality of providing satisfaction. This potentiality, it is claimed, belongs to it even if no one ever digs it up and enjoys it. And it is a property of the gem just as real and objective as its physical hardness or specific gravity, which are also potentialities of experience although of experience of a different kind. All properties of objects are in fact such, so that value properties are in no sense unique. The existence of such properties is expressed in contrary-to-fact propositions. For example, salt has the property of solubility in water. We may therefore express it as: "If this salt had been placed in water, it would have been dissolved," in this way indicating that the property exists even if no one tests for it. Similarly, the property of beauty in the gem may be expressed as: "If anyone had seen the gem he would have had an aesthetic experience." This concept of value as a property assumes importance in the eyes of C. I. Lewis as a way of saving the "objectivity" of values.

The view is intriguing but will not, I believe, stand up under vigorous analysis. For one thing there is a crucial difference between "value properties" and the properties studied in the physical sciences, namely, that under standard test conditions the former are not always observable, whereas the latter are. Given standard test conditions *everyone* will have the specifiable experiences of the chemical and physical properties of the gem, but not everyone under those same conditions will experience it as beautiful. For example, if I feel that diamonds are a senseless luxury of the rich, I may experience repulsion instead of attraction toward the gem. Now of course it is true that we can, as Lewis attempts to do, specify further conditions for the experience of beauty in the gem—one might be the absence of the kind of prejudice mentioned. But now observe, this sort of condition would be a potentiality of the brain. So, I would remark, would be the color of the gem, which is closely bound up with its beauty. In short, when one is concerned with the so-called "beauty" of valued objects—and this would be true to an even greater extent of works of art—the potentialities are "located" rather in the brain than in the so-called object. But to assert this is to assert in different language all that anyone has ever meant by the "subjectivity" of beauty. Everyone has recognized that if we specify a sufficient number of "brain conditions," we can predict the probable existence of an aesthetic experience of a general type in any individual. We never can, however—and this is an important point—predict the full aesthetic experience without taking into account the *individual brain;* which means that we can never state *in general terms* what the full aesthetic experience would be. In this respect, value potentialities differ radically from physical potentialities, which can always be expressed in adequate general terms.

The recrudescence of the concept of the potential under the name of "property" is one of the startling *volte-faces* of contemporary philosophy. It is especially interesting in that it is due largely to empiricists and logical positivists—thinkers most loud in their repudiation of the Aristotelian and scholastic categories. And when *all* the properties of things are interpreted as potentialities, a step has been taken beyond Aristotle himself. One begins to wonder what the thing is that *has* these properties; what, for example, it is to which beauty is ascribed? Is the thing a mere *x*, a *Ding an sich,* the analogue of Aristotle's matter; or is it perhaps just the class of properties (or powers, in the Lockian sense)? That a thing must be something more than a class of potentialities seems to me evident, for every potentiality must have a basis in actuality. And if this is so, it becomes clear that a potentiality (or a property so interpreted) is not itself a real quality or character of anything, but the expression of a well-based expectation that a certain entity exerting control over experience will, under specifiable conditions, probably cause, or could have caused under similar conditions, a certain effect in our experience. Formally stated, if it is true that when A and C have constantly interacted under specifiable conditions an effect B (say beauty) has regularly appeared in C, to say that A has the property of beauty means nothing more than the expectation that B will probably occur again under similar conditions; it does not mean that A has some B-ish character. So, to say that "a gem of purest ray serene" *is* beautiful does not imply *any* special element in the gem above its physical and chemical nature, and to ascribe beauty to it as a property is, to say the least, misleading. The physicochemical nature of the gem is the sole and sufficient basis for the effect of beauty, in co-operation, of course, with the percipient of the gem.

More fundamental, however, than any of the considerations so far advanced against the identification of value with the object, either as something actual or as something potential, are two further points: first, that value positive or negative does not arise until desire is assuaged or frustrated; and second, that there are values without objects. The mere fact that there is desire for something does not create value either in the subject, as true value, or in the object, as what I call "attributed" value. A value is either positive or negative, it is either a good or an evil, but mere interest in, or desire for, an object does not establish the one or the other. The polarity of value is potential in interest but becomes actual there only as desire is assuaged or frustrated. Wanting something *seems* to give it attributed value because I commonly anticipate (hopefully) that it will be mine; that is to say, it will assuage my desire. Before I get it, then, I possess it imaginatively; this imaginative satisfaction *is* its value. Similarly, a thing is not evil merely by being in relation to desire; it becomes evil by frustrating desire. When it seems to be evil before it actually frustrates me, that is because I anticipate frustration: I experience imaginative frustration. For example, suppose that I want to make an ally of A, who has been neutral in a conflict in which I am engaged. A then comes into relation to my desire or, in Perry's language, becomes an object of interest. But so far there is no value to be attributed to A, either positive or negative. The most one could say is that A would be valuable as my ally, but then one could also say that A would be evil as an enemy. But A *is* a value (to use Perry's language) only when A joins my team and an evil only when he joins the other team. If again A seems to have great (positive) value while I am wooing him (her, or it) that is because I am getting imaginative satisfaction in anticipating success and objectifying this satisfaction in him.

A final point that can be made against the theory that value is the object of interest, or a predicate or property of the object of interest, is the seeming existence of values without objects. This evidence is perhaps not conclusive but is worth assessing. Usually, as will be noted in the chapter on the analysis of value, desires are directed toward objects, but in certain unusual ex-

periences of depression or elation, whether normal or pathologi-
cal, there occur longings and satisfactions or dissatisfactions
which seem not to be longings for anything or satisfaction or
dissatisfaction over anything. If you ask the depressed or elated
person who or what his depression or elation is concerned with,
he will often say that he does not know—that he is just merry
or unhappy. Sometimes also we know that we want *something*,
but what we want we do not know. Among normal experience
of this kind, the best example is absolute music. The musical
experience is, as Schopenhauer has phrased it, the expression of
pure will apart from representation or idea of any objects; it is
objectless emotion—objectless happiness or objectless despair.
Of course, when there is a program, as in song or opera, these
emotions are given definite ideal objects. The happiness in
Mozart's Symphony No. 40 and the despair in Tchaikovsky's
Pathétique are pure objectless value. It is wrong to say that it is
happiness *over* the tones, for it is happiness *in* the tones; they
are media, not objects of the primary musical experience, even
as my happiness is not *over* or *about* my words, but *in* them
when I say, "How happy I am!" To be sure, I may make the
music, reflectively, an object of critical aesthetic approval or
disapproval, when the satisfaction or dissatisfaction does have
the tones as objects, but that is a secondary not a primary musical experience.

So far as I can judge, the only way to try to destroy this evidence would be to allege that there are *subconscious* objects of
desire in all cases of seeming objectless interest or desire.

When there is pathology, psychoanalysis seems to reveal such
objects. A highly successful businessman, honored by his asso-
ciates, finds that when he attends a meeting of directors he is
beset with a feeling of inferiority, insecurity, and guilt for which
there is no known reason in any of the circumstances of his life.
All of his dealings with other businessmen have been exem-
plary; in fact he is regarded by them as a model of probity and
kindness. In his relation with his family also there is no taint.

Analysis reveals, however, that when a boy on the farm where he was brought up he committed what most people would regard as a grave sin. His feeling of guilt or inferiority was not therefore, it could be alleged, an objectless emotion after all, for it had an object, only a forgotten one. Following this analogy one might claim that musical satisfactions and dissatisfactions are, as it were, the emotional residues, experienced in summary form, of countless attitudes toward objects, long forgotten but now reawakened and embodied in tones.

It is doubtful, however, whether the evidence from objectless values can be destroyed in this way. After all, what psychoanalysis reveals is only their history. It shows that without objects they never would have arisen; it does not prove that as they now exist they have objects. This seems to me to be particularly true in the special case of music, in the experience of which the individual may far transcend any of his own past object-tied emotions.

The question as to whether there are values without objects has a bearing on the last statement of the theory of value which I am considering—the statement namely that value is the existence of an "interest relation" between a subject A and an object B. If this statement is merely equivalent, as it is asserted to be, to the definition of value as a relational predicate in B, when A is interested in B, then we have already dealt with it. Formally considered, it cannot be equivalent, for, although a relational character is always acquired by B, when there is a relation of any kind between A and B, the existence of the relation means more than that.[3] Although it may seem to some readers that we shall be indulging in useless subtleties, it will be worth while in the end to consider the definition of value as the existence of an interest relation for its own sake.

[3] Even in the case of so-called external relations, such as spatial relations, it can be shown that this is true. See *Experience and Substance* (Ann Arbor: Univ. Michigan Press, 1941), Chs. X and XI.

The first matter to decide is whether interest is a relation. That in most cases where interest exists there is a relation, and that we often speak of it as if it were a relation, there can be no doubt. If A loves B, we speak of a loving relationship between A and B. Notice that in those cases A's love has an existing object B. We also speak of there being something between A and B, where "between" obviously signifies a relationship. Notice that both A and B are affected by the relationship. Observe further that there is a special tie or bond between A and B, which creates through its tension a dynamic configuration or *Gestalt* in which both A and B participate. This situation contains all the features characteristic of a relationship: at least two elements, each of which "acquires" a character due to the situation, and a unity between them. Moreover, there is no doubt that A's love *creates* the tie and therewith the relational predicate of B. Finally, such words as "love," "hate," etc., are relation words: words such that if they are used in such a phrase as "A loves" (or "A hates," etc.) the phrase is incomplete and must be supplemented with some term like B in order to complete it.

On the other hand, there is evidence that interest is not itself a relation, although I would insist that it creates a relation or depends on a relation (language in recognizing such words as "desire," "loves," "is interested in," etc., fails to make this distinction). If there are interests without objects, as I have claimed there are, then interest is not by itself a relation, for there is no relation without at least two terms. Further evidence to this same effect is provided by desires which have not yet found or created objects, for example, my desire to build a house. Obviously, I cannot want to build a house if I already have a house. To be sure, in this situation there is a concept of a house and perhaps an image of a dream house, but I do not want either. An image or a concept of a house would hardly give me shelter from the cold or provide me a bedroom, study, bath, and kitchen. I desire *through* the concept or image. I do not desire them. In such cases desire cannot be a relation, but it is clear that in seeking or trying to create objects, desire tends to create a relationship between the person who has the desire and its objects, when they come into existence. And when the situation "A is interested in B, where B is a real object" does exist, we could call the interest an interest relation, meaning the kind of relation between A and B that is determined by the interest.

Now if one wishes to call this situation value, that is at one's pleasure. But it is open to all the objections alleged by us against the alternative interpretation of value as a relational predicate of an object when interest is taken in the object. The most telling of these objections holds—that value positive is the assuagement and value negative is the frustration of the interest: the mere existence of the interest does not as such create value. I feel in reading both Perry and Prall that when they use the term "interest" they are thinking of it as either assuaged or frustrated.

Since G. E. Moore has very largely repudiated his own theory, one might think that there was no need to discuss it. If this were so, we might be thankful, for his theory has in my opinion lain like an incubus upon ethical discussion for the last half century. One could, in fact, say of him, what James said of Bradley, that "he messed up philosophy to such an extent that it would require a generation to get it straight again." Yet interestingly enough, there are thinkers (in England) who accept the younger as against the older Moore's beliefs (and why shouldn't they: it has not been proved that philosophers grow wiser as they grow older); and even if a person such as myself finds little in the younger Moore's theories to applaud, he has to admit Moore's service in providing rigor of thinking in a field where it has been notably lacking. I shall not, however, cover the entire ground again, since it has been thoroughly gone over in the Moore-Schlipp [3a] volume, but will limit myself to showing how it stands in relation to the theory defended in this book.

According to the younger Moore, value or the good is an objective, nonnaturalistic, simple, indefinable predicate. In charac-

[3a] *The Philosophy of G. E. Moore,* ed. Paul A. Schlipp (Evanston: Northwestern Univ. Press, 1942).

terizing the good as objective, Moore's theory is the same as one or the other of the foregoing views and is accordingly subject to all the criticisms that can be directed against them. I shall not try to determine with which of these it is identical. The uniqueness of Moore's theory is expressed in the last three characteristics: "nonnaturalistic," "simple," and "indefinable." The first of these is the most challenging to thought and has been widely commented upon. I shall interpret it as meaning that when I ascribe value to an object, I am not ascribing to it any predicate that can be found by a "scientific" study of the object: "The rose is beautiful" is not a sentence to be found in books of botany. Although this is true, as we have had many occasions to remark, it is not true because "good" expresses a peculiar property of the object, but because it expresses *no property* of the object but merely as Kant would say "how I take it"—my attitude toward it reflected into the object again in the words of Kant it is not a logical but a reflective property. Understood in this way I myself would assert that good is a nonnaturalistic property and would insist that the natural sciences, insofar as they study the properties of things apart from their relation to centers of feeling, cannot decide questions concerning aesthetics or morals. I cannot help feeling that Moore had a partial awareness that this was the state of affairs when he characterized the good as "nonnaturalistic."

The problem of the definability of "good" can be solved only after deciding which one of these four meanings of definition is intended: (1) Ostensive, or definition by pointing. (2) Aristotelian, or definition by assigning the genus and differentia; as, "Man is a rational animal." (3) Relational; as, "Truman is the President of the U.S.A." (4) Analytical; as, "A brother is a male sibling."

Since, according to Moore, good is analogous to yellow, we can test the indefinability of good by testing that of yellow in the various senses of definition offered. We immediately see that: in sense (1) yellow is definable, since we can point to

somebody's tie and say that it is yellow; in sense (2) it is indefinable, since although we can say that yellow is a color, thus
giving its genus, we cannot assign any differentia to yellow that
would distinguish it from green or blue, except by using definitions in sense (3); in sense (3) yellow is definable as the one and
only color caused by a certain vibration rate; and in sense (4)
it is indefinable if it is simple, as Moore takes it to be. This last,
I may remark, is probably the sense in which Moore means that
both the good and yellow are indefinable (for only such a concept as brother, which combines the two concepts of maleness
and a common parentage, can be analyzed).

The question whether good is definable ostensively is not so
simple as it seems. If definition were a purely first-personal
process, then, from our point of view, it would be definable because each individual could point to satisfaction in himself and
say to himself, "That is what I mean by value." But having done
that, how could he tell another by pointing that that was what
he meant by value? In the case of yellow, it is claimed that I can
define the term by pointing because when I point to a yellow
surface my fellow man will also see yellow if he is not color-
blind; whereas I cannot point to anything that he will experience when I say "That is value" but only to a behavioral expression of value. I can point to the look of contentment on his
face but not to contentment itself. Similarly, I cannot point to
frustration and say *that* is evil; I can only point to tears and
wringing of the hands and drawn lines on his face. This, by the
way, is the basis of the demand for a behavioral interpretation
of value.

There is, however, a curious fallacy in this line of reasoning.
It assumes that the so-called behavior of a person is more capable of being pointed out than are his feelings. But his behavior, strictly speaking, consists of visual and tonal configurations in my own experience. Hence when I point to his behavior
I point to something that lies within my experience just as my
own satisfaction does. Of course, I assume that he has similar

configurations in his experience, so that when I say "wringing hands" he hears something similar to what I hear and sees something similar to what I see; hence the words "wringing hands" mean to him what they mean to me. But I also assume, and in general with as good right, that when I say "wringing hands" he will get an experience of sorrow. The child in fact learns the meaning of the word "sorrow" just as he learns the meaning of "wringing hands." Take the simplest case. How does he learn the meaning of the word "pain"? He burns himself, he hurts himself, he is spanked; on each occasion I say "pain." I hear the word, he hears a similar sound, and that sound is associated with a common factor in his experience, a factor just as real and immediate as the sound "pain" or the sensations involved in seeing the pin that pricks, the fire that burns, or the rod that chastises.

My conclusion from this discussion is that value can be defined ostensively, just as yellow can. We are left then with the problem as to whether it can be defined in senses (2) and (4), in which yellow—and therefore good—are assumed to be indefinable. Both these senses are easily seen to be one, for Aristotelian is a species of analytic definition: "Man is a rational animal" is an analysis of man and is formally the same as the analytic definition of brother as male sibling, in which sibling is genus and male is differentia. And from our standpoint it is evident that good can be defined analytically; our definition of generic good as desire being assuaged is an analytic definition in which desire is the analogue of sibling and being assuaged is the analogue of male. The notion of good, unlike yellow, requires *two* concepts for its explication: desire and assuaging. Nevertheless, as Santayana remarked some time ago, there is a kind of simplicity, and to that extent indefinability, in good. But this simplicity and indefinability is no different from that which attaches to any definable or analyzable complex and expresses the form or *Gestalt* quality, as Ernst Mach called it, of the complex as a whole. The good (and the evil too) does have its peculiar tang, as unique as yellow or the taste of a lemon. This is the element of truth in Moore's view.

Another theory of value which contrasts in many ways with my own is that of John Dewey. This is a far more complex theory than Moore's. Many of its facets will engage our attention in other parts of this treatise; at the moment only that one of its aspects which has to do with value in the generic sense will be considered.

Dewey rejects desire as the fundamental value fact in favor of need or lack on the ground that desire has its roots in need or lack. My desire for food, for example, depends on a certain lack of nutriment in the organism; my desire for water on a need for water. However, while no one would deny this relation of at least the "bodily" desires to organic states, it is hard to see its relevance to a theory of the essential nature of value. For it is the satisfaction of these dependent desires that is value, not the mere relief of the need. The mere replenishment of the body with food or water would no more be productive of value without the experience of desire and assuagement than would the stoking of a furnace with coal and the filling of the attached humidifying pan with water. And while these *urgent* needs and their removal are closer to desire and satisfaction than is the air we breathe and the sunshine we bask in, the last are as necessary for the existence of human values as are the first; yet no one would dream of identifying value with them *per se*. For the practical enterprise of creating values it is, to be sure, important to realize the dependence of desires on needs, for in order to satisfy the desires we must minister to the needs. But if we were to ask, why minister to needs, the answer is inevitable—in order to provide felt satisfaction—thus showing that satisfaction is the end, the value, and the ministering to need is merely a means to that end. We could ask the same question with regard to clothes and air and sunlight; we should get the same answer, and it would be sufficient.

For another reason also Dewey insists that desire and satisfaction are not ultimate; namely, that both are appraised in terms of the cost of the means required for their fulfillment. If this cost is too great, they may be judged as foolish or extravagant, and therefore as far from being good. Genuine good or value, he tells us, consists rather in the resolution of conflicts among desires leading to a "co-ordinate or unified organization of activities." [4] More explicitly, he says in another place: "Good consists in the meaning that is experienced to belong to an activity when entanglement of various incompatible impulses and habits terminates in an orderly release in action." [5] In the *Theory of Valuation*, Dewey says to the same effect: "Ends in view are appraised as *good* or *bad* on the ground of their serviceability in the direction of behavior dealing with states of affairs found to be objectionable because of some lack or conflict in them." [6] One may think of this process as occurring either within an individual, between individuals, or between groups. In the end, however, social conflicts and adjustments issue in individual conflicts and adjustments and, for all his stressing of the social, it is there, I believe Dewey would agree, that the good is born. Now no one, least of all myself, who will try to show its transcendent importance, would question the good of harmony; still it is essential to realize that this good is not the generic good, but, as we shall show, an aspect of the highest order good and that its own goodness issues from the fulfillment of desire, which therefore stands as the generic good. For what makes the resolution of conflict a good is the fact that, through conciliation, compromise, and integration, competing desires, frustrated through mutual interference, acquire some measure of assuagement. This is "the meaning that attaches to an activity when it

[4] *Theory of Valuation* (Chicago: Univ. Chicago Press, 1939), p. 49.

[5] *Human Nature and Conduct* (New York: Henry Holt & Co., 1922), p. 211.

[6] P. 47.

terminates in an orderly release in action." And the assessment of a desire in terms of cost is always in the interest of some other desire that would be frustrated by a too lavish expenditure of means. We abandon the costly desires in order that we may have some means left for the fulfillment of those that are for each one of us more important or higher.

Moreover, this sort of definition of good is subject to a further defect—its failure to provide for a hierarchy of values. I can explain how great this fault is in the following way. Let us think of a band of "aggressor" nations beset with conflicts of interests among themselves. Let us next imagine their making the necessary compromises in order that a grand strategy may be worked out capable of finding "an orderly release in action," resulting in the conquest of other peoples. Would the harmony so attained be good? Yes, from the point of view of the alliance, since it would provide its members maximum satisfaction; but not from the point of view of those who would condemn it as evil in the specifically moral sense of that term. One might, to be sure, demur that no "true" resolution of conflicts would have taken place in the imagined circumstances unless room were found for the welfare of defeated nations. But why this should be given any consideration is hard to deduce from Dewey's principle. The decision to extend the resolution of conflicts to the interests of others besides one's own rests on a preference for love over selfishness; apart from charity, apart from tenderness toward the dream of each individual, no alien interests can claim consideration. The only possible reason for admitting the claim on Dewey's principle would be that otherwise the neglected interests would find strength later on to renew the fight. A permanent resolution of conflicts, a secure peace, must provide some satisfaction for all desires. But suppose we destroy the alien interests, even as the S.S. tried to do when they set up their murder factory at Maidenek. The Poles were trouble makers in the Nazi harmony—was it not right therefore to "liquidate" them? One cannot answer this question in terms of an ethics based on harmony alone.

Another important point in Dewey's theory of value is his conviction that the good, defined as a harmony of interests, can be secured through the instrumentality of the social sciences. Many would regard this as one of his great contributions to philosophy. It would seem in fact that according to him ethics will become a sort of synthesis of the social sciences. But this faith in science "dates" Dewey as belonging definitely to the nineteenth rather than to the twentieth century, where it is on the decline. His belief in the efficacy of discussion as the method whereby the knowledge embodied in the social sciences can be applied to the resolution of conflicts is another rationalistic note in his philosophy. I judge by recent statements by him that the war has not dimmed this faith, because he feels that the social sciences were too young, that their prestige was not sufficiently well established to permit of their being fairly tried in the crises that led up to World War II. *Il faut pardonner beaucoup à la jeunesse!* But it is very clear to me that ethics cannot be identified with any organization of the social sciences, and that there are definite limitations to the use of discussion as a method for the realization of the good. Why and how ethics is true will be shown in our chapter on the Relativity of Values.

The last theory that I wish to contrast with that of this volume was derived historically from Kant's distinction between the categorical and the conditional imperative, was represented in Germany by Rickert and Windelband, and is now professed by such thinkers as Ross and Ewing in England and by Urban in America. Inevitably, there are differences between the views of these and other writers, some clinging more and others less to G. E. Moore, who has strongly influenced this school in England, and others breaking more completely with him. We may call the theory the "right" theory for a brief characterization; the theory that value cannot be expressed without the use of an imperative term such as "right" and that this term is unanalyzable and "nonnaturalistic." The good, it is said, is not what I want or the satisfaction of want, but what I ought to want, even as beauty is not what I enjoy in art but what I ought to enjoy, and truth not what I believe but what I ought to believe. One can see from this brief statement of the theory that the polemic against the kind of view called "naturalistic" is very important in the eyes of these writers. I shall accordingly begin my consideration of it by examining the objections to the "desire theory," as they have been formulated by a recent writer, A. C. Ewing.[7]

1. It is claimed that such a definition of good as "what satisfies desire" or "the appeasing of desire" is invalid because it can be denied without self-contradiction. In other words, it is conceivable that something else might be good. To my thinking, however, this is a mistake, when by good is meant "generic good." It *seems* to be true only when "good" is used in some *specific* sense as morally good, when the satisfaction of some desires is not good in that sense, although it is still good in the generic sense.

2. No collection of statistics can settle the question as to the nature of the good. Of course not, since the good is always individual. But that the good is an indefinable imperative does not follow.

3. Obligation cannot be derived from desire because I may be obliged to do what is contrary to desire. We have already discussed this objection and shall have more to say in rebuttal in our chapter on Moral Values. To summarize briefly what has been said and what will be said: obligation is a complex concept, analogous to the moral good, expressive of a specific desire in response to the desires of other persons; it cannot therefore be defined in terms of desire *as such,* but nevertheless can be derived from a specific desire. I am, therefore, never obliged to do what is contrary to *all* desires, but only what is contrary to

[7] *The Definition of Good* (New York: Macmillan, 1947), pp. 74-75.

some desires. Hence when I say, "I ought to," I do mean "I want to." It is impossible and inconceivable that I ought to do anything that someone else does not want me to do and that I myself do not want to do in response to what he wants. You cannot find the ought outside the circle of desire and satisfaction. When I tell someone that he ought to enjoy Haydn's Quartets, I am saying in effect, "I want you to enjoy them since I am interested in your happiness, and if you expose yourself to them and study them carefully, you will enjoy them." But if he shows that he *cannot* enjoy them, it is meaningless for me to say to him that he ought to enjoy them or for him to say that he ought to. Even so, if I say to an alcoholic, "You ought to stop drinking," I am saying, "I want you to stop drinking because you will be happier if you do stop," and if he says to himself, "I ought to stop drinking," he is saying in effect, "I want to stop drinking (although at the same time I also know that I want to drink) because if I stop I shall be happier and those whom I love will be happier."

4. Another point made by Ewing against the interpretation of obligation in terms of desire is that whereas the former depends on the properties of objects, desire does not. It is conceivable, he says, that with regard to any object, I may not desire it, but it is inconceivable with regard to some objects that I should not have a duty toward them. Now the first part of this statement strikes me as very strange, to say the least. If I desire food, it seems to me inconceivable that I should not want an object that has the properties of food. Of course, I may not act upon this desire but that is another matter. I fear Mr. Ewing commits the fallacy of regarding the ego as something apart from desires, and of viewing desire as unrelated to the things that might satisfy it. Since for me duty is expressive of a kind of desire, I can accordingly agree with him about the latter part of his assertions, properly qualified. To see just what he means let us examine some of his illustrations. He says, "I ought to

dislike cruelty," "I ought to love good parents." [8] Seemingly the obligation to dislike cruelty or to love good parents depends upon the nature of cruelty itself and of good (kind?) parents as such. Merely by knowing what cruelty is or by knowing what good parents are I can deduce my obligation to hate the one and to love the other. This would be a case of the synthetic a priori in the field of ethics. Now I do not doubt that for Ewing this is true. He is by tradition and environment subject to the demands formulated in the Christian code of morals. The very thoughts of kindness in parents and of cruelty induce a love of the one and a dislike of the other in his kindly and grateful nature. His saying that he ought to feel so is only another way of saying that he does feel so. But a person not brought up thus, or a person not so responsive to love as he is, would not necessarily feel so. One might, of course, say that he ought to feel so. But in saying this I am making a demand upon him, even as Ewing would if he said so; I am trying to awaken horror of cruelty and gratitude to good parents. I am asserting my own sense of values, seeking to make them effective in the world. Yet if I could get no response, if I had to do with a person utterly cruel and indifferent to kindness, I should cease to say that he ought, for it would be meaningless to say so, as it would be meaningless to say to a tiger that he ought to dislike cruelty. That obligation, like desire, is two-sided, depending not only on the nature of objects but also on the nature of men and their circumstances, is admitted by Ewing, surprisingly, when he tells us that the holding of slaves in antiquity was not necessarily wrong. In other words, we could not *deduce* its wrongness from its mere nature.

Let it not be supposed, of course, that I am arguing that Ewing or myself should not dislike cruelty or should not love kind parents. Of course, we should! What I am arguing is that obligation is personal—a deed or choice of the individual self

[8] *Op. cit.,* p. 120.

with relation to objects, no doubt, but not out of relation to subjects. To infer, as Ewing does, that I could just as well *not* be obliged as I am obliged is utterly to fail to understand obligation. I might as well infer that, being in love, I could not desire to be near my beloved or, being hungry, I could not want to eat the food that is placed before me. And the same is naturally true of all persons minded like Ewing and me.

5. Finally, Ewing tells us that ethics cannot be stated in terms of desire because its concepts are generically different from those of psychology or any empirical science, and desire and satisfaction are empirical psychological concepts. This thesis contains some error but also, I believe, a grain of hidden truth, but a truth from which the doctrines of Ewing and his school cannot be deduced. I have tried to show that obligation is a species of desire, and I shall presently show that his "fittingness" is also. So, if these are the basic ethical concepts, and desire and satisfaction are psychological concepts, it follows that ethical concepts *are* of the nature of psychological ones. One reason why Ewing thinks they are not is because of his obsolete view of psychology He thinks of psychology in its associationist phase, as represented say by James Mill and Alexander Bain; he is seemingly unaware of dynamic and *Gestalt* psychology, in which such a matter as desire may come alive and be presented in its relation to other desires in a complex structure of demand and response. Another reason, I believe, is that Ewing feels, although he does not say as much, the difference between science and life, knowing and doing. Now, as has already been shown, it is one thing to know about a desire—or an obligation—and another thing to feel a desire or an obligation, or as I might perhaps better say, be a desiring or an obligated person. Ethics is not psychology, not knowledge; it is an expression of living deeds and choices, and while its stuff is the same in both, it is one thing to know that stuff, another thing to be it. The notion of nature and consequently of naturalistic is a strangely limited

one. But nature as the mother of us all contains both our deeds and our descriptions of those deeds.

Perhaps enough has already been said in criticism of the notion of obligation as basic to value theory—or if enough has not yet been said, more will be said in the chapter on Moral Values—yet it remains to say something concerning the relatively novel concept of "fittingness," which Ewing regards as underlying obligation.

It is interesting to notice that Ewing breaks definitely, though reluctantly, with the view of G. E. Moore that there is an indefinable, objective, nonnatural predicate "good." In his own words, "We are not clearly aware of an indefinable non-natural goodness, but we are of fittingness and obligation." [9] Moreover he thinks he can define good in terms of ought or fittingness as "a fitting object of a pro-attitude"—a pro-attitude being a favorable attitude, one that tends to bring the object into existence or to conserve it. One may, I believe, translate this definition into our own language, and get rid of the barbarous term "pro-attitude," as "good is a fitting object of desire." Moral obligation is not the same as fittingness, for " 'fittingness' stands for a relation between an action and its environment, moral obligation is something analogous to an imperative on the agent." [10] The morally obligatory is further defined, showing its dependence on fittingness as follows: "It is morally obligatory for an agent to do A where he thinks A the most fitting action in his power and where it is both possible for him to do and also possible for him not to do A." [11] If we ask why an object A is the fitting object of a pro-attitude, we are told that it lies in the natural, factual characteristics of A itself; for instance, the characteristic of pleasantness possessed by certain experiences or the characteristic which certain acts have of being the fulfillment

[9] Ewing, op. cit., p. 178.
[10] Ibid., p. 133.
[11] Ibid., p. 135.

of promises. This does not mean, however, that because the object is fitting for a pro-attitude that one does, as a matter of fact, take this attitude; it remains fitting for the attitude whether it is taken or not.

In exchanging the property of intrinsic goodness for the relational property of fittingness one does not, however, avoid any of the fundamental difficulties of the former. For it is just as hard to see how a thing is a priori fitting, apart from a real context of wishes, expectations, and circumstances, as to see that it is intrinsically good. This is revealed very clearly in Ewing's own discussion of promise-keeping and other prima facie duties, where it is shown that the mere fact by itself that I have made a promise does not make it obligatory or fitting that I should always keep it. For example, he says, "There would be no point in keeping a promise if it did not give any satisfaction at all to anybody, even the promisee." [12] It is even admitted that it was fitting and morally right for the German soldier to fight in the last war if he thought he was doing his duty.

Although fittingness (why not fitness?) is a genuine thing, as is obligation, a few examples will show that it is not a priori or unanalyzable. Let us begin with the obviously conventional level, where, however, we shall see that a moral aspect is not entirely absent. It used to be fitting for widows to dress in black for some time after the death of their husbands, and it is still fitting for them to dress in black at funerals. But that this fitness is not a priori is shown by the fact that in China not black but white is the color deemed appropriate in mourning. It is fitting in our culture, therefore, for the widow to dress in black at a funeral because people desire and expect it and are accustomed to it. For us it has become a symbol of sorrow, which the mourner wants and her friends want to express. If the widow appeared at the funeral dressed in a gay red she would disappoint and pain her friends: there would thus be a certain aspect

[12] *Ibid.*, p. 208.

of the selfish and immoral in her behavior. That fitness on such occasions is not purely "subjective" follows from the fact that it is based on the expectations of members of the individual's group, and expectations are as real as sticks and stones.

There is another sense of fitness, which is not so much conventional as "natural." To want pleasant food, to desire the female of the species, is fitting, not because of convention or custom but, as we say, because these desires are natural and to fail to have them is "unnatural," "abnormal." Especially unfitting are the cases in which desires are fixed on unwholesome substances, as sometimes happens among children, or on persons of the same sex: these we say are "perversions." But such kinds of unfitness are clearly relative to what we call the purposes of nature, self-preservation and species preservation. If we deny the existence of these purposes, as most materialists do, there is nothing unfitting in the desires specified except insofar as custom—which is a tissue of expectations and desires on the social level—forbids them. These materialistic views regarding sexual deviations are in fact becoming so common that "abnormality" and "perverseness" are denied of them—anything that is, we are told, is natural.

On the more explicitly moral level let us examine Ewing's own example that we "ought to love good parents," where obligation rests on the fittingness of love for good parents. This is an excellent example, because it involves more than one level of fittingness. For not to love good parents would be regarded by most people as "unnatural"—contrary to nature—as well as "wrong" in the strict moral sense. It is unnatural because it is unexpected, unusual, since kindness ordinarily inspires gratitude; and it is unnatural in a richer sense since not to be kind to those who are kind to us defeats our desire for our own welfare, which may depend on the help of our parents who need our help. There is an underlying purposiveness in returning kindness, even as there is a purposiveness in feeling resentment at injuries, since the resentment seems to injure those who injure us and hence to protect us. We reach the strictly moral level when we realize that it is wrong not to love kind parents because the failure to do so violates *our own* love for our parents. It is clear from Ewing's book that he loves his parents; he stands in that love and wishes all children to love their parents, even as he does. Once more we find duty as the expression of a demand, a desire—not as something irrelevant to desire.

Thus far, I have tried to show how fittingness is meaningless in abstraction from desire, but have said little or nothing more about the relation itself. However, the relation seems to me to be essentially the same as that which philosophers from the time of Pythagoras have called "harmony," which will be examined carefully in a subsequent chapter. In order to complete the argument of this chapter, let us anticipate by stating that harmony (and therefore fittingness) signifies a "co-operation" of such a kind as to realize a purpose and therefore to create a value (satisfaction). So, to reinterpret the examples already cited, there is co-operation between the widow who wears her weeds and those who demand that she do so, from which arises the cathartic value of the funeral rite; there is co-operation between male and female when they desire each other, from which the joy of a new life may come; co-operation again between the kind parent and the grateful child by means of which the happiness of both parent and child is created and maintained. Whether on the conventional, natural, or moral level, the most fitting thing or act is the one which co-operates most effectively to realize some purpose. But co-operation is in no way "non-natural"; it is, as we have shown, deeply rooted in universal nature.

CHAPTER III

THE EXPRESSION OF VALUE

IT IS not without significance for an understanding of the general approach to problems characteristic of modern philosophy that, beginning with Kant, the nature of value has been studied through an analysis of value *statements.* At first sight, at least, this would seem to be a curiously roundabout method; for why not study value directly? One could, I suppose, study roses by investigating the sentences botanists and poets have used concerning them; but, in the end, one would have to leave the library for the garden. So one would expect the philosopher to pass eventually from scrutiny of expressions of value to scrutiny of value itself as it is lived or directly discovered. Yet there is good reason why the analogy drawn is not entirely valid. For if (as we all believe) other people as well as we ourselves experience values, we can come to know or share their values only by way of their expressions. I can presumably go into the garden and find the same rose that you find, but I cannot go there or anywhere else and find your values. If the rose has beauty for you, I cannot discover that fact along with the rose in the gar-

60

den, but only when I hear you say "How beautiful!" Similarly, if I wanted to know your moral judgment about a man, I could not find it anywhere in the world except through some expression of disdain or qualified admiration. Or how could I study the moral sentiments of the ancient Hebrews except by reading the text of the Ten Commandments, the Prophets, or the Book of Leviticus?

There is another reason also. Philosophers have been more interested in knowledge than in anything else—a prejudice, doubtless, yet undeniable. Hence in their study of values, of aesthetics, and of ethics, their interest has centered largely in comparing these fields with science. Now science, mathematical, physical, and historical, is achieved and preserved through such expressions as "7 plus 5 equals 12," "$G = \dfrac{m_1\, m_2\, K}{D^2}$," "Caesar crossed the Rubicon." It has become a matter of great importance, therefore, to compare such expressions with the kind that occurs in morals, in poetry, and in law.

The comparison between scientific expressions and value expressions has, indeed, been a favorite starting point for the investigation of values ever since Kant introduced this approach; and to follow him in it will serve us very well, too.

Accordingly, let us begin by setting side by side two expressions: (1) The earth is roundish. (2) The earth is beautiful. Structurally, they seem to be very much alike. Both have subjects, apparently the same in each—"the earth." Both have "predicates"—"roundish" in the one, "beautiful" in the other. And the predicates are applied to the subjects by means of the same connective—"is." But it would be a mistake to infer from this formal similarity that the two are of the same essential kind. A circumstance that leads us to suspect that they are not is the fact that the one belongs to science and the other does not. You can find "roundish" in books on geography and astronomy, but not "beautiful." No man of science would admit it among the sentences in his work; or, if he did, its presence would cause surprise, or even some loss of reputation. On the other hand, one might find it in a book of poetry or essays without its arousing the least bit of astonishment or censure. And if we reexamine the two sentences we can easily see why this is so. Obviously, the reason cannot lie in the subjects, since they are the same, or in the connective, which is also the same; it must therefore lie in the predicates. In the one case, the predicate describes the subject and thereby expresses its nature; in the other case, the predicate does not tell us anything about the subject's nature but, as Kant said, how we take it. The one communicates something about the earth as it is for itself; the other about ourselves, in relation to it. Since, therefore, astronomy and geography are concerned with the earth and not with the way we feel toward it, the first sentence belongs to those sciences but the second does not. Since poetry and essays are concerned with how we feel, the second sentence might properly belong to them.

There is a whole class of similar sentences in which we should find the same situation—sentences formally like "The earth is roundish," but unlike it in the kind of predicates they contain, all of which express our ways of feeling or attitudes rather than the nature of the subject of the sentences. Examples of this class are: (3) "Stealing is wrong"; (4) "Smoking is pleasant." In these cases, too, the predicate is, as G. E. Moore would say, nonnaturalistic, which we may define in our own way as, "not expressing the nature of the subject (object) independent of its relation to us," which is contrary to what the natural sciences would demand, or at least what they hope to achieve.

There is another difference between the two types of sentences: the one is a complete meaning, the other is not but has to be supplemented in a very revealing fashion. "The earth is roundish" says exactly what is necessary, and that is that; but "the earth is beautiful," while tied—so to speak—at one end, the subject end, is not tied securely at the other end, but—again so to speak—is a little loose at the mooring, for the earth might not be beautiful to you. Hence, in order to complete the sentence,

I must add "for me"; or I could add "for you," if that is what
I meant, or more generally, "for you or me," or still more generally, "for somebody." On the other hand, when I say that
"the earth is roundish," I do not mean that it is roundish for
me, or for you, or for somebody—I mean it is roundish *an sich*,
just roundish, independent of you and me, and that is the end
of it. Hence, I do not have to complete its sense by saying for
whom it is roundish. Naturally, I am not saying that the sentence is *true:* I am merely explicating what we mean when we
assert it.

It is true that there seem to be certain value expressions,
notably the ethical, which it appears artificial, or perhaps even
absurd, to complete in this way. To say, "Murder is wrong for
me," sounds inept; for is not murder wrong, wrong in itself,
even as the earth is roundish in itself? *Could* we say, "Murder
is right for you"? Here, as Kant observed also, there appear to
be certain value expressions which behave like scientific expressions in this regard of being complete in themselves. And yet
the wrongness of murder is no "objective" predicate, like
"roundish." The situation is thus paradoxical. The solution of
the paradox is as follows: "Murder is wrong" is no more a complete sentence than is "The earth is beautiful"; only, instead of
completing it by saying, "Murder is wrong for me," we mean to
say, "Murder is wrong for me and you, that is to say, for us."
But it still is not just wrong in itself; to suppose it wrong apart
from the whole human context would be senseless, for what on
earth would that mean? Its wrongness always has reference to
somebody—for the murderer, or for one of us who know about
it, or perhaps for God.

One might, however, suppose that the difference between the
two types of sentences could be softened in the following way.
Suppose we try to re-express "The earth is beautiful" as "Under
certain conditions some people feel the earth to be beautiful,"
or "Murder is wrong" as "Under certain conditions some people
feel murder to be wrong." Notice that formally, at least, either

sentence is changed, for now it has a different subject; instead of being about murder or the earth, it is about people's feelings. And this difference remains even if we try to eliminate the purely formal difference by restating the sentences thus: "The earth is felt to be beautiful by some people under certain conditions"; "Murder is felt to be wrong by some people under certain conditions": for although murder and the earth are re-established as the subjects of the sentences, the predicates "beautiful" and "wrong" are not ascribed to them respectively as theirs independent of any attitude toward them, but as explicitly dependent upon an attitude. The transformation in the sentences is now very similar to that which occurs when, instead of saying "The earth is round," I say "The earth looks round," for roundness is now no longer ascribed to the earth as an independent property but is made dependent upon some person's perspective upon it. Notice also that the sentence "The earth looks round" is as incomplete in the way explained as "The earth is beautiful"; for in order to make it complete, I must specify for whom it looks round—for me, for you, or for somebody.

These transformations are significant in at least the following ways: In the first place, insofar as they make the predicates dependent on feeling, they appear to re-establish value statements as a species contrasting with scientific statements. The predicates, as already indicated, no longer are accepted as belonging to the object independent of feeling, but as dependent on feeling. There are, however, two possibilities of interpretation. 1. The predicate may be regarded as a genuine, though variable and relational, property of the object. Such properties, it might be pointed out, exist in other situations besides the valuational. The potential energy of a particle of water in a waterfall is variable, for it is never the same during the descent of this particle from the top of the fall to the moment when it reaches the earth, since it depends on the distance from the ground. Value then might be a function of feeling but would not itself

be a feeling. According to this interpretation, the value statement "murder is wrong" or "the earth is beautiful" would be
as scientific in its way as the statement "the earth is roundish."
It might even be claimed, indeed it has been claimed, that all
scientific statements are of this character. Even the shapes and
sizes of things, it may be said, are relational in a determinate
way. They, too, exist only relative to some frame of reference.
A statement that a body has a certain size and shape would be
as incomplete without reference to a frame as would a value
statement without reference to someone for whom a thing is
good or beautiful. If then by interpreting value predicates as
relational, they move in the direction of the scientific, the interpretation of scientific statements as relational would cause
them to move in the direction of the valuative. Hence the two
kinds would tend toward coincidence.

There is, nevertheless, a good reason why this interpretation
cannot be accepted: namely, because the relational property
that supervenes upon an object when it is valued is not itself
a value predicate. For if, as I have claimed, value is a satisfaction of desire, a thing does not necessarily acquire satisfaction
by being prized, loved, desired, or by contributing to the as
suagement of the activity of prizing, loving, desiring. The food
by being stored satisfies my acquisitive interest or by being eaten
satisfies my hunger, but it is not known that it thereby takes
satisfaction in being stored or eaten. It is true that a man when
loved finds joy in being loved, and a child when rocked is pleased
by being rocked, but it is one value to be rocked and loved and
another to love and rock. In social situations there are these
values, which I have called reciprocal. But they are not the
values that thinkers have in mind when they talk of value as a
relational predicate. For them, the relational predicate is something that accrues to things merely by being desired or prized.
But to say that a thing has the predicate "being desired" when it
is desired is merely another way of saying that it is desired—no
new property is designated.

Or to say that the bread, because it is good to eat has a value predicate, "being good to eat," is to be misled by language, for the bread is good to eat not because it has a value predicate but because of its already existing chemicophysical properties. No new property is added. The fallacy is like that which Molière immortalized in his play. The doctor answered the question why opium makes a man sleep by saying that it has a dormitive property—*virtus dormitiva*. We now know, however, that the opium causes sleep not by having the property of being able to make a man sleep, but by having a certain chemical constitution. And to return to our original illustrations, the earth does not acquire any new properties by being felt by us to be beautiful, for it is on account of its actual constitution that we feel about it in that way; similarly, murder is what it is, and the fact that some people feel it to be wrong does not give it a property of "wrongness." The way we feel about it may alter the feelings of a person who commits murder, causing him perhaps to despise himself for committing it, or to fear the retribution we shall exact, but these are *all* the changes that supervene—there is nothing more—not a property of "wrongness."

However, let us see if the alternative way of reinterpreting "The earth is beautiful" or "Murder is wrong" as "Some people feel the earth to be beautiful" or "Some people feel murder to be wrong" will serve to prove that, after all, value statements do not differ from scientific statements. This alternative (2), instead of putting the sentence in the passive voice and saying "The earth is felt by some people to be beautiful" or "Murder is felt by some people to be wrong," thereby making the earth or murder the subject of the sentence, keeps the original form and preserves the statement as a straightaway declaration about how some people feel. But surely when one says "Murder is wrong," one is not saying that some people feel it to be wrong. One would still say that murder was wrong even if some people did not feel it to be wrong. The fact that some people do feel it to be wrong confirms the conviction that it is wrong, but to say that it is wrong is not the same thing as to say that some people feel it to be wrong. Similarly, if some people felt the earth not to be beautiful, one might still say "The earth is beautiful." The innovator in the field of ethics or aesthetics is not merely stating how some people feel—he is trying to create a new way of feeling. "Some people feel murder to be wrong" is a statement of anthropology or history; it is not an ethical statement. In the same way, "The earth is beautiful" is a genuine aesthetic statement, whereas the statement "Some people feel the earth to be beautiful" is again history or anthropology. The moralist and the aesthetician are not historians or anthropologists.

No change in the matter occurs if one restates the sentence as "We feel murder to be wrong," with the intention of making a descriptive statement *about* our feelings. For we could then rephrase the sentence; as, "It is true that we feel murder to be wrong." But how would this sentence be challenged? By trying to prove that we did not really feel murder to be wrong—that we were either deceived about our feelings or were trying to deceive others about them. That is to say, one would make the counterstatement, "It is false that you believe murder to be wrong" and would present evidence to show this. On the other hand, to challenge "Murder is wrong" one would not try to prove that we did not really think or feel murder to be wrong; one would not say, "You do not really feel murder to be wrong—you misrepresent your own feelings, and here is the evidence." Rather you would say, "No! Murder is right," and you would then offer an entirely different set of reasons.

It will not be better if, as has been suggested, you rephrase "Murder is wrong" as "Murder disrupts the unity and integrity of a group of persons" or "Murder does violence to the feelings of the leaders of the group to which we belong" or some similar purely descriptive statement. Any one of these sentences would indeed be true, but none would be the same in meaning as "Murder is wrong." To see that they are not the same, one need only say in response to them, "Well, what of it?" or in our vernacular, "So what!" The fact that you would be shocked by such a comment shows that when you said "Murder is wrong" you were not merely describing a state of affairs, either sociological or behavioral, but were yourself feeling in a certain way toward it, and this expression of feeling, obvious in "Murder is wrong," is lost in the rephrasal.

The kind of argument given in the last few pages might, like a spider's web, be spun more widely and finely to show that the distinction between the two types of statement, of fact and of value, stands. Value statements, I shall maintain, are vectorial currents of feeling which overflow into expressive media and as such are neither true nor false. They are forces tending toward goals and must be so conceived and treated if one is not to go grievously astray in one's philosophy of value. I wish now to discuss whether they are a unique class or whether they may not have parallels in the whole field of expressions. That they are a species of a genus of nonpropositional expressions can easily be shown and has been the contention of many contemporary writers. The existence of this genus, however, had not escaped the attention of Aristotle. For he had already noticed the difference between ordinary judgments and such expressions as threats, entreaties, and commands. In *De Interpretatione* he wrote, "Every sentence has meaning . . . yet every sentence is not a proposition; only such are propositions as have in them either truth or falsity. Thus a prayer is a sentence, but is neither true nor false." [1]

Although nonpropositional expressions are today commonly called "emotive," I shall venture to rename them "volitional," thus avoiding the barbarism of the former term. Moreover, "volitional" is a better description of their essential nature. We may classify volitional statements as follows:

1. Lyrical, nonpractical communications of feeling:
    a) Interjectional: "Oh dear!" "Alas!" "Oh!"

[1] See 4, 17a, 1-6, *The Works of Aristotle,* trans. by E. M. Edghill, (Oxford, 1928), Vol. I. Cf. *Poetics,* 1456b, 8-11.

   b) Declarative: "I love you," "I wish the war would end."
   c) Aesthetic: Musical-Tonal: any piece of lyric music.
                    Poetical-Verbal: "My luve is like a red, red
                       rose." "The fog comes on little cat feet."
                    Iconic: Giorgione's "Tempesta," Michel-
                       angelo's "Moses."
                    Functional: Notre Dame de Chartres, La
                       Miniatura of Frank Wright.
2. Practical expressions:
   a) Commands, entreaties: "Help!" "Shut the door!"
   b) Legal: "Whoever commits burglary shall be punished
        with imprisonment from five to twenty years."
   c) Ethical: "Thou shalt not steal," "Love thy neighbor as
        thyself."

Examples 1*a* and 1*b* belong together as pure utterances of feeling, yet differ insofar as the former contain, in their simplest
form, no concepts, no denotations or descriptions. In "Oh!"
and "Alas!" surprise and sorrow are expressed, but there is no
indication or characterization of what one is surprised or
grieved at. The transition from 1*a* to 1*b* is illustrated by "Con-
found it!" where some object, although indefinite, is indicated.
In 1*b* the presence of the concept, and even of the proposition,
is explicit. In an expression like "I love you," there is a definite
denotation of an object in the words "I" and "you," with some
description of the object; the words connote, for example, a
human being. In an expression such as "Would that the war
would end," I shall show that there is a proposition "that the
war will end." The 1*c* aesthetic expressions differ from 1*a* and
1*b* in important respects, which, owing to their complexity, will
be considered by themselves presently.

   Lyrical expressions differ as a class from 2, practical expressions, in that no explicit intention to cause action is present,
whereas in practical expressions this intention is explicit.
"Help!" is a good example of practical expressions. They pos-

sess, it is true, a lyrical aspect—the communication of pure feeling—but this is not the end but the beginning of their purpose, which is to induce or prevent action. It is noticeable also that in such expressions, as in lyrical expressions, the conceptual, propositional element may be more or less explicit. In "Help!" it is at a minimum, whereas in "Shut the door!" it is explicit. The second expression is easily seen to be equivalent to "I want *that you will shut the door,*" in which the part italicized is a proposition. The fact that lyrical and practical expressions may contain propositions is very important, as we shall see, both for their understanding and their misunderstanding.

Aesthetic expressions, 1c, are a highly significant and controversial class. That they are primarily lyrical in character, although in most cases full of conceptual and propositional factors, can I think be shown. Yet they have constantly been misinterpreted as scientific expressions aiming at truth, especially by philosophers and philosophical poets. To show this in detail would require a separate chapter, but the general strategy of the argument, illustrated by one or two examples, would be as follows. Let us fix our attention upon two lines of the poem by Burns:

> Oh, my luve is like a red, red rose
> That's newly sprung in June;

Now if poetry be, as has been so often maintained, merely a popular or pleasant form of truth-saying, the *gáia scienza* of Renaissance critics, we could transpose the first of these lines, neglecting the second for the sake of shortening the argument, into "My love is like a red rose," which has the appearance of a simple proposition, either true or false. Well, it is true that the poet's love, whoever she be, being a woman, may be pink but is surely not red as a rose, nor does she smell like one nor have thorns nor grow in a garden. Following this line of thought, one would conclude that what we have here is simply a false proposition, from which we might justly infer that Plato

and many others were right in condemning the poets as pur-
veyors of untruths. Yet the strange thing is that the poet seems
to be enjoying his falsehoods, although except where they are
useful in the service of private ambitions or as propaganda,
people as a rule prefer the truth. Moreover, the falsehood is so
simple and obvious, it is strange that the poet should take the
pains to utter it. It is not anything that he could readily get
away with, and what ends, private or public, would be promoted
if he could, are not clear. How preposterous, therefore, that he
should be interested in telling the world this particular untruth!

However, it might be suggested that, after all, the proposition
really is true, for to say that one thing is like another is to say
something very general, in this case meaning only that the poet's
love is like a red rose in some respects, and so, to be sure, she is.
She, like the rose, is made of cells, respires, grows, and so on.
But it would seem to be as difficult to see why the poet should
be interested in telling such obvious truths as in telling equally
obvious falsehoods, on the supposition, just entertained, that
the proposition is true. And it is very certain, I think, that the
poet's intention, and ours when we read these lines, is very
different. Once the sentence is viewed as lyrical, as a kind of con-
ceptualized music, like music an expression of feeling but, unlike pure music, formulated through such lyric concepts symbol-
izing happiness as "red rose," "newly sprung," and "June," the
entire matter clears up. For now we understand that what the
poet is trying to do is to communicate to us how he feels toward
his sweetheart, as if he said simply, "How I do love her—as I love
a rose! As I love the spring!" In music, feeling is expressed directly through tones, in poetry indirectly as it shines through
certain concepts.

That such poetic lines as these are not practical expressions
is as clear as that they are not scientific. There is no intention to
arouse responsive action. Perhaps there was on the poet's part,
if he sent his verses to his lady, but not on our part, as we read
or recite the poem. To be sure, if the term "practical" is used

in so inclusive a sense as to mean causing any effect whatever, then all expressions are practical; for all do have effects and are intended to have at least such results as are involved in communication. But that is a different matter from intending a responsive action. Sometimes, indeed, lyrical expressions tend toward the practical, as in "I love you," which may aim at some responsive action on the part of the one to whom it is addressed. But not so pure lyric poetry and music.

If we were writing a treatise on aesthetics, we could show that the iconic (imitative) arts, and even the functional arts so far as their value is aesthetic, are lyrical expressions, not scientific or practical. Just to indicate the line of argument that would be followed, I shall analyze a single telling case. Suppose we consider a still life by Cézanne, representing apples on a plate. If this were scientific expression we could translate its meaning into words somewhat as follows: "Here is a plate and here are apples on the plate and these apples are red." But, if a proposition at all, that would be a false one, for surely there are no apples or plate there. Our argument would follow the lines we took in discussing the verses cited from Burns. Why should one be interested in telling such an obvious untruth? Not one of the motives for deception is plausible. One could not interpret the picture as stating not a singular but a general proposition to the effect perhaps that "all apples are red." For again the objection is inevitable: why state such an obvious untruth?

And surely the picture is not practical expression, for it is not saying, as a real apple says to us, "Come eat me!" for no apple is here. Only as lyrical expression is the picture intelligible; for in the first place it is pure music in color and line, communicating feeling as directly as is done by tones; and in the second place it is feeling communicated *through* the concept of an apple, even as the poet's feeling is communicated through that of a rose. The poet communicates a roselike feeling, the painter an applelike feeling. That in the one case the concept is expressed verbally and in the other iconically makes no essential difference; for both are alike, not descriptions of objects but communications of feeling. The artist does not say, "Here is an apple," but "Let us *imagine* an apple and feel in an applelike way!"

Yet I suspect that some who acknowledge the distinction may still harbor doubts as to the absoluteness of the distinction between value statements and scientific statements, between ordinary lyrical and practical expressions and scientific expressions. Arguing for the doubter, we may put the matter in this way. Consider first the lyrical type of expression. Take a simple expression such as "I love you." Would it not be plausible to assert that in addition to its function as expression of feeling, it has also the purpose to describe the lover's state of mind to the beloved? He tells her how he feels at least as objectively as when he writes her from a distance and describes the room he is living in, saying perhaps "The wallpaper is blue." In each case he would be using concepts, only whereas, in one, he is referring to and characterizing a thing (the wallpaper, blue), in the other he is referring to his own feeling (love). If this were so the distinction between the two kinds of statements would not be a distinction in kind at all, for both would be descriptive; but rather a distinction between the objects to which the descriptions refer— in the one, inner states, in the other, external things. In art, also, one might claim that the artist is *describing*, not things, to be sure, but his own sentiments.

The same sort of analysis might be used with regard to such practical expressions as commands or requests. Take, "Shut the door!" One would analyze it into two propositions: one, "You will shut the door," and the other, "I have a wish." The one would be a proposition, true or false, about the future; the other a proposition, true or false, about my state of mind or attitude to such a proposition. All such propositions would therefore be descriptive but partly psychological in their nature.

Such an argument has much plausibility, and yet I think it can be shown that it does not suffice to destroy the distinction.

For, in the first place, it would have to be admitted that there are some lyrical expressions such as music that are not cognitive. Music aims, through the instrumentality of ordered sounds, complex and highly organized, to create in communication a kind of balanced emotional experience—not to *describe* that experience. In pure music there are no concepts. Poetry and all the fine arts, so far as they really are fine, must, as Pater said, be understood with music as a clue. They are not efforts to describe the artist's feelings but to arouse in the appreciator an orderly experience analogous to the artist's own. The concepts employed, as in the example from poetry cited, do not function as descriptions of feelings but as lures for feeling. The poet is inviting *us* to imagine a rose and a woman, and in so doing to feel toward the one as toward the other. Or, to express the same thought differently, the concept in its cognitive function is a substitute for feeling; in its aesthetic function, a bearer of feeling. In all cases of description, two things are present, the object and the concept; in poetry, there is only one, the concept. The concept is there, not in order to describe an object, even a feeling, but on its own account as a lure for feeling.

Let us next try and see if this kind of analysis will work as suggested if applied to practical expressions. Taking as our model the request "Please shut the door," we are asking whether it can be analyzed into two descriptive statements, (1) "I wish," or "There exists in me a wish," describing my present state of mind; and (2), another proposition, predictive in character, "You will shut the door." That the second is a proposition has already been admitted. It is clear, however, that if the original statement consists of these two propositions, they are not unrelated, for the second one formulates my wish in setting forth its objective, and their relation must be included in the restatement. One might perhaps think that this relation could be identified with the relation between a condition and its consequence, so that the whole proposition would become: (*a*) "If you will shut the door, I shall be pleased." In this way, it might seem, we would have an exact transposition of the request statement into a propositional statement. But that this transposition cannot be made without loss of meaning can I think be shown as follows:

Consider a sentence which, like (a), expresses a conditional empirical proposition, but which cannot be construed as a request: (b) "If someone shuts the door, the room will get warm." The difference between (b) and the original request statement is entirely clear and will serve to exhibit the difference between the latter and (a). (b) is a mere statement of causal relation, intended only to predict what will happen. Not so my request. It is intended to influence your conduct, to be a factor in determining that something shall happen, not merely to foresee what will happen. It aims not merely to state a condition (shutting the door) for something to happen but at being itself one of the conditions; it aims to make the proposition true. And it purposes to make the proposition true in a very specific way: by making my wish your wish. Or to express the matter in still another form: when I say, " I wish you would shut the door," or "Please shut the door," I intend an effect which *you* might formulate as "*I* wish that I shall shut the door" (assuming that if there is no obstacle to your shutting the door, since you wish to do it, you will do it). In fine, what I aim at in a request—and the same thing applies to a command such as "Shut the door!"— is not so much to state a fact about my own wish as to create in you a corresponding wish.

Thus far, however, I have been studying volitional expressions from the standpoint of the intended results, but when they are studied for themselves internally, they reveal differences from descriptive statements no less important and dramatic. I can bring this out by comparing the statement "I love you" with the statement " He loves her," uttered by a bystander watching the drama between lover and beloved and overhearing the lover's tender phrase. The expression "I love you" is part of a process that includes the love of the lover. Indeed, his love is part of the very content of the expression, literally part of its meaning. This can be shown by analogy with a proposition such as "This visual patch is red," uttered by one who is looking at the patch. The subject of the proposition, meaning by subject what the proposition is about, is clearly the patch, but the patch is also a factor in the mind of the one who utters the proposition, since, as the demonstrative "this" indicates, he is looking at it so that *the patch is a very part of the proposition itself*. As C. H. Langford has claimed,[2] in similar fashion, when the lover says "I love you," in using the word "I," which has meaning only through connection with himself, he puts himself into the proposition, in the specific way, of course, of being lover of *you*. Or, if it be thought that there is no self apart from the flux of feelings, and that the word "I" has no real counterpart, then the phrase "I love you" means "This love is for you," where again the word "this" covers the love of the lover and is one with it. Hence the statement is no mere description of a state of mind, but part of it—part of an act or current of feeling, not a mere report on how the current is flowing.

Now let us consider its counterpart, "He loves her." It is noticeable that exactly the same situation is designated and described: the word "he" (the counterpart of "I") refers to the lover; "her" (the counterpart of "you") refers to the beloved, "loves" to the love of the lover, not only designating it but also describing it as love directed to the woman. If two statements refer to the same objects—if their referents are the same—and if these objects are described by the same concepts, one might with reason claim that they are the same. And descriptively, that is to say so far as their propositional elements are in view, the two statements are identical; yet it is certain that they are far from being identical. Moreover, the difference has been indicated: the one is a mere report, giving information *about* a situation;

[2] See C. I. Lewis and C. H. Langford, *Symbolic Logic* (New York, 1932), pp. 319-20.

the other is an utterance *of* that situation, and a very part of it. The one reports *upon* the love of the lover, the other *contains* that love; his words are like an envelope holding something precious within or, to change the metaphor, like a pipe through which a current is flowing. The matter is the same in all practical and lyrical expressions—they are not mere descriptions of feeling but currents or acts of feeling.

I do not mean that for the person expressing a wish or a satisfaction there may be no cognitive element in his expression. To clothe a wish in words is equivalent to clothing it in concepts, for the words and the concepts are one unrent garment. Expression may contain self-knowledge, but knowledge by acquaintance, not knowledge by description. And in knowledge by acquaintance what is known is present to the concepts that know it. It is again the difference between "I love you" and "He loves her." In the first, as we have noted, the lover's love is a warmth in his words and a force there trying to kindle a like fire in the beloved; in the second, love is absent, and there is left only a cold description—not utterly cold, since all concepts are echoes of primary experiences, but the warmth is not that of the lover but of the embers of the spectator's love remembered. The possibility of combining feeling with knowledge of feeling is, I have argued, characteristic of the aesthetic expression,[3] but I think it can be shown, in the way here illustrated, that it is also characteristic of all lyrical expression. But in propositions—pure descriptive expression—the lyrical element is minimal or has vanished.

I shall now, in conclusion, try to show that legal and ethical expressions belong among practical expressions, as I have indicated in the general classification of expressions given.

It is true that both seem to differ in several ways from the simpler kinds of practical expression already analyzed. For one

[3] "Wish Fulfillment and Intuition in Art," in Melvin Rader's *A Modern Book of Esthetics* (New York: H. Holt, 1935).

thing, they seem to differ in being impersonal, in which regard they simulate scientific expressions. No definite persons seem to be wishing or commanding, but this impersonality is actually a sham. For consider a simple example of each: "Burglary is wrong [ethical]," and "Whoever commits burglary shall be punished by imprisonment from a period of from five to twenty years [legal]." Take the last statement first. Suppose one tries to interpret it as a mere prediction or proposition: "If anyone commits burglary he will be punished." This obviously would not do, for no one can claim that everyone who commits burglary will be punished since some may *get away with it.*" The law does not read as it would read if it were a prediction, "If anyone commits burglary and is apprehended and convicted, he will be punished, etc." This statement is, to be sure, true, but is not what the law says, for the law says nothing about apprehension and conviction. Moreover, it uses the word "shall," not "will"; and "shall" connotes command. As in the simpler commands, there are the two parts to the expression—the pure volitional part and the propositional part concerning the future. In effect the law says "We, the constituted authorities, wish [volitional part] *that those who commit burglary shall be punished* [propositional part]." The use of the word "shall" brings the two parts together. And that the law is not a *proposition about* a wish, but the expression *of* a wish—not something to be verified, but a decision to act in a certain way, therefore something to be acted on by whoever confronts it—is clear for the reason that a potential burglar is not in doubt what the law is, and that the officers who enforce the law are not concerned with whether it is the law but with enforcing it. To be sure, it may happen that there is a question as to what the law is. But then we are not dealing with the same expression but with a correlative propositional expression of the form, "It is true that they—the constituted authorities [notice the change from "we" to "they"]—wish that burglars shall be punished." The one is the expression *of* a value; the other is an expression *about* a value.

The analysis of ethical expressions follows closely that of legal expressions, although, as we shall see, there are important differences. The fundamental theme of this analysis was stated by Russell [4]: ethical expressions are commands, or, since commands are wishes, let us say simply that they are wishes. "Stealing is wrong" is equivalent to "Thou shalt not steal." It is not an accident that the basic moral code of our civilization is the Ten Commandments. One critical difference between legal and ethical commands is that ethical commands do not assign penalties for their violation, or when they do, as is sometimes true, it is well recognized that they acquire a legalistic tinge. The law says, in effect, "We want you to do or refrain from doing something, and if you don't, we want the officers of the law to punish you"; the moral injunction says simply, "We want you to want to do or refrain from doing so and so." The one aims to create an act through fear, the other aims to create a wish for the sake of the intrinsic satisfaction that the fulfillment of that wish will bring. The moralist does not merely desire that people shall not steal, but that they shall wish not to steal. This is the "disinterestedness" of morality. And the basis of such a wish is liking for a way of life which the wish sustains and for the persons who participate, with oneself, in that way.

But if ethical and legal expressions are commands, whose are they? The legal are primarily the commands of the "constituted authorities," and secondarily of those citizens who support the authorities out of approval of the law. They express a desire for a way of life which "crimes" tend to disrupt. Ethical expressions originate in the desires of religious leaders or other innovators in the realm of conduct but have now become the commands of parents and teachers who seek to build up in the mass of the people desires similar to their own. The legal and the moral tend to coincide but never do so. The impersonality of these

[4] Bertrand Russell, *Religion and Science* (London: Oxford Univ. Press, 1935), Chapter IX, especially pp. 247, 249.

expressions is therefore merely apparent, as I have suggested, and is due to the fact that they are the commands of many persons rather than of a single one. When I say to the child, "You should honor your father and mother," I am not saying to him, "I want you to honor your father and mother" in the same fashion that I would say to him "*I* want you to run this errand for me," but rather, in effect, "*We* want you to honor your father and mother," meaning by "we" a group of persons that includes me. At the moment I am a spokesman of that group. And, eventually, the command of the parents and the group becomes my own command to myself—the wish of the higher interests in competition with the lower.

The attempt by Professor Lepley in his book, *Verifiability and Value,* to reduce ethical to scientific expressions can now, I think, be shown to be impossible. Adopting his general procedure, we might seek to re-express "Stealing is wrong" as a scientific proposition of some such form as this: "Stealing disrupts the social and economic organization of a society." But were I to say this to a hardened thief, his answer would be "What of it!" Unless he desired to preserve the way of life sustained by the economic organization of our society, or unless he identified himself with the frustrations of persons who had their goods stolen, such a Lepleyian transposition of our sentence would have no *ethical* meaning for him. It is well known that the early Bolsheviks partly supported themselves by the use of counterfeit money, but *for them* this practice was not wrong, for they did not wish the economic organization to continue. Those who think the transposition adequate presumably do wish the economic organization to continue, and this wish is covertly embodied in the expression, thereby destroying its purely scientific character.

To designate ethical expressions as commands, however, may have the appearance of making them too external. This seems strongly to be the case when a man says to himself "I ought"; it may then seem far-fetched to say that he issues commands to himself. And yet, in effect, that is what he does: he takes the part of the wish which constitutes what we call his conscience and tries to strengthen it against conflicting wishes. As we have already shown in our discussion of value as the expression of an imperative, the "ought" is always the voice of a wish in conflict with other wishes, our own or another's. This wish comes to verbal expression when, communing with himself or with a friend, a man says "I ought" or, equivalently, "I should." And then, as in any expression of value, the wish is actually contained in the very words that express it and acts as a force in the tense situation, pointing the way to its resolution.

A consideration of one of Lepley's own examples will bring to light another aspect of the same matter. "Promises ought generally to be kept" is transposed as "The keeping of promises produces effects which upon careful and continued examination of consequences are felt (by those who make this judgment) to be very important." But, on the contrary, anyone who says that promises ought generally to be kept is not saying merely that he or anyone else has certain feelings, that such feelings exist; he is not stating a proposition about his feelings which his auditors would be interested in verifying. He is expressing his feelings, in order to win the sympathy and excite an appropriate action on the part of his auditors. And generally, no statement as to how certain persons feel or have felt (whether in books on anthropology, psychology, or history) can ever be equivalent to an ethical expression, for the reason that the latter contains the attitude of the speaker or writer as a living, active force; whereas the former does not contain it, but simply affirms its existence, or, insofar as some of the attitude lingers there, ceases to be a purely scientific and becomes a volitional statement.

Although we have, I believe, shown that ethical and legal expressions belong to the same genus as practical expressions, it is clear from what has been brought out concerning them that they are a distinct species. There is obviously a world of difference between the entreaty, "Please shut the door," or the command, "March!" and a legal or ethical expression. One difference is the generality of legal and ethical expressions as compared with the particularity of the ordinary command or entreaty. The first refers to a whole class of acts; the second refers to a single act only. Nevertheless, there is an interesting group of practical expressions which would not at first sight seem to belong among ethical expressions but which also have a general import. I refer to such warning signs as "Poison!" on a medicine bottle or "Dangerous Passing" on a road barrier. That these are not mere descriptive expressions stating certain consequences from drinking a liquid of that kind or driving on such a road follows from their intent to influence action and from their inspiration in a wish to keep people safe. In fact, the difference between such expressions and ethical expressions is not sharp. Many ethical expressions are, in effect, warnings against the consequences of acts of a certain sort; for example, "The wages of sin is death." In expressions of this class, the untoward consequences predicted are usually natural; in the legal, they are artificial, that is to say, man-made.

Some ethical expressions are more of the nature of promises of rewards than of threats, such as "Honor thy father and thy mother that thy days may be long in the land that the Lord thy God giveth thee," or "Be ye merciful, that ye may obtain mercy." These may be compared with promises of reward for useful or heroic acts, like medals of honor or prizes. So far as such expressions are inspired by a regard for the interests of others, they are akin to the ethical but more so to the legal in seeking to influence conduct by rewards or predicted ill consequences rather than by building up an attitude. Being motivated by love in a broad sense is the second prime characteristic (the first being generality) differentiating the ethical and legal from ordinary practical expressions, which are selfish.

Ethical and metaphysical expressions have been classified by logical positivists as "poetical." If this is meant merely as a way of distinguishing them from scientific expressions, it is valid;

if it is meant as a slur, it is undeserved, for what could be better than the poetical? But is it correct? If by poetical is meant aesthetic lyrical expression in verbal rather than in iconic symbols, it is certainly incorrect. Ethical expressions are not "lyric cries." It is a mistake to interpret "Thou shalt not kill" as "Would that people would not kill!" as Russell has done. Ethical expressions, as we have noted, are practical, not lyrical; they are intended to cause action, not just feeling. On the other hand, if "poetical" is taken in a larger sense, as is often done, to include the intrinsic values of action, then it has meaning to speak of ethical expressions as intended to build up these values in a way closely similar to that of the poet in creating imaginative values. The true moralist is not envisaging the useful results of action alone, as does the merely practical man, but its resident values as well. When he says "Love thy neighbor as thyself," he is trying to create the values of doing kindly deeds in the experience of whomsoever will listen to him. When he says, "The pure in heart shall see God," he is seeking to inspire purity as an end in itself. The poet's words are acts creative of imaginative values; the moralist's of values in deeds. That is why it is often hard to distinguish the great moralist like Christ from the poet. By giving to poetry this enlarged meaning, it is possible to call ethical goodness the poetry of action and the Beatitudes a poem.

Our study of value statements will be complete if we can show that the highest generalizations of ethics and aesthetics are volitional in character. It will suffice if we can prove this with regard to ethics. Two of the most famous ethical generalizations are those of Henry Sidgwick as restated by Hastings Rashdall, "The greater good should be preferred to the less," and "The good of one man is of equal worth with the like good of another." From the first quotation it is believed that one can deduce the principle that the highest good is the greatest good of the greatest number. A respectable group of moral philosophers regarded these or similar generalizations as axiomatic, rational truths, self-evident like the principles of logic or arithmetic.

Now I once maintained that the apparent self-evidence of the ethical maxims depended on their being mere tautologies.[5] "The greater good should be preferred to the less," seems to be a tautology because what we *mean* by the greater good is the good which should be preferred or, equivalently, what we mean by what should be preferred is precisely the greater good. Similarly, "The good of one man is equal to the like good of another" is tautologous because, of course, if the goods in question are like, they are equal. And so interpreted, the two statements are, indeed, self-evident but also trivial. Yet it is clear that, whether true or not, they are not trivial. One can see this by construing the first, as everyone would allow it may be, as "The good of more people is to be preferred to that of the few" or, in other words, "If we are to decide between an act which benefits only a few persons and one that benefits many, we should choose the second rather than the first." "The interests of the majority should be served rather than those of the minority" is not a tautology. We can see that the other so-called axiom is not a tautology by construing it as "One should not act in such a way as to benefit a rather than b, when a and b are in parity of circumstances." For example, workmen in the same shop who produce the same amount of goods should be paid the same wages. And if these principles are not tautologies, they are not mere analyses. From the mere fact of the interests of more people you cannot deduce that you should further them rather than the interests of a few, just because more are greater than few. So, because a and b are in parity of circumstances, or are capable of a like degree of happiness, it does not follow, by mere analysis, that I should treat them alike, not preferring to make a happy rather than b, say by paying a for the same amount of work more than I pay b.

[5] *Human Values* (Ann Arbor: Wahr, 1931), Ch. VI.

Although, as thus interpreted, the statements are not tau-tologies, are they self-evidently *true*? But in what sense true? Surely not as reports of fact. As reports of fact, they would mean that people sometimes prefer the greater to the lesser good; and that sometimes they treat *a* and *b* alike in parity of circum-stances. Yet if that is what they mean, they are not self-evidently true but empirically true. And they certainly do not mean that. If they did mean that, one would have said that; one would not have said, "You should treat people in parity of circum-stances alike" when one meant that sometimes you do treat them so. To say to people that they should be just and should prefer the interests of a majority to the interests of a minority is not the same as to say that some or all people do so, even though to remind them that some people do may be cited as reason why they should do so. These statements are therefore not true as categorical statements—as reports of matters of fact.

However, it might be held that these statements are true in another way—as conditional statements. For example, instead of saying, "Prefer the greater to the lesser good," you might say, "If you prefer the greater to the lesser good you will be happier than if you prefer the lesser to the greater good"; and instead of saying, "Be just!" you might say, "If you treat people in parity of circumstances alike, you will be happier than if you discriminate between them." Now, leaving undecided, for a moment, whether these new statements are equivalent to the original ones, it is clear, I think, that they are not self-evidently true, if true at all, but empirically true. One could not know them to be true merely by understanding them, but by observa-tion that when one is, for example, just, one is happier than when one is unjust, or by observing this to be true, perhaps, in the case of people one knows or has heard about. The proposi-tion would be true empirically, as a generalization from experi-ence, not true a priori.

Granting this, let us consider whether these restatements are equivalent to the original expressions. If they are equivalent, then our whole conception of ethical expressions as volitional would be false, for ethical statements would turn out to be empirical, conditional scientific statements. Moreover, if ethical statements are of this character, it would become likely that all value statements are so; and our entire point of view would be shown to be false. The matter would seem to deserve, therefore, the most careful consideration on our part. We have, however, already laid the foundations for a rejection of the theory that ethical statements are empirical statements rather than volitional statements; and we have exhibited, in addition, the reason why the confusion between the two has arisen. For in our analysis of commands and imperatives generally, we observed that an empirical proposition is part of their meaning but is not the whole meaning. We showed that, for example, "March!" means, "I want *that you will march*," where the italicized phrase is a simple, predictive proposition, and where the whole proposition is not a simple prediction but an efficacious, expressive act. And for the same reason a statement of command cannot be re-expressed (or transposed) as a conditional empirical proposition to the effect, "If you march, I shall be pleased." The commanding officer is not making a prediction as to his own future state of mind, but trying to influence his men to do something.

Now the situation is logically the same in the case of ethical propositions. If I say, "Be just!" I am not stating a conditional proposition to the effect that if you are just both you and I will be happier than if you are unjust; I am giving voice to my desire *that* you shall be just, and *that,* by being just, you will be happy—and the expression of this desire is, as in the case of a command, an efficacious act intended to make it true that you will be just and will be happy. I believe I can make my point of view more convincing by an analogy. Suppose I am giving a friend advice regarding some simple practical affair, say, advising him not to lend someone money. I say, "Don't lend that money to John!" Now, am I merely saying, "If you lend that money to John he will not repay you and you will be unhappy"? Certainly not! For when I give him my advice, I am expressing (1) my interest in his happiness and (2) I am trying to deter him from acting in a certain way. I am, therefore, uttering a volitional expression and am very far from merely making a prediction. There is, indeed, a correlative conditional proposition, already stated, to the effect that if he lends the money he will regret it; but the intent of my expression is to *make* the protasis of that proposition untrue. In my expression there is love for my friend and the efficacy of an act; in a mere proposition there is neither love nor efficacy. It remains true, therefore, that ethical expressions are volitional in character. If they were not, one wonders why they are stated as they are, using *should* or *ought*, and are not given the simple propositional form, either categorical or conditional.

Nevertheless, it is of the utmost significance that corresponding to every practical volitional statement, there are one or more conditional predictive, empirical propositions. This we have seen to be true of simple commands; and it is also true of legal and ethical expressions. Even as corresponding to "March" there is the empirical conditional proposition, "If you march I shall be pleased," and "If you do not march you will be punished"; so corresponding to "Don't steal!" there are the propositions, "If you steal, probably you will be punished (legal)," and "If you steal you will probably be unhappier than if you do not steal, and I also will be unhappier (ethical)." There are also certain correlative factual propositions to the effect that "There exists in me a wish that you march," "that you do not steal," etc. (The precise character and evidence for the correlative propositional statements in the case of ethics we shall study in the chapter on ethics.) This general correlation between value statements and propositional statements has a twofold significance: it explains the persistent confusion between the two types, and it shows that values do not exist in some hypostatic realm of their own but have firm residence in the world of fact—in existing desires and in prevalent conditions for their realization.

As a fitting conclusion to this chapter we may ask, "Of what sort are the statements it contains, omitting, of course, those in quotes?" Are they volitional or are they descriptive? My answer is, unhesitatingly, that they are descriptive. For in this chapter, I am not desiring, advocating, appraising; I am studying value statements, not making them, and with the sole intent of discovering their general character. My discourse is *about* values, not *of* values. I am not speaking as one who loves or hates, suffers or is happy; as one who commands or preaches or gives advice; or as one who writes poetry. What one may derive from reading this chapter is not inspiration to action or to imagination, but information as to how values are expressed. Not all the statements I make in this book, however, are equally detached. But I promise to let the reader know when they are not. When I am writing poetry, in the broad sense of that word already defined, I shall try to give notice; otherwise I shall be writing prose. One great fault of writers of value theory is that they do not know when they are writing prose or poetry.

CHAPTER IV

THE ANALYSIS OF VALUES

SECTION I. ESSENTIAL FACTORS

In our first chapter we sought a definition of value, and in our third we offered a study of the way values are expressed. We found that, generically considered, value may be defined as the assuagement of desire, and that, as we should expect if this definition is correct, value is expressed in volitional statements. Now, making use of all we have learned so far, we wish to probe more deeply into the nature of value. A value is complex, we shall see: we desire therefore to discover, if we can, its multiple aspects. The method to be employed is the one in use wherever knowledge by acquaintance is possible: the scrutiny of experience itself, as we suffer or create it, to the end of finding concepts that will fit those aspects of it in which we are interested. We then express these concepts in words, communicating them to the reader, and ask him to examine his experience as we have ours and discover for himself if our descriptions apply. We start with this or that value experience, then look to see if the concepts which fit it will fit any other that may be offered. An adequate study of any one value would suffice, since its general characters would be the same in all: even as, if we knew the constituent aspects of a single tone, as loudness, pitch, and timbre, we would know those of all tones. Yet we can hardly do with the study of a single case, because, without the contrast of something specifically different, a generic quality can with difficulty, perhaps never, be noticed. So, if we had heard none but tones of the horn, and never tones of violins or trombones, we might not have been able to discern that generic character of tones we call timbre.

When the reader tests our analysis by confronting the concepts used with his own experiences, three cautions should be carefully noted—one, to remember that we are analyzing generic value, not, say, moral or aesthetic value, and that therefore he should not look in this analysis for the characteristics peculiar to any one or another species of value; and two, that no description or analysis can convey the distinctive, unique flavor of any individual value. This peculiarity of analysis and description is not restricted to the field of values. As we have already noted in discussing the views of G. E. Moore, every value is indefinable in this one sense, that we cannot embody in any description its unique tint. But that is no defect in the description, for we are not concerned with uniqueness, but with generic qualities. Finally, in the analysis of value about to be presented, we shall have in mind the simpler kinds. But everything that is true of the simple is true of the complex.

A careful analysis yields, I submit, the following essential factors:

1. *Desire.* The term "desire," as was said, is used in the most general sense to indicate whatever such words as "wish," "interest," "will," "purpose," "determining tendency," "instinct," "drive," "habit," "urge," "libido," and the like have in common. Being elementary, desire cannot be adequately described, yet can be and is denoted, and what is denoted in my experience is generically the same as what is denoted in yours; and, al-

though not capable of *adequate* description, there are concepts which apply to it and give a partial description of it. Three are very significant, because they serve to mark off desire from contrasting experiences—vectorality, tension, and efficacy. A desire is a vectorial experience, that is, it is asymmetrical and directed. We can depict it graphically by means of an arrow: $\ggg\!\!\longrightarrow$. In this regard it is like movement and like time. This is no accident, as we shall see, because both time and movement owe their asymmetry to desire. Desire, so to speak, is a one-way street. It is also a tense experience; we can apply with truth such words as "restless," "uneasy," "disequilibrium" to it, and compare it to coiled spring. And here again the aptness of such words or phrases is no accident; for what they indicate is rooted in desire as we see when we penetrate to their essence. Finally, it is an efficacious experience, an activity, one which changes or might change the course of events. If, for example, I am hungry, then I am wound up, I am all set to act, and, if nothing prevents, I will act, and my activity will produce and will control a series of events. And this, too, is no accident; for to the vision of an adequate cosmology, all causality, all natural necessity is that of desire. The value of these descriptive terms can be brought out if we contrast the experience of desire with that of color. I choose color, but any other pure sensuous quality would do, as a tone or a savor. In color, there is no pointing at anything, no asymmetry; there is no tension and no efficacy. It may, to be sure, release a change, as when we see a green traffic signal, but it does not generate a change. On the other hand, even a mere wish, using the term "wish" not in its broader sense as I shall be using it but in its narrow sense, is efficacious, for, although ineffective actually, it would produce a change if occasion offered.

It might, however, be thought that although desire is a condition of value, it cannot be a constituent of it, if value is, according to the definition accepted by us, the assuagement of desire. When satisfaction arrives, desire would appear to cease; it would come before, it would not be copresent with satisfaction. And yet, paradoxical as this may seem, that is not true. For, in the first place, even when satisfaction does come after desire, it is contiguous with it; owing to the general contiguity of the process of experience, there is no gap, no break between them. The one follows on the heels of the other. In letting go of desire, we keep contact with desire. The reality is comparable to the experience of letting go of the hand of a friend; at the moment of releasing it, his hand is still in contact with one's own hand. So when satisfaction follows upon desire, desire remains at the heart of satisfaction. Moreover, desire is not satisfied all at once or entirely in a pulse of experience, and therefore remains copresent with the continuing, later, and even final phases of desire. Hunger is not appeased all at once, but in the process of dining, of eating, or of drinking. So as the desire is being appeased, it persists along with its assuagement. A way of summarizing this matter would be to say that satisfaction comes to us *as* an assuagement of desire.

2. *A goal or objective.* The satisfaction comes to us, further, as the realization of a goal or objective. How often, when happy, we say, "Now I have what I had wanted!" Usually, we express the objective as a desire *for an object,* as when hungry we say, "I want something to eat," or when lonely we say, "I want my friend." But, as a matter of fact, the objective of desire is never an object but an activity or passivity, usually with reference to an object. It is not bread that I want, but to eat the bread; not just a friend, but to talk with or play with the friend. The miser may think that he wants gold, but what he truly wants is to contemplate his gold, and, of course, the normal man wants to spend it. All these multitudinous things that we say that we want—a car, a house, a garment, a yacht, a pen and paper—these we want, not as such, but to use; and to use is to be active or passive with reference to them: to drive the car, to sleep or dine in the house, to wear the garment, to sail the yacht, to write with the pen and upon the paper.

All my illustrations of objectives have been of activities, but equally I may want passivities with regard to objects, and my satisfactions will be in these passivities. If the mother wants to rock the child, the child wants to be rocked; if the boy wants to kiss the girl, she wants to be kissed. And if we want to praise others, we want more, perhaps, to be praised by them. However, there is no absolute contrast between activities and passivities; for every activity involves a passivity and vice versa. One cannot rock a cradle without adjusting one's hand to the rhythm of its motion; and one cannot get satisfaction from being rocked unless one consents to it, and that is activity. All experience has these two faces—control and countercontrol, activity and passivity—neither can exist alone, and we call it one or the other according to its relative dominance in degree.

It might be thought that the objective could be some mere event or happening. Thus, during a war we all wish that it would end. But if we think about it we shall see that we are not wishing for the mere ending of the war, but rather for all the activities and passivities that the war interferes with or makes impossible. The young man in service wants to return to studying or transacting business, or to the pursuits shared with wife and children. The householder wants to buy groceries without the hindrance of rationing, to drive a new car, to repair his house. Even to military leaders, the occurrence of an armistice is only a symbol of victory, the realization of the will to triumph; for the masses of men it is never willed for any other reason than as a means.

Technically, an objective is a proposition about the future, as is shown by its linguistic expression. Thus the objective of my hunger is "that I shall eat bread"; the objective of my longing for my absent friend, "that I shall play with and talk with X"; the objective of the little boy about to go to bed, "that I shall be rocked to sleep by Mother." It is a prediction of some activity or passivity to come. What we want is *that* this activity or passivity shall occur. That the goal is a proposition is clear from the fact that it is something to be verified or refuted, something to be proven true or false.[1] But while the objective is a proposition, the entire expression of which it is a part is not one, as I have already argued.

The objective is not always in the forefront of consciousness, either in the case of satisfaction or of desire. When a drive is assuaged by habitual activities, it is commonly in the background. If while I walk I am accustomed to swinging my arms, I do not have the objective "that I shall swing my arms" clearly in mind. When I experienced the satisfaction of writing this sentence, I did not have explicitly formulated the goal that I should write it. Yet that the proposition was somehow there emerges when, if the desire is frustrated, we protest, saying for example to the one who interrupted us, "I did want to finish that sentence"; or when, if the desire is fulfilled and someone inquires why we are so contented, we say, "Because I was able to finish that sentence." It may be true that the proposition seldom comes into the focus of consciousness unless there is blocking of the impulse or delay in its realization; yet since these two conditions are usually present to some extent, we may infer that the proposition is present in some degree.

That the objective belongs to satisfaction as well as to desire follows from the same considerations that led us to place desire itself in the bosom of satisfaction. Satisfaction comes to us *as* the realization of the objective even as it comes *as* the fulfillment of desire. We are aware that we are being satisfied *because* the objective is being verified. Satisfaction is the turning of desire into assuagement, and just as the desire is still *there* as it is fading into satisfaction, so the proposition that *I shall* be active or passive with regard to an object is still in mind as it gives way to the proposition that *I am* active or passive with regard to a certain object. But more of this under 5.

[1] That, being a proposition about the future, it is not *now* true or false, I have argued in *Experience and Substance* (Ann Arbor: Univ. Mich. Press, 1941), pp. 160-62. *Now* it is only probable.

3. *A complementary object and perhaps means object.* That an object enters into value would follow from our definition (the assuagement of any interest in any object), from our characterization of desire itself as vectorial, and from our description of the goal of desire as an activity or passivity with reference to an object. There are, to be sure, possibly objectless satisfactions, as in music and certain morbid states, and, as we shall see, certainly in the case of what we shall call "higher order satisfactions," but in the simple, typical cases, desire is directed upon an object, and satisfaction is *in* and about an object. The energy of desire flows through and around the object and is released by it. The self dips into and momentarily fuses with the not-self. The object is primarily what has been called a complementary object but may also be a means object. A complementary object is one with which desire is directly concerned and with which it is involved in the activity or passivity which assuages it. A means object is one with which desire is not directly but is indirectly concerned, only for the reason that it is causally necessary for the existence of the former object. If I desire to eat bread, the bread is the complementary object, whereas the knife with which I cut off a slice of desirable thickness is a means object to that desire, although it is the complementary object to the desire to cut it. A means object that is means to one interest is a complementary object to some other interest; it is never a mere means object. The distinction between means and end is, therefore, tied up with the fact that some interests are dominant and others subordinate in a system of interests. But since we are now studying relatively simple desires, we are not concerned with this matter at the moment.

It is interesting to notice that although the complementary object of *satisfaction* must always be an individual, since I can be active or passive only with regard to something which exists and only the individual exists, the object of *desire* may be either indefinite, generic, specific, or individual. In certain moods of restlessness and in the musical experience, I may merely want *something,* I know not what. Of course, the psychoanalyst will believe that he knows what definite thing I want, but phenomenologically I do not want anything definite. It is probable that all desires are originally for indefinite objects—they merely point without pointing at something—and have to learn by experience what the objects are that would appease them. The babe has originally a drive just to suck but has to be taught that it is the breast it wants. Or the object of desire may be generic; being lonely, I may want someone to talk to, and any human being will serve. Perhaps, however, I want someone to talk philosophy with; then my object will not be the *genus homo,* but the rare species, *homo philosophicus.* On the other hand, a young man may wish to get married (genus); he may wish to marry a girl who is rich and pretty (species); or he may wish to marry Sally (individual). But obviously his desire in any one of these cases can be appeased only through Sally or Jane, or some other individual girl. Nevertheless, so far as *that desire* is concerned, the particular traits of the individual involved in its assuagement do not count as such when the object wanted *is* generic or specific, although the desire itself may later undergo a transformation of a kind to make them count—having first wanted the generic or specific we may come to want the individual which we are now possessing and enjoying. The kind and diversity of satisfactions obtained from marrying Sally will be different from those we would have had if we had married Jane.

At this point I wish to remind the reader how important it is, in order to avoid serious pitfalls in theory of value, to realize that when the object of desire is generic or specific, there is no existing object concerned. If I want *a house,* there is no such thing as *a* house; there exists no mere colonial house as such, although, of course, there are many individual houses in the colonial style. Only the individual house, this or that or the other house, is real. This truth becomes perfectly clear when we want *to build a house:* obviously the house does not exist until it is built; if it did exist, I could not want to build it! Hence there is no relation between desire and its object in such cases, because there is no object. There is only a concept of an object. And even when I desire an individual, as when I want to marry Sally, there is no relation between herself and myself involved, for she does not enter bodily into my experience of desire; only the concept of her enters there. But in satisfaction, of course, it is otherwise; there she does enter in person.

A popular treatment of the part played by the object in satisfaction might dodge the epistemological issue, but a philosophical treatment cannot. We must raise the issue as to *how* the object enters into value (satisfaction)—just as we have asked how it enters into desire (and found that it enters through the concept). Is it a mere condition of satisfaction separable in existence from it, or does it enter as a constituent factor in satisfaction? If it is a mere condition, it would no more properly belong in our present analysis than do other important conditions, such as the organism, which is obviously an omnipresent condition of all satisfactions, so far as we know. The matter is clearly metaphysical. We must begin our discussion of it by distinguishing two kinds of objects, imaginary (ideal) and real. By the latter I mean such objects as this friend I am talking with, or this piece of bread that I am eating; by the former, I mean such objects as the fictitious incidents or characters in a story or play that I am reading, say Carrie sitting alone rocking in her chair in Dreiser's masterpiece, *Sister Carrie.*

Now it is certain that my friend and the piece of bread enter directly as constituents of the satisfaction. Whatever we may mean by "mind," they are in it when interest is appeased through them. There is no difficulty in such cases because the *esse* of these objects is *percipi*—their being is their being perceived. Carrie has no existence except in the minds of readers of Dreiser's novel. And if I obtain satisfaction from Carrie, she enters directly as a factor in the immediacy of my satisfaction. In desire also when the object is generic or specific, the object

enters as a constituent, for a genus and a species exist, as we
have said, only by way of concepts, and these are present in desire. To revert to one of our illustrations, if we want *a* colonial
house, the concept of a colonial house is present in our desire.
Even when what we want is individual, as when we want that
colonial house on Main Street, the individual is present in the
desire through the concept of it—that is the only way it can
enter, as we have noted.

When, however, the satisfaction is in real individual objects,
the way they enter into satisfaction is not so clear. Those who
follow the Cartesian tradition of separating the mind from the
body and the whole "external" world would assert that, say
in eating bread, only sensations of sight, taste, smell, and the
kinesthetic sensations involved in biting and masticating are
present in the satisfaction; the real physical bread would be
thought to lie outside of the satisfaction somewhere in the physical space of the mouth. But the consensus of contemporary
opinion is against this view. We cannot isolate the organism
from the environment, even from the standpoint of strict physical and physiological theory, especially when there is interaction
between them; there are exchanges of energy between them,
there is a contact of the two, and no clear line of demarcation.
Furthermore, we can no longer separate the mind, and therefore
desire and satisfaction, from the organism; it is as genuinely in
contact with the organism as this is with the environment.

This picture of the situation is confirmed from the side of
experience. The sensuous surface of our experience has an
ambiguous status. On the one hand, it consists of events which
are clearly mental; the taste of the bread is a given new event
in my experience when I eat it. On the other hand, these same
events belong to the thing; the taste is the taste *of the bread*
and is determined by "forces" belonging to nature. My very
hunger is determined in my stomach, and my satisfaction is
somehow "there" also. In the process of acting upon or "suffering" with reference to an object, the control of the situation,

which is my control, is met by the countercontrol of the thing, with the result that the satisfaction penetrates its surface or, to put it the other way round, the being of the object "overflows" into the satisfaction itself. My conclusion is, therefore, that the very object itself—or at least its surface—is a factor in the satisfaction.

4. *A judgment or series of judgments concerning the fitness of means objects or the complementary object for the realization of the goal.* In order to reach the goal it may happen that many means objects have to be sought and used, with regard to each of which a hypothetical judgment asserting that if I use a thing of this kind my aim will be furthered, or a predictive judgment asserting that this will further my aim may occur. If, while walking in the country, I am hungry and I see a restaurant across a little lake, and there is a boat for hire that I can use to get over, then I may make the judgment, "If I use that boat, I will get to the restaurant"; and after I have arrived there I may make a new judgment to the effect that, "These strawberries will assuage my hunger." Such judgments may not be explicit in the sense that they are put into words but may become so if someone asks *why* I am hiring that boat or eating those strawberries. Like the objective of desire, they may or may not be formulated.

There are students of the theory of value for whom these judgments are value judgments and the only value judgments. And that they are judgments relevant to values, there can be no doubt. Taken abstractly, they are simple empirical judgments: "This boat will take me across this stream" (or "If I take this boat, I will cross this stream"); "These strawberries will satisfy my hunger" (or "If I eat these strawberries, my hunger will be stilled"). These are propositions no different in kind from "This piece of iron will rust" or "If this piece of iron gets wet, it will rust." Their importance, no less than their relevance, is evident; apart from the possibility of making them, no complex actions and no complex values are possible at all. And I fear that this importance for values has misled students into identifying such judgments with value expressions. But by themselves, they are not value expressions at all, although they may be elements in value expressions. I can show how this is so by means of a simple example. Suppose I say to a friend, "Oh, I am hungry, those strawberries will satisfy my craving," or, " I want to cross that lake; this boat will take me over." Now both these expressions are volitional, taken as wholes; and the empirical propositions, "those strawberries will satisfy my craving" and "that boat will take me over" are parts of them; but, I repeat, considered as separate elements by themselves, they are not value expressions. How and why this is true, I have shown in the chapter on "Value Expressions."

5. *The assuagement of desire through the realization (verification) of the objective.* Since the objective is an activity or passivity with reference to an object, the realization of the objective is the activity or passivity itself. But by itself this is of no value; it must assuage a desire, there must be satisfaction. Merely to do or to suffer something is obviously no value, as action under compulsion or mere endurance or suffering attests. We have therefore two factors here, and, taken together, they constitute in a sense the satisfaction: pleasure and the realization of the objective. Yet while distinguishable, they are not separable, for the pleasure is in the activity or passivity desired and cannot occur without it. The great mistake of the hedonist is to suppose that they can be separated.

The matter seems very simple as I have stated it, but actually it contains several problems. One is whether the activity must be my own or whether it may be another's. Prima facie, it would appear that the activity may be another's. I may wish my friend to run for election, and if he does and is elected, I am pleased and there is value. Or I may wish the happiness of my daughter, which means wishing that her desires be satisfied through appropriate activities or passivities of her own, and if these occur there is value for me as well as for her. The issue between altruism and egoism would appear to depend upon how the answer is given to this question.

To me such examples as those given prove that the objective of desire may consist of activities or passivities which are not my own. Desire and satisfaction, although always someone's own, may therefore be unselfish. The desire and the assuagement are mine, but *what* will assuage it may yet be the activities or passivities of another person or persons. However, it does not follow that no activity on my part is involved. On the contrary, a very specific act occurs in me in such cases—the imagination of the activities or passivities of the other, which are the objective of my desire, together with belief that they are occurring (or have occurred). Imagination is an inner imitation or picturing of the activities desired, but this is not enough; it must be supplemented with belief, for otherwise the value would be akin to what we get from fiction, where we imagine activities but merely make believe that they are occurring. Moreover, the objective of desire and of satisfaction is not the imagination or the beliefs themselves—I am not desiring that I shall imagine or believe I am not interested in my own mental processes, but in activities that should happen outside myself. In these cases, imagination looks beyond itself to what is not itself. Nevertheless, as factors in my value, the imagination of the activities desired, which is their surrogate in my experience, together with belief, is necessary.

But with regard to all this, we must be very circumspect. For imagination together with belief, when well based, is knowledge; hence in the circumstances where value for me arises through the imagination of the activities of other persons, it would seem as if this value were a value of knowledge. And yet that this is not so becomes clear when we reflect that we may imagine and believe in the existence of the activities of persons in whom we are not much interested, and therefore have the specific value of knowing them, but this value is not the same

as that which we have when we are interested in them and wish
for their success. It is one value when I know of the successes of
my enemies, and another when I know of the achievements of
my friends. It follows that the first is a pure knowledge value
and the second, although also a knowledge value, functions as a
means to the assuagement of a particular desire, the desire that
such be the case as I imagine it. That this distinction holds becomes even clearer when we reflect that the value in knowing
that something is so may mediate the frustration of a wish that
it may not be so. Even to know bad news is as knowledge good;
but on that knowledge may depend our profoundest sorrow.

It is of great significance that this same specific value in knowing may accompany other values; those that result from the
realization of goals requiring activities of our own as well as
those that we have just been considering which require activities of other persons. Being satisfied is one value, knowing that
we are satisfied is another. Yet one satisfaction at least cannot
have attached to it the satisfaction of knowing that it is there—
the satisfaction in knowing that I am satisfied; otherwise experience would be infinitely complex. Moreover, there is no evidence
that this knowledge value must accompany any other values
than itself. There may be unknown satisfactions, even when
they are our own.

6. *Anticipatory and memorial satisfactions.* The analysis of
value so far given is complete for what I would call its active
phase. But there is a dimension of satisfaction that we have
neglected, which I would call its imaginative or, if you prefer,
its poetic phase. It has two forms, anticipatory and memorial.
The former is contained in desire itself. It has already been said
of value that desire is at its heart. Yet with equal truth it should
be said that satisfaction is at its heart. This is satisfaction in the
objective itself in contrast with satisfaction in the realization of
the objective. With the very positing of the objective, desire
finds an anticipatory assuagement—a satisfaction before satisfaction. It might be thought that anticipatory satisfaction must be

quenched when realization arrives; but that would be a mistake comparable with the view that desire disappears with satisfaction. The fact is rather the fusing of the imaginative with the active phase of satisfaction, whereby the latter acquires a new coloring of satisfaction, like the overtones of a tone or the base note of a chord. And, as everyone knows, it often happens that anticipatory satisfaction is more intense than the satisfaction that comes through action—"anticipation is better than realization."

The memorial phase of imaginative satisfaction I would call satisfaction after satisfaction. It is of more than one kind. The simplest is a memory echo following the active phase of satisfaction; it is like an echo or a tone that continues itself in the mind after the vibrations of air and tympanum have ceased. Values do not like to die. This echo then recedes into the background of experience, but even so gives it a special coloration of happiness or contentment and is seldom if ever entirely lost. Such echoes become the material out of which anticipatory satisfactions are built: satisfactions after satisfaction become the material of satisfactions before satisfaction. It may be true that all past satisfactions echo in any present satisfaction, especially those of the same kind, but of this we cannot be sure. What we can be sure of is that the present satisfaction is modified by past satisfactions of the same sort. Finally, there are the satisfactions which are voluntarily recalled, like arches of triumph set up by victors or memorial celebrations. Values thus show themselves to be complex like a chord or musical tone, not simple like a pure tone, devoid of overtones; or to continue the comparison, values are a three-part musical composition, a running melody, with a base accompaniment of echoes and a treble of anticipations. One might object, however, that this complexity cannot be a universal characteristic of all values, as it could not hold of utterly novel satisfactions. The infant's first drink of milk may be remembered but cannot be anticipated. On the other hand, the utterly novel is rare; and an adequate analysis of value cannot limit itself to minimum factors but should rather be limited just to maximum possibilities.

SECTION II. DIMENSIONS OF VALUE

One of the facts most baffling to any attempt to bring order into the field of values is their multidimensionality. If values were linear or planar or even voluminal, with one or two or possibly three dimensions, the task would be relatively easy, but, as we shall see, they are even more highly dimensional than our space. The mathematician, to be sure, works with ease in spaces of higher than three dimensions, but for two reasons: one, the relations defining the orders of the three dimensions are all homogeneous (they can, in fact, be reduced to a single relation, that of *between*); and two, the orders of higher dimensions contain as elements the orders of lower dimensions. Thus the order of points on a line is homogeneous with that of lines on a plane, and volumes consist of planes which are similar orders of planes. But the relations of greater and less in the dimension of intensity of values is not homogeneous with that of height or what we shall call volume, and height and volume are not series that contain intensities as elements. Moreover, in one dimension at least, that of quality, it has so far proved to be impossible to arrange the variations in any order. Because of these facts concerning values, mathematicians might object to our use of the term "dimension." There seems, however, to be no term so appropriate. As we shall use it, we shall mean a range of variations of a kind which may occur independently of another range and may or may not be susceptible of serial order.

When dimensionality is defined in this way, values show themselves to be at least six-dimensional, varying in: (1) intensity, (2) duration, (3) volume, (4) quality, (5) height, (6) harmony.

For those to whom such analogies are significant, we can

correlate the dimensions of value with those of tone, as follows: intensity with loudness, duration with duration, volume with volume, quality with timbre, height with pitch, and harmony with consonance. Some explanation must be given to each, especially to the last three.

1. *Intensity.* Variations in intensity of satisfaction are correlative with variations in intensity of desire. I may want something strongly or weakly, or more or less strongly, and when, and if, I get it, my satisfaction will, in general, be strong or weak. If I am only moderately thirsty, my pleasure in drinking will be moderate. If I am very thirsty, it will be intense. If, full of honors, I am awarded a new one, my satisfaction will be slight, because I now have very little eagerness for it; but the value of the first honor was vivid in comparison. However, the correlation between intensity of initial desire and intensity of satisfaction is not strict, because oftentimes, desire will be stimulated by the process of satisfaction itself. We may have had little desire for the music, but now, beginning to hear it, we have much. Few if any, I believe, would deny the existence of this dimension.[2]

2. *Duration.* This also, being a general trait of all existents, does not admit of controversy and is recognized by everyone. It is a commonplace that satisfactions may be more or less fleeting, more or less lasting. Moralists have invariably recommended the more lasting. Yet despite its obviousness, no attribute of experience is so difficult of interpretation and no term which we use to designate it more ambiguous in meaning. We may mean by "duration" a character of a pulse of experience of such a kind that one pulse may exist along with the rise and fall of others. Thus, the sound of the word "perfect" when

[2] From the time of Plato (*Protagoras,* 356A-E) this attribute has been recognized by all students. For some physiological speculations concerning it, see Ralph B. Perry's *General Theory of Value* (Cambridge, Mass.: Harvard Univ. Press, 1926), pp. 626-32. Plato also recognized duration and number, as evidenced again by the *Protagoras, loc. cit.*

we read the lines, "Perfect as the rose/ In its proud repose," comes to us as one item of fact, longer in this sense than either the syllable "per" or the syllable "fect." But this is not usually what we mean when we talk of one satisfaction as being more enduring than another; for we are usually comparing experiences that persist through more than one such pulse. Rather we are comparing the satisfaction that attends the gradual realization of a plan requiring months or years for its execution, or the remembered satisfactions that may recur again and again, with the momentary or almost momentary satisfactions of sense or sexual passion. The former satisfaction is assumed to have the same duration as that of the plan. Or the satisfaction attending the playing of a whole symphony would be another example of a satisfaction relatively enduring as compared with that of a whiff of perfume. It is assumed that the satisfaction in the symphony is one even as the symphony itself is one.

We admit the validity of the assumptions, which are those of common sense, but they are full of difficulties for metaphysical analysis. For example, the satisfaction obviously changes or grows during the musical experience; how can it remain one nevertheless and have one duration? And worse, the satisfaction that attends the realization of a long-term plan is intermittent during sleep; how now can it be one despite this? For those who interpret experience as a succession of droplets (with Whitehead) a long satisfaction is reducible to many satisfactions, and duration ceases to be an attribute of a satisfaction and becomes (as number) a property of a class of satisfactions. But, on the contrary, I shall try to show that experience cannot be interpreted as a succession of droplets but as a relatively stable and recurring matrix, about which new items arise and perish; hence the values attending the fulfillment of a plan which itself is an element of the matrix have the duration of the matrix. The proof will be given in the analysis of what I call the matrix self. And this is, I believe, in accordance with intuition (sometimes called common sense), which testifies to the persistence and recurrence of what we know as ourselves. Or, to put the matter in another way, if satisfactions are inseparable from their objectives and their objects, they have the duration that belongs to the latter.

3. *Volume*. Values (satisfactions) may be classified as massive, as voluminous, or as thin and small. And these distinctions run along a one-dimensional line. Compare the satisfaction in eating a piece of chocolate candy with that of welcoming home a son who has been away in combat! These, of course, are extreme examples, employed for the purpose of bringing the attribute into focus. A less extreme example would be a comparison between the satisfaction in playing bridge and that of reading a poem, say "Abraham Lincoln Walks by Night." These illustrations show, I think, that volume is the same as complexity. Moreover, complexity bears some relation to the number of distinguishable (though not necessarily distinguished) sensuous and active factors in the experience, as follows from the definition of value in terms of activities and passivities upon an object. The experience of eating chocolate is simple compared with that of welcoming a son. Or to use a very elementary illustration, the experience of drinking coffee is more complex than that of drinking water, for the satisfaction in drinking coffee is not merely a satisfaction in assuagement of thirst, but also in flavor. But it is not merely the number of elements that is determinative, but their variety also, for if they are too much alike, they tend to fuse and lose volume. The satisfaction in the chord c-e-g is more complex than the satisfaction in the chord c-c'-c''. Yet that a voluminous satisfaction may be concentrated upon a slender thread of sense experience is shown by the example of a violin solo. This illustration shows that in the end volume depends rather upon the complexity of the pattern of desire than upon the complexity of the pattern of the object, although the two are roughly correlative.

4. *Quality*. Satisfactions are as diverse in quality as sounds and colors. They too have their tints and timbres. The satisfac-

tion in tasting tea is a different kind of satisfaction from that of tasting wine or milk or coffee. The satisfaction of jazz is different from that of a work by Mozart; the value of love is of a different sort from that of hate; beauty has one flavor, bodily exercise, as swimming or playing tennis, another. All of these statements would seem to be obvious. They are, however, in contradiction with a long tradition for which all satisfactions are utterly homogenous. The great exception is Aristotle, who in the *Poetics* declared that the pleasures of tragedy are of a different kind from those of the epic. Although so strong a tradition must be viewed with respect, I am nevertheless convinced that the failure to perceive differences in quality is due entirely to the opaque screen of theory—the theory that satisfaction is an entity that can be isolated from the other factors in value, and as so isolated is the same in all values. But, on the contrary, although the various factors are distinguishable, they are not isolable. The satisfaction is in the activity or the passivity upon the object, apart from which it simply does not exist. To ascribe the differences in values to differences in these and then to hold off the factor of assuagement as something separate is to fail to recognize the integrity and unity of the experience. In fine, the satisfaction is colored by the activity, and itself becomes different according to the differences in the activities.

5. *Height*. This dimension is the most puzzling of all. Yet prima facie it seems to be as genuine an attribute of values as intensity or volume. We distinguish values as higher or lower with as much confidence as we distinguish them as more or less voluminous or intense. Thus, for me, my interest in poetry or philosophy is higher than my interest in bridge, my love of my children than my interest in professional advancement, and the enjoyment of a melody than the enjoyment of a perfume. This is as obvious as that my satisfaction in tea is more intense than it is in coffee. Nevertheless, the tendency has persisted to deny the reality of the dimension. Among the ancients, Aristotle

clearly recognized it, but the testimony of Plato is ambiguous. In the *Protagoras* Plato allows only the dimensions of *near* and *far, many* and *few, more* and *less,* although in the *Symposium* differences of height are clearly recognized. Among the early utilitarians no place was given to this dimension. However, in the case of J. S. Mill, as is well known, a surprising reversal of opinion occurred. Yet the originality of his view was only relative to the climate of opinion to which he belonged, for from a more universal standpoint, he simply reaffirmed the classical tradition. Today the tendency is widespread to question differences of height as intrinsic to desires and values, and to regard them as mere conventional marks of social status no more firmly based than the preference of the "upper" classes for white collars. Such differences of opinion would in themselves induce caution in accepting height as a bona fide dimension.

In the interest of simplicity, one would like to reduce it to complexity or intensity, or perhaps to a combination of both. And that it is not independent of these is certain. The higher tend to be more intense than the lower—my satisfaction in philosophy than my satisfaction in bridge, my satisfaction in a melody of Mozart than in a perfume. Yet certain organic desires, like hunger and thirst, if starved can attain to an intensity and yield a corresponding satisfaction difficult to surpass by any "higher" value. And, on the other side, even when the intensity of satisfaction of a higher value is low—as when tired, I listen to music—I still recognize it as higher than the bridge that I am enjoying with such zest.

That height is not unrelated to volume is also clear. Love between man and woman is felt to be higher than crude sex impulse, and at the same time is more voluminous because it comprises, in addition to sex, devotion and beauty. A melody of Mozart, besides the pleasantness of pure and consonant tones, comprises in addition the expression of subtle and complex objectless emotions. The strongest case for the reduction of height can, in fact, be made on the supposition that it is nothing more than an *evaluation* of a value in terms of its complexity. Besides complexity, harmony might enter in as a determining factor in the rating.[3] Thus of two melodies, the one which satisfied more desires in the imagination, provided they were well integrated, would be a "higher" melody than one which satisfied fewer, or than one which, while satisfying many, left them in unresolved conflict. Mere complexity would not suffice, for otherwise the rank of a musical composition would be enhanced merely by adding a few scattered bars unrelated to the whole, or our admiration for St. Francis would be increased if we knew that he had had a liking for fine clothes (the illustration is T. S. Eliot's).

Indeed, the very terms "higher" and "lower" would appear to substantiate the suggestion that height is rather an evaluation of values than an intrinsic property of them: they have a connotation of appraisal, of ranking, as when I say of something that I rate it very high or give it a high rating. Height, then, would be just a synonym for rank and would accordingly disappear from our list of dimensions of value. The temptation to accept this view would be strong since it would clear the theory of value of a very troublesome problem. Against this hypothesis, however, there stand certain facts. One such fact is that low values may be rated very high because of their effects on other values and still remain intrinsically low. The value of eating is a telling case of this sort. And, on the other hand, high values, such as the aesthetic, may be rated low in times of crisis when life itself is in peril. In emergency, the rating scale may turn the scale of height upside down. Yet the scale of high and low is not abolished in these circumstances; it remains intact. On the other hand, in favor of the identification of height with rank it

[3] For an interesting attempt along these lines, in the aesthetic field, I would cite George Birkhoff's *Aesthetic Measure* (Cambridge, Mass.: Harvard Univ. Press, 1933), with its formula for aesthetic valuation, $M = \dfrac{C}{O}$, measure equals complexity divided by order.

could be argued that height is nothing more than an evaluation of values when all the factors determining rank (intensity, volume, harmony, and, what is most significant, importance in terms of effects on the whole system of one's values) are taken into consideration. Thus, the high value attributed to moral values, like love and courage, would derive from the fact that another's courage protects, and his love promotes, all my values. In similar fashion, the high value of art would be explained away as a rating due to its efficiency in propaganda for so-called useful ends, or as means of promoting altruistic sentiments, beneficial in the end to myself.

In an effort to decide the issue, one should begin by admitting that rank and height are easily confused, partly because height is ambiguous, meaning either, and partly because height may itself be a factor in determining rank, if it is an independent variable of satisfaction. Thus for those who appreciate beauty, its height is a factor, along with its complexity, harmony, intensity, and importance in terms of effects, in determining its rank. Moreover, as we have seen, height is not unrelated to intensity, complexity or volume, and harmony. Both love and beauty are experiences of the greatest intensity, the greatest volume—absorbing the whole man into them—and also confer a wonderful harmony; their height may therefore seem to be nothing more than a synthesis of these dimensions. Yet that there is some unique dimension of values, referred to by the term "height," which is an intrinsic attribute and not a mere evaluation or rating, I for one am convinced. That height cannot be reduced to an evaluation in terms of effects is proved by the cases of love, beauty, and courage. For anyone in love, it is not the fact that someone else's love is beneficial that confers its dizzy height, but something in the experience itself. For, as Aristotle said, "It is better to love than to be loved"; and who that appreciates beauty in poetry or music or painting or architecture is appraising them in terms of their effects? With courage, it is no different. The height of its value is in the activity

of being courageous oneself, not in enjoying the fruits of somebody else's courage. The question then is, what, if any, intrinsic
attributes have the high values in greater degree than the lower,
over and above the dimensions of intensity, complexity, and
harmony, which admittedly they possess in great degree?

In order to answer this question, we should revert to a problem already raised by us when we were discussing the objective
of desire, namely, whether the objective could be the assuagement of another person's desire; and we resolved this by answering, "Yes." The objective of love, in its many forms, is unselfish in the specific sense of aiming at a value that is not one's
own. Here is a desire that is at the extreme of a dimension to
which we may give the term "self-transcendence." In love, desire takes us definitely outside of ourselves, bringing us into
union with another's life. At the other extreme lies the animal's
interest in food—or our own for that matter under some circumstances—where only the present good of ourselves is sought. Yet
even where self-transcendence is minimal, as in this case, it is
not completely absent, for in satisfying hunger the animal looks
to the future, even if short, and thus transcends its present self.
And the degree of self-transcendence may be great when long-
range plans for the acquisition and storage of food are projected,
leading far into the future and involving an increasing area of
control and absorption of external substance. Such desires are,
it is true, destructive of values in animal and plant life, but this
destruction is compensated for by the building up of a larger
and temporally more extended life in one's self.

Vanishing in degree of self-transcendence are the autoerotic
desires of men and animals. Compare this with normal sexual
intercourse which requires physical union with the body of
another and, in man, a desire to cause pleasure in the partner
to the act, as well as perhaps an interest in the creation of a new
life. Thus in this one interest, we find an ascending series of
degrees of self-transcendence and union, from autoerotism,
through animality or lust in sexual intercourse, to love in its—

notice how we inevitably use this term—"highest" forms. Even the interest in food is capable of ascending degrees of self-transcendence from the animal's lonely eating to the sharing of food with another or with a group when desire is centered on the satisfactions of others, as well as of oneself, and brings one into union with them. The greatest self-transcendence is obviously attained by the hero, the patriot, and the saint, where the individual's desire brings him into union with the lives of thousands or millions.

Of particular interest with regard to self-transcendence are the values of knowledge, art, and religion, all of which have commonly been thought of as "high." The appreciation of knowledge as high is undoubtedly partly an evaluation. Knowledge is the supreme means to the realization of any desire, and the respect for it since the Renaissance has largely been owing to this fact. But among the Greeks it is interesting to notice that this respect was inversely proportional to its value as a means. Even today knowledge is felt to be intrinsically "high," owing to its "disinterestedness." But disinterestedness is a phase of self-transcendence. In the first place, it is not an interest in one's self, in one's own satisfactions, but in the world external to one's self. It brings one into union, directly in knowledge by acquaintance and indirectly through the concept, vicariously, with that world. In the second place, it is a value that can be, and is, shared with others, both in its pursuit in co-operation with fellow workers and as an attainment to be communicated and enjoyed with them. Research and teaching are essentially social enterprises and satisfactions today. There is nothing in the value of knowledge that prevents another from having a like joy with one's self.

Like scientific value, beauty also is high in the evaluative sense, not because of its beneficent effect, but for other reasons such as intensity, inclusiveness, and harmony. Yet it, too, has usually, but not always, been regarded as disinterested, and as high intrinsically. When it has not been so regarded, emphasis has been placed on its circlelike, seeming self-sufficiency, leading to its condemnation by moralists as being selfish, "autoistic," and even as a form of autoerotism. But this way of viewing art is one-sided. For it is forgotten that aesthetic enjoyment does not depend on private conditioning, as the enjoyment of a keepsake does, and that the lover of beauty wishes others to have a like enjoyment with himself and feels frustrated when this desire is not realized. Art is communication, not mere self-expression. Moreover, insofar as art contains conceptual elements, as it does in poetry, prose literature, drama, painting, and sculpture, it is like science in giving us vicarious imaginative union with the pageant of nature and human experience. And even when art is pure, as in music and abstract painting and ornament, the artist feels himself in union with the basic rhythm of the universe. Since there is an abstract element in all art, the so-called imitative included, a music of sheer color and line and shape, art remains high as self-transcendent and unifying.

Like science, religion may be evaluated high as a means, magical rather than manipulative, for the achievement of personal or social ends; and if it were not high in any other sense or for no other reason, it would not be long in the present discussion. But even the most pragmatic religions were forms of self-transcendent union with the powers of nature, and in the performance of the rite brought the believer into union with other members of his group. And, in what are once more revealingly designated its higher forms, service, not of oneself, but of God, or in the mystic faiths, direct union with God or the universe, is sought. Here self-transcendence attains to what is perhaps its highest degree, justifying the judgment of religion as the highest value.

Such then is our vindication of height as an intrinsic dimension of values. We admit that sometimes intrinsic height is confused with rank as an evaluation on grounds other than intrinsic height—although that, too, may play, as we shall see, an important role in evaluation. But we have found that in dis-interestedness or what we prefer to call self-transcendence, there is a genuine intrinsic dimension of values, like other dimensions capable of degree and arrangement in a scale. And even as the other scales may be reversed, ordering the items not as they are more or less but as they are less or more, so in the case of self-transcendence, one can arrange the degrees according to selfishness, for even the most heroic or purest religious or aesthetic experience—the supreme sacrifice of the soldier, the celebration of the Mass, a toccata of Bach—are somebody's satisfaction, rooted in personal desires not wholly to be transcended or shared with another.

6. *Harmony*. This is clearly a structural characteristic, and as such differs from intensity, duration, and self-transcendence which might belong to simple values, if there were any. Yet since there are probably no simple values known to us, this difference is not important. Moreover, harmony is more or less present in every experience, for insofar as even the simplest act depends upon the co-operation of many impulses, there is some degree of harmony within it, despite elements of waste and conflict. By harmony is meant precisely the co-operation of diverse strains of desire toward a single goal or satisfaction. It reaches a high level in the experience of mastery, where all forces of the personality are integrated to a given end, in courage where they are marshaled to meet some imminent danger, or in beauty and in that infusion of the whole self with tenderness and sexual desire which we call being in love. It attains to its highest level in the attitudes of faith, resignation, or heroism, whereby even the disharmonies of personality are resolved in a difficult happiness.

It is important to realize, however, that any low degree of harmony is not a mere absence or privation—as a lower degree of intensity is a privation of a higher degree of intensity—but that any absence of harmony involves *disharmony*. For insofar as any partial impulse merely fails to co-operate—not to say conflicts with—the other partial impulses, it is a drag on the system and a cause of frustration. Once again I think the analogy with tones is enlightening: two tones that do not harmonize are discordant. So in the self, it is difficult for two impulses to remain merely side by side, as it were, unintegrated, without conflicting in some degree. The tendency of any interest is to pervade the entire self, so that unless another interest can be brought into co-operation with it, a struggle between them for time and energy is inevitable. Prima facie, gardening and doctoring do not conflict, but the former will interfere with the calls of desperate patients. As an interruption, every vacation is a disorganization, although in the end it promotes integration. Illustrations of the more serious forms of disharmony are as easy to provide as are the conspicuous cases of harmony. The state of soul of the woman who because of "incompatibility" wishes to leave her husband but does not, owing to loyalty to her children or fear of an untried way of life; the ambivalence of the attitude of the Christian who as patriot hates his enemy yet remembers the admonition of Christ; the enjoyment of the "forbidden" lusts of the flesh; these are well-known examples of disharmony.

Since disharmony stems from a conflict of impulses that cannot be resolved, of such a nature that the satisfaction of one entails the frustration of others, it might seem as if disharmony were not *within* a value, but rather between a satisfaction and a frustration, between good and evil in the whole of experience. If this were true, disharmony would not parallel harmony, which is an attribute of a value, where the satisfactions of the diverse interests fuse into a single whole of value. Nevertheless, it can be shown that actually disharmony qualifies satisfaction itself. This follows from the fact already noted that every desire creates an anticipatory, imaginative satisfaction of itself, so that, even when frustrated, it is, thus far, satisfied. Now this satisfaction is inharmonious with the satisfaction of the victorious impulse in any case of conflict. For example, the satisfaction yielded by the forbidden lust is side by side and inharmonious with the incompatible remembrance of the satisfaction of innocence; or if the temptation is resisted, the satisfaction in conforming to duty is accompanied with the inharmonious imagination of the assuagement of lust, which still persists. Or the satisfactions of the woman who remains with her family—pleasures in the round of accustomed duties—are intermingled with inharmonious imaginings of escape. These satisfactions belong to one whole of experience; they constitute a single complex value; hence it remains true that conflicting desires create inharmonious satisfactions. The subtle implications of these facts will be of decisive importance in some of our later chapters.

SECTION III. THE THEORY OF EVIL

It will be fitting to conclude this chapter with a brief discussion of evil—brief because almost, if not quite, everything that may be said of evil is a simple corrolary of what has been established concerning value.

First, if assuagement of desire is generic, intrinsic good, then frustration of desire is generic, intrinsic evil. Or, even as desire and fulfillment go together and are what we mean by the good, so desire and frustration go together and when together are what we mean by evil. So, corresponding to goods or valuables which promote assuagement, there are evils that hinder assuagement and promote frustration, but these are not intrinsic good or evil, but what are often called extrinsic or contributory good or evil, respectively. Correspondingly also there are direct or complementary evils and indirect or means evils: the rope that ties me and against which I struggle to be free is a complementary evil; the man who tied and then left me is a means evil. Frustrations have the same dimensions as the parallel satisfactions: intensity, quality, volume, duration, height, and harmony. This statement is I think obvious; the only difficulties concern the last, but it will be better to delay the study of them until after the study of another important matter.

This matter is the following: evils, both in the sense of objects that cause frustrations and frustrations themselves are connected with negative desires (aversions), of escape from (fear) and of destruction (hate); and also with the positive interest which we may identify in a general way with what is ordinarily called "intelligence"—the activity of devising ways and means to achieve an end, in this particular case, the avoidance of evils. This last interest, since it is connected with satisfactions as well as frustrations, may be neglected for the moment. Confining our attention therefore to the first two, we see that we could define, as Professor R. B. Perry does, evil as the *object* of negative interests. An interesting objection to his general definition of value "as any object of any interest" may be derived from this fact; for, accepting this definition, it turns out that evil, as object of interest, is a value! Surely a paradoxical result, yet not without its truth, for the assuagement of negative interests is a patent good: the thrill of escape, as one shoots the rapids or takes a nose dive in a plane, and of all other dangerous pleasures so dear to adventurous youth; the satisfaction of hate in the destruction of the enemy. Moralists do not like to recognize the values of hate, but no understanding of human nature is possible otherwise—the fascination of war, for one thing, becomes unintelligible. But negative interests are as real as any, and their satisfactions are values as genuine as those which arise from the "positive" interests. Moreover, adopting the conventional though not too appropriate terminology, they may become extrinsic goods. For in providing occasion for the devising of means of escape or destruction, they may be the source of some of the sharpest joys. Or, as we shall see, they may become occasions for finding substitutes, sublimations, and compromises, and in that way also become creative of values. I would, however, stress the fact that frustrations are in themselves never values in the proper sense, but at best means to values. Hence when negative interests fail through the frustration of our interest to escape or destroy the evil, evil is added to evil.

The imaginative values of negative interests are also rich and important compensations for evil or the threat of evil. The joy in hating is an imaginative value arising from the thought of revenge exacted—the secret delight of slaves and conquered peoples. Masters and victors nourish it unwittingly to their eventual cost.

Although the problem of evil in connection with harmony will be investigated later, we must set down certain elementary generalizations at this point in order to give some completeness to our present discussion. The most elementary of all generalizations is the possibility of the coexistence of frustration and satisfaction. This may exist even in the simplest appetition, for frustration due to delay coexists there with the imaginative satisfaction of anticipated fulfillment; and on the highest level of personality we may find the satisfactions attendant upon the carrying through of a professional interest appearing against a black background of sorrow or inhibited sexual desire. The Plato of the *Gorgias* was right, therefore, in maintaining that pleasure and pain may coexist, but wrong in inferring that the one is not the generic good and the other generic evil because (so he thought) their coexistence would be a contradiction.[4] It is, of course, true that the frustration and the assuagement of the same impulse cannot coexist on the same plane of action or imagination. That this is true is as evident as the law of contradiction. But they coexist on different planes, as when all the time a desire is being frustrated I may sustain myself with the imagination of its fulfillment. Another important generalization—no less important although obvious—is the dissonance of satisfaction and frustration. And yet, as we shall see, it is possible, as in music, to turn this dissonance into harmony.

But while satisfactions together with frustrations are always dissonant, frustrations may be either harmonious or dissonant with each other, as in the parallel case of satisfactions paired

[4] See 496A-497A.

with satisfactions. Thus, the moral frustration which is experienced as guilt is in some curious way felt by the child or the religious adult to be harmonious with the pain of physical punishment or of a sacrificial gift. As an example of dissonant frustrations, I would cite the felt inappropriateness in oneself of slight annoyances, as well as slight pleasures, in the midst of a great sorrow.

CHAPTER V

THE ORGANIZATION OF VALUES

THUS far in our analysis of values, we have been chiefly concerned with single desires and satisfactions, and the impression might easily arise that we believed them to be actually separate and separable facts. But such an impression would be entirely erroneous. For there are no simple or isolated desires. Even such a seeming unit as the desire for food is really a patterned cluster of propensities: the interest in seeing the food, in smelling, tasting, masticating, and swallowing it, and so on. Usually, what is commonly called "an interest" is largely a linguistic device for a whole constellation of activities. Consider, for example, what might be called a professor's "interest in philosophy." This is no simple matter, but covers at least the following: an interest in studying the writings of other philosophers or teachers of philosophy, a habit of conversing with colleagues about philosophy, a desire to expound and communicate one's ideas to students, an impulse to write controversial letters, or books and articles. And the assuagement of each of these impulses provides a different and characteristic satisfaction. On the other hand, these linguistic devices are not purely fictitious. There is a certain truth in talking about *an* interest or *the* interest in philosophy, for all the various activities mentioned are held together as contributing to, and are intertwined with, what I shall call a desire or interest of "higher order"—in this case, the recurring interest in solving certain problems called philosophical. Moreover, the satisfaction of this interest of higher order is also unique and characteristic and cannot be completely identified with the relatively "lower order" interests mentioned.

Or consider another example, the interest of the good housekeeper in keeping her home looking attractive. This is again no simple matter, for it depends on a large number of relatively distinct activities, such as sweeping, dusting, scrubbing floors, arranging furniture, making and hanging curtains, and the like. And if the housewife enjoys housekeeping, as she probably will if she is a young bride in her own new home, each of these activities will yield a peculiar pleasure for her. But none of these pleasures can be simply identified with her pleasure in seeing her house look attractive; for it is only through all these activities taken together that she gets it. Yet the desire for it and the imaginative anticipation of it will inform and organize the whole round of housewifely doings, stringing them like beads on a thread.

We can state the difference between what we are calling desires of higher and lower order as follows, recognizing that the distinction is relative, except for any basic appetitions of zero order and any desires of highest order which we may discover. The objective or goal of a relatively first order desire is activity on a single or a limited small group of objects, and the desire is appeased in a single terminating process of satisfaction. Thus, if when thirsty I want to drink, my desire will be assuaged if I drink this glass of water, and the process of satisfaction will be a self-terminating one. To be sure, many glasses of water may be required, but even so the process runs a rounded course. Or if I want to play a game of tennis with a friend, then I shall want to win *this* game through a limited number of activities on a limited number of things—racket, balls, court, and net, and my desire will issue in a single triumph or defeat. This illustration is interesting, however, in showing that even relatively first order desires are not of lowest order; for the desire to win this game controls many plays in the game—the serving, returning, or placing the ball in such a way as to contribute to victory, each of which, being well directed, has its own objective and yields its peculiar modicum of satisfaction, distinguishable from that of winning the game itself, which comes only after all the plays. Yet the latter is not entirely separate either, since the hope or anticipation of winning colors each play, and the memory of each good play gives body and richness to triumph when it comes. That first order desires are recurrent does not affect their general character; for when the desire recurs, it terminates, for the time being at least, in a single satisfaction, and then becomes quiescent.

In contrast, a high order desire cannot be satisfied by a self-limiting activity on a single object or small number of objects. No single satisfaction or course of satisfaction can bring it to quiescence. Your love of your young daughter is not assuaged by giving her a new doll on her birthday or on Christmas, by providing her an education or trousseau, a layette for her infant, or by any other act expressive of your love. True it is, of course, that each of these acts will cause you pleasure. But your desire does not terminate in any one of them. A whole series of acts extending through the years is necessary in order to assuage the desire. What we call the desire for knowledge is of this sort, for it cannot be appeased by knowing this or that fact. Sometimes the series of activities is infinite, or "open," as in both love and curiosity. Such desires are, as we say, insatiable; they are not satisfied through any limited class of activities. Sometimes the series of activities is of ascending intensity, as in the case of the ambition of the politician, beginning with the county office, then rising to state and eventually to national appointment.

There may even be a climax or end point to the series in which it terminates, as when the office seeker wins the presidency. On the other hand, when the series is open, there can be no climax. There is none in love or in knowledge.

The heart of the contrast between first and second order desires is clearly in the objective of each. For convenience of discrimination in discourse, let us call the objective in the case of the former a goal; in that of the latter a plan. A plan of campaign, a plan of education for self or child, these are objectives that require a series of acts, each of which will terminate, but in terminating will not assuage the desire, for it is a desire to *perform acts of a kind or class;* or, alternatively, a satisfaction in satisfactions of a *sort.* On the other hand, as we have seen, the objective of a first order desire may be a goal quickly reached. Hence in tabular form, we have the following:

1st order desire	*2d order desire*
Goal—single activity	Plan—series of activities
Complete assuagement in a single act	Incomplete assuagement in a single act

It follows that, in second order desires, the satisfaction, until the end, if there is an end, is a restless satisfaction, and when the series of assuaging acts is open, it remains restless. It is obvious, furthermore, that second order desires may require acts of very different sorts, as love does. We may, therefore, give them another appropriate name, system-desires.

I believe I have already made it clear that first and second order desires are not separate. Yet the matter may perhaps need emphasis and further elucidation. Generally speaking, as has been noted, second order desires are unifying threads among the miscellany of first order desires. So the love of the daughter unites and organizes the various acts performed by the father with reference to her, each of which is the expression of a first order interest. So the birthday party he gives her is the expression of an interest that terminates when the party is over, yet is bound together with the interest, also self-terminating, in buying her a new frock or giving her a graduation present. In similar fashion the desire for fame and power of the politician organizes the various acts of consulting with party chiefs, speech-making, letter-writing, and fund-raising, each of which realizes a first order objective, terminating when that particular goal is accomplished. Moreover, the second order desire chooses among possible acts, thus becoming the basis for decision, accepting some and rejecting others.

On the assumption that this theory of the hierarchical order-ing of desires is correct, the question becomes inevitable whether there is a desire, and so a possible satisfaction, of high-est order, a supreme value, a desire and value of the self as a whole. In order to answer this question we must try to answer a preliminary question, "What is the self?" Obviously, we can-not study this problem exhaustively, as would be done in a book of metaphysics, but only insofar as is necessary for our purpose in hand.

I have found it convenient to distinguish between what I like to call the focal and the matrix self. By the former I mean the total ongoing pulse of experience, which is always centered in some desire or appetition, some activity or passivity seeking assuagement. No philosopher or psychologist today would think of this pulsation as a mere bundle of miscellaneous and sepa-rable items, as Hume seems to have thought of it, but rather as a highly organized system—in our own language, a stratification of higher and lower impulses, the higher controlling the lower in the fashion described. The total ongoing activity of writing the present sentence of this essay would be what I am calling my focal self; the total experience of the tennis player as he returns the ball directed to a certain spot on the court would be his focal self. The course of our experience from its beginning to its end is a series of such focal selves, pulsations or waves of activity, rising and falling. But this series is certainly not all that we mean by the self, for if it were there would be no meaning for personal identity, and no unity in our various activities. The pulses come and go, rise and fall, but the self remains in some sense the same carried over from moment into moment, from day to day, and through the years.

This other aspect of the self, contrasting with the focal self, I call the "matrix" self. It is not anything occult or transcendental but is as genuinely given and empirical as a color, a tone, a longing. It is compresent with all our activities, with all the sensuous and imaginal items that constitute a person's experience. Although interwoven with their texture, it yet survives their comings and goings. It is the basis of personal identity, and when it is shattered, one ceases to be one's self. It corresponds to the Aristotelian essence, the τὸ τί ἦν εἶναι of a person. It overarches long stretches of our experience the way a plan overarches and is carried through and gives sense to the activities that fulfill it, as for example the plan of this book is carried along from sentence to sentence or chapter to chapter, or as the conductor's knowledge of a composition continues through and survives each note, each figure, each phrase and movement of the whole. The simplest alternative designation of what I mean by the matrix self is perhaps the "life plan," a phrase prominent in the writings of Josiah Royce. All our focal activities flash in and out of the matrix self.

Although possessed of unity, the matrix self is highly complex. Within it we may distinguish, although we cannot separate, conceptual (intellectual) and volitional components. The former constitute a kind of map or basic orientation, of spatial, temporal, psychosomatic, and social relations, each with a center and a horizon. In space the center is the "here" of each person, that is to say, at the body, while the horizon consists of those positions "there" to which he may be interested to move. So for me, the here is this room. The horizon consists of interesting points like the campus, Detroit, and New York, to which I may wish to move. The spatial map enables one to get around without confusion in one's world. How important this orientation is every traveler realizes who arrives in a strange city without having in mind its ground plan. Such a plan is, of course, only a detail of one's master spatial plan. Yet the master plan is made up of smaller plans of this kind—the plan of one's house, of one's garden, of one's town, of one's country.

In time, the center is the "now" of each person's ongoing activity, the horizon is two-directional, the *has been* and the *to be,* past and future, consisting of important ordered events, remembered on the one hand, and anticipated on the other. Without temporal orientation it is obvious that no effective planning is possible. The temporal aspect of our matrix self is our personal calendar of events, of which a schedule of appointments for a day or week or year is an illustration in little. Maps, calendars, and histories are interpersonal extensions and aids to our spatial and temporal schemes, meaningless, however, apart from the personal. To explain how such interpersonal schemes grow out of our personal spatial and temporal orientation would be an interesting development of our present line of thought, but we cannot pursue it here. How important the integrity of spatial and temporal orientation is to the preservation of the ego is clear to anyone who has watched the disintegration of personality in mental disease.

In psychosomatic orientation, the center is "me," vaguely located somewhere in the head (the brain?), the horizon is my members—hands, legs, mouth, eyes, ears, and so forth. The vagueness of location of the me is largely due to the fact that the connection of the personality with the body is so close that we tend to confuse them, and spread the ego, so to speak, all over the latter. The psychosomatic is the smallest of all our maps in range, but in importance it ranks as high as any. It may, indeed, be regarded as the central part of the spatial map, but there is good reason for distinguishing it from the latter. The reason is that what appears to be direct control over regions of space is confined to the body—beyond, control is indirect through the body itself. I can, seemingly, raise my hand directly, but I can raise my cane only through my hand. Moreover, some of the desires topmost in rank in anyone's life plan are what are known as "bodily"—localized in the body both as impulse and as satisfaction, notably food and sex. With regard to such interests, the body is not merely a tool, but apparently a participant—satisfaction is in the body itself. The psychosomatic map enables us to find our way around the body as spatial orientation permits us to find our way about in space. It is something which the child must learn; and it is subject to disintegration like all our other maps. A slight degree of disintegration is shown by the left-handed, who remain to the end of their lives uncertain which is the right and which is the left hand or foot; and such disorientation within the bodily field easily affects the wider spatial field, as is illustrated by the uncertainty of such a person at the table, as to whether the napkin or glass is his or his neighbor's.

Finally, in social orientation the center is again *me,* the horizon is *they.* Most important is the scheme of family relations— the recognition of certain persons as father, mother, brother, sister, wife, husband, son, and daughter. Next in importance is the professional map—superior-subordinate, employer-employee, teacher-student, or the reverse. Less significant, but still significant, is orientation in the friendship and civic fields. It needs no argument or illustration to show how essential to the organization of experience these schemes are, and how disastrous is failure of their functioning. Suppose I no longer know who is my wife, or my child, or my friend!

That the spatial, temporal, psychosomatic, and social orientations are not separate is evident. Let me illustrate. A child's spatial plan of the house in which he lives locates a certain room as *his* bedroom, another room as *our* playroom (his and his brothers' and sisters'); yet another as father's and mother's; still another as belonging to all of us (the dining room)—where he accomplishes the delicate psychosomatic job of co-ordinating hand and mouth. Each of these persons and places, moreover, fits into a time schedule. So, for the child, his playroom is "where I go after my nap" and "after my breakfast," whereas the dining room is "where I go from my bedroom after I wake up," and so on. Similarly, for the businessman, the office is "where I go after breakfast and meet my colleagues" and the club is "where I go on Saturday nights to play cards with my friends."

These maps are never matters of mere knowledge and recognition, however, for they mediate patterns of desire and action. The spatial pattern, as we have noted, is a pattern of possible movements to be executed in order to fulfill our desires, or to be prevented for the same reason; the individuals and bodily members which are the important anchorages in our map of social-psychosomatic relationships are objects of special interests and habits or resolutions to action. The matrix self is thus seen to be essentially a plan of action expressive of fundamental desires. It is the master objective in which all objectives find their places. But it should not be thought of as a mere pattern exhibiting how events or actions actually occur in obedience to desire; for like all lesser objectives it is itself regulative of actions, not static and inert but functional and creative. When we say "I decide," it decides, determining what shall be done and what shall be left undone; for "I" and "it" are one and the same thing. It is a selector of possible interests and acts, initiating and cultivating some and forbidding others according as they do or do not further it. Thus the student's plan to get his degree impels him to renounce certain amusements, keeps him long hours in the library or at his desk. It is the basis of decision.

Although the matrix self is a plan of and for our desires and undoubtedly emerges out of their objectives in the development of the individual, it attains to a certain independence of some desires. The relationship here is comparable to that which we have already established between any desire of higher order and the desires of lower order which it controls. Only this is the desire of highest order, the desire to realize the objective of highest order—the life plan. In it our major long term interests alone are represented, not the passing interest or passion. The latter must either be fitted into the plan, suppressed, or accommodated in some way. The life plan obviously includes our organic needs, such as those for food and sleep, our highest professional and cultural aims, and the interests bound up with our more permanent social relations—those concerning husband or wife, parents and children, and very close friends. However, the life plan is a general scheme—it cannot include all the details of our life, which no one can foresee. It includes the plan to eat three meals a day, but not to eat this particular food at this restaurant tonight. It includes the desire to educate one's children, but not the courses they will take, which are matters of their own choice. It dictates that I shall wear clothes, but not this suit on this occasion. All these special acts and interests are provided for in the life plan, but are not there before they occur. The situation is the same as in the game of tennis: the aim to win the game controls all my plays but cannot foresee them all. And just as the satisfaction in winning the game is not the same as the pleasure in making this or that good stroke, so the satisfaction belonging to the realization of the life plan is not the same as that which attends the assuagement of this or that subordinate interest, although these latter make their contribution to it.

That there is a specific satisfaction and emotion attendant upon the realization of the life plan—and a correlative evil attendant upon failure—incapable of being attached to any desire of lower order than the highest, is another indication of the relative independence of the matrix self. What is ordinarily called happiness is, I believe, this specific value, and unhappiness is the specific evil. The adult human being is not happy because he has won a game of cards or bought a new car. These achievements contribute to happiness but do not constitute it. But winning the girl of one's choice or securing some long-sought professional honor comes nearer to happiness, because these are elements in the life plan. On the other hand, a man may be happy and be in pain, if the pain is not too intense, or be continually uncomfortable (*crede experto*) and still be happy, if his life plan is being realized. Again, a man may be happy and lose money on the exchange, for that will not necessarily give him the feeling of being a failure. There is a vast difference between failing now and then and being a failure, even as there is a vast difference between having a current pleasure and being happy. Being a failure or being happy belong to one's self, not to some constituent of one's self. The feeling of inner peace and security, or one of anxiety and conflict, belong clearly to one's self, not to this or that passing interest of one's self. All these feelings carry over from moment to moment, from wave to wave of experience, giving to it a dye which it does not easily lose.

I have suggested that what people have always called happiness is the specific value or satisfaction belonging to the matrix self. That this value is complex rather than simple can, I believe, be shown, as one would expect from the varying descriptions of it in both popular and philosophical literature. Fundamentally, happiness is the satisfaction arising from the assuagement of the desire to realize one's life plan. This follows almost analytically from the definition of the self as the life plan, and the analysis of satisfaction as the verifying or realization of an objective. Naturally, however, since the realization of the plan requires years, and since happiness is not something that merely occurs once in a lifetime but pervades a long course of experience, the satisfaction is in the *realizing* rather than in the *final realization,* although there may well be some dramatic end moment, as victory in war for the general, when achievement becomes triumph. That this is so is in accordance with the general nature of satisfaction, already noted by us, as a process. Essential to happiness, then, is the experience of achieving, rather than of achievement.

Moreover, since desires of higher order, although distinguishable from, are not separable from desires of lower order, the experience of achieving cannot be independent of the realization of the objectives of such desires. The life plan, as we have noted, is the overarching plan of and for such objectives—not of all these, but only of those that are dominant in one's life. So long as the plan as a whole, along its main lines, is being realized, partial failures do not destroy happiness, and some failures do not count, since, being unimportant, the relevant objectives are not embraced in the plan. So, to make use of illustrations already employed, failure to win a game of bridge with friends who happen in of an evening will not destroy happiness since the goal, "that I shall win this game," is no part of my life plan, but "that I shall win this girl" may be. In the latter case the winning of her will color my happiness, or my not winning her will discolor it, and give me a permanent sense of being a failure, depending on how far I have set my heart upon her and whether I have replaced the desire for her with the desire for another.

The extent to which the life plan is realized obviously depends upon many conditions, some of which may be external to and beyond the control of one's self. Sometimes an element of sheer luck appears to enter. *"Der Mensch muss Gluck haben,"* said Goethe. But there is an essential condition within the sphere of control which is so important that it has been identified with happiness itself—I mean what has been called, ever since the term was used by Pythagoras and later by Plato, harmony. The happy man is the man at peace within himself, one whose desires have been brought into harmony among themselves, and with the desires of his fellows and the exigencies of the environment. To win this peace is one of the major tasks of the self, and the methods by means of which it may be accomplished will be one of our most important topics for study. That the life plan cannot be realized when there is chaos within the self is evident. The existence of a plan implies some reconciliation and adjustment of rival and diverse desires.

Yet there are good reasons why harmony and happiness cannot be simply identified. One is that happiness depends upon the sense of achievement, the forward-looking realizing of the life plan noted by us. Merely to feel at peace is not enough. Another reason is that happiness is possible when there are grave internal and external conflicts—happiness, as we shall see, may be a difficult, even a tragic happiness as was, for example, that of Lincoln. Conflicts, both internal and external, insofar as they provide an opportunity for and a challenge to intelligence and imagination may be a means to happiness. As Heraclitus said, conflict is the creative principle of life, and it is interesting to recall that Pythagoras, who introduced the concept of harmony into philosophy, thought of it as a mixture of opposites, a mean between extremes, as the harmonic intervals, the 4th and the 5th, lie between the extremes of a tone and its octave. And yet if the self is torn to pieces by conflicts, there can be no happiness; there must be some resolution of them, either by thrusting them into the background of the mind or by reconciliation on a high level. When harmony is achieved a unique satisfaction, inner peace, pervades the self, giving to happiness, as the onward self-realization of the life plan, a unique coloration.

In passing, let me mention some obvious points which we shall develop later, that harmony may be the result of co-operation of desire with desire within the self, the union of the desire of one's self with that of another in what we call mutual understanding or love, the solidarity of the activities of the self with those of the physical and organic environments, as exemplified in health on the one hand and the efficient use of tools on the other hand.

There is a third component of happiness than can be deduced from the essential nature of desire—I mean the experience of power. Insofar as every desire involves the use of an end object for its assuagement, and of means objects on the way to assuagement, and as all such objects, which may be human or animal as well as physical, are somewhat resistant to use and manipulation—their countercontrol opposed to our control—their resistance has to be overcome, and the desire arises to overcome it. This desire, the so-called will to *power,* is accordingly intermixed with every other desire. It must consequently appear on the highest level of desire, where all means are marshaled for the realization of the life plan. What we call the feeling of power, the sense of mastery, is the satisfaction of this desire on this level.

We are inclined to view harmony as the typical classical conception of happiness, expressed by Plato in many places in his *Dialogues* and inherited from Pythagoras. But we forget the championing of the theory of happiness as power by Socrates' interlocutors, Callicles, Polus, and Thrasymachus in the *Protagoras, Gorgias,* and *Republic I.* And, as usual, the truth is to be found not by siding with Socrates against his opponents, but by a synthesis of his view with theirs. In our own time, the most forthright expression of the identification of happiness with the feeling of power is Nietzsche's, in the following passage of his *Antichrist,*

"What is good?—everything which increases the feeling of power, the will to power itself in man.

"What is evil?—everything which stems from weakness.

"What is happiness?—the feeling that power is growing, that an obstacle is being overcome."

On the other hand, John Dewey has in effect denied the importance of the will to power on the ground that it is not primary, but arises only when desires are frustrated. But both views are in error: Nietzsche's because it defines happiness in terms of only one of its facets, neglecting achievement and harmony; Dewey's because it overlooks the fact that every desire is partly balked, if only through delay in satisfaction or through necessity for overcoming the countercontrol exerted by means and end objects. Without an obstacle—the *Anstoss* of Fichte— there is no desire, therefore no experience and no existence;

and without its overcoming and the feeling of power in the overcoming, no happiness.

Power has two sides, passive and active, security and mastery, each of which should be defined. Security depends more on the environment, social or physical; mastery, more on one's self, although the two aspects cannot be separated. Security presupposes a relatively stable environment, enabling one to predict with high probability the circumstances one must meet in the future. Nothing gives a greater feeling of insecurity than a rapidly changing, unpredictable future. Yet it is not enough that the environment be predictable—it must be in relative harmony with the demands of the self. A man feels secure when he can count on the permanency of his job and his home, and on the constancy and fidelity of his wife, each providing expected satisfactions. But besides, the man must be capable of counting on *himself;* he must have the capacities to meet the exigencies of his life and realize his plan. Without this, the most favorable and stable environment will leave him a prey to a feeling of insecurity incompatible with this aspect of the supreme value.

The essentials in the analysis of power on its positive side have already been adumbrated. Mastery depends on awareness of capacities to meet and overcome obstacles, social and physical, offered by the environment and standing in the way of the realization of the life plan. This awareness both precedes and accompanies the experience of overcoming obstacles. Although based on experiences of triumph, it is not necessary that there be triumph in every case, but only in the large majority of cases or with reference to our major interests. And, although dependent on these individual successes, the satisfaction in mastery is a satisfaction of the self as a whole, of what I am calling the matrix self. It is a satisfaction not in any single experience of adequacy, or in any sum of these, but in the select few which belong in the life plan, enriched, however, by the echoes of all other experiences.

The positive and negative aspects of the experience of power, namely, security and mastery, may appear to be antagonistic. And it is true that those who seek security primarily are a different type from those who seek opportunities for the adventurous exercise of power. Yet the distinction is not absolute. For security is mastery of the environment already achieved by one's self or secured as a gift or inheritance; and without security as a basis no adventurous seeking for power is possible. One has the feeling of being in power either through the ease of adjustment resulting from mastery achieved—that is to say, through security—or by the actual overcoming of obstacles. Finally, mere security soon stales and is always precarious; hence the feeling of power has to be fed and renewed through its active exercise.

It might be objected to the analysis of happiness that I have been giving that it is no more than an eclectic putting together of three dominant points of view in the history of ethics. To this I would answer that I have tried to show how each of the three aspects is essential to desire and satisfaction as they lie at the foundation of all value. My whole argument rests on the success of this attempt. In other words they are not three things, but three aspects of one thing. Moreover, it would be strange if there were no truth in the prominent historical theories of the supreme value. Philosophies are not products of the imagination, nor are they ever wholly wrong; they arise and endure because of some element of truth which they contain. That achievement, harmony, and mastery or power are not three separate items which, when put together, add up to happiness, but rather three inseparable facets of it, can I believe be shown by the analysis of an example.

Let us consider the case of a man who has the plan of writing a book. This desire and this plan will be an essential part of his life plan. As the writing proceeds, bringing him nearer and nearer to his goal, he will have the happiness of achievement, which will, however, reach its climax only when his task is performed. This plan, moreover, is a good example of a desire of high order, for it will control many activities of lower order such as gathering of data, fitting them together, writing and filing notes, and typing chapters, each of which will yield its own modicum of satisfaction as he proceeds but will not be equivalent to the happiness of achievement itself. But now, in order to accomplish this purpose, a harmony must be established among the man's impulses. For he will, of course, have desires other than to write this book. He also wants to do his duties, to advise and play with his children, to see his friends, to talk to and assist his wife, and so on. He must therefore find some way to reconcile, that is to say harmonize, the desire to write that book with all these other interests. For they will compete and distract and conflict unless he does, and, without the establishment of order in his life with reference to this plan, the book will never be written, and a feeling of failure will result. But when order is established, to the sense of achievement will be added the feeling tone of smooth functioning, of peace within. Finally, in order to achieve his goal, our author must overcome many obstacles: his own fatigue, beckoning him to relax and postpone or relinquish his aim, the difficulty of finding time, the difficulty that attends the solution of any intellectual problem, the difficulty that comes from discouragement in any large enterprise.

But now, in overcoming such obstacles, who does not feel himself a master? Even in achieving a harmony between this plan and one's other interests, the experience of mastery arises. A sense of harmony, a sense of mastery, a sense of achievement, these are the inseparable aspects of happiness. The satisfaction that comes from the assuagement of any desire, however low in the hierarchy of desires, is happiness in miniature and exhibits the three aspects of achievement, harmony, and mastery. For when the objective of the desire is attained, there is achievement, when the obstacles in the way of attainment of the goal are overcome, there is the feeling of power, and since in order to realize the goal, the desire in question must be brought into adjustment with other desires, competing and conflicting, the experience of harmony attends upon achievement.

That, nevertheless, the three moments in happiness, while inseparable are yet distinct, can be seen from the two following facts. First, in any process of assuagement of desire, if the obstacles are great, then the feeling of mastery will dominate happiness; if there are many competing and conflicting interests to be harmonized, then the sense of peace will become prominent; and, if the goal is very important, the experience of achievement, of triumph, will relegate the other factors in happiness into the background. Second, in the lives of some persons, harmony counts for more, in others, power, in still others, achievement. So, in some gentle souls, and in most women, in whose lives there is no plan of action to be effectuated, a harmonious sweetness will be the dominant note in their happiness; while in others, the success of some brilliant plan will overshadow inner peace, forcing its way to victory despite conflicts and agony of soul, as in the case of Lincoln, already cited, whom we judge to have been happy despite our knowledge of unresolved conflicts; and for still others, nothing will seem quite so important as the exercise of power, the feeling of control, whatever be the plan to be achieved. Yet in no happy life is achievement of some sort, harmony to some degree, mastery of circumstances to some extent, completely absent. With regard to many, we are at a loss to decide whether they are happy or not, so great is the defect in one or another of the aspects of happiness. Of Van Gogh we wonder: Did the unresolved discords of his inner life prevent him from being happy, despite his shining achievement in art?

Corresponding to the values of the matrix self there are the following evils: to achievement, failure; to inner peace, agony of soul; to security and the sense of mastery, a feeling of insecurity or ineffectualness. Like all evils, these are species of frustration, in this case, frustration of the aim of the matrix self for realization of the life plan. That these are evils of the matrix self dependent upon its frustration, rather than current or haphazard evils, arising from the frustration of this or that desire, has already been indicated. A man does not feel himself to be a failure because this or that want remains unsatisfied, but only when the life plan as a whole is unrealized; nor does he have a sense of weakness and insecurity because he cannot meet this or that obstacle, nor agony of soul by reason of one or another conflict unresolved. It is only when some dominant purpose of the life plan is frustrated that he feels himself a failure; only when he is powerless to overcome the resistances to it that he is plunged into despair; only when he is torn to pieces inwardly that agony of soul sets in. When the entire life plan collapses, suicide or some escape such as alcoholism or dissipation may occur, unless certain saving compensations intervene.

Both the distinctive values and evils of the matrix self take on a special character when its social nature is prominent. Thus pride and self-esteem arise when achievement is recognized by one's fellows, and the sense of power and security becomes self-assurance under the same circumstances. Harmony becomes love in one's relations to one's fellow men or women; it becomes religion—the peace that passeth all understanding, in one's relation to God or the universe. Similarly, the evil of regret becomes humiliation; ineffectualness becomes what is now so commonly called a feeling of inferiority; and when it is a violation of love, disharmony becomes remorse.

Within the satisfactions of the matrix self we can distinguish, as in all satisfactions, an active from an imaginative (memorial and anticipative) phase. One might indeed be tempted to regard happiness, as distinguished from mere pleasure, as being wholly imaginative, especially memorial. Is not the happy man, one might say, he who possesses memories of achievements, of mastery of circumstances, of reconciliations, inner and outer, which he has effected? Is it not these funded satisfactions which constitute abiding contentment? And do not these provide the menstruum (matrix) within which the flashes of focal satisfactions occur? Contrariwise, is not misery precisely the continuing presence of memories of a frustrated life plan, conflicts unresolved, weaknesses unconquered? Or, making provision for anticipation, may not the substance of happiness be the confident and persistent looking forward to success, verified by each new present achievement? And is not misery hopelessness?

Certainly no student of the psyche would question the very great share of this imaginative phase in happiness. And since all current satisfactions are related to it, happiness cannot be independent of the treasured memory of any past enjoyment. Memories give dimensionality to anybody's happiness, if they be of pleasure; or, if they be of frustration, to anybody's misery. Hence, if one has been happy in childhood, it is hard to be utterly miserable ever; and if, on the contrary, one has been miserable in childhood, happiness at any time becomes difficult.

The only intelligible meaning which can be given to the concept of a sum of pleasures is the happiness resulting from the retention of traces of satisfaction in the matrix self. Nevertheless it would be a mistake to identify the values of the matrix self with its imaginative values, and to deny all present values to it. For there are occasions when focal and matrix self coincide, and then the values of the one are those of the other. This occurs when a current objective achieved is an element in the life plan, as the plan has been formed after deliberation and decision—in other words, when the whole self participates in an ongoing act. This may be equally some great climactic achievement, crowning a series of anticipated accomplishments, as when the ambitious career man is appointed to a post long coveted, or some inconspicuous and intrinsically unimportant act which, nevertheless, is recognized as the necessary means to the fulfillment of some cherished end. In both types of cases, there is a power as well as a success value, since either is a token of mastery over difficulties and adjustments of means to ends. And, although inner peace is compact of memories and anticipations of conflicts resolved, together with the echoes of the satisfactions that result, providing the happiness of peace even in loneliness, it has its active phase in the experience of union with one's fellows, and of conflicts brought into resolution. There is a time, however, when at least the value of achievement exists almost wholly in its memorial phase—I mean when a man retires from active life. And generally in old age, much of happiness consists of happy memories—and achievement, if important at all, is that of love in building up and living on imaginatively in the lives of children or others near and dear to one. The great problem now becomes that of harmony—adjustment to a life of restricted activity and scope, and then, finally, the supreme adjustment to the prospect of death.

In concluding this chapter, I wish to follow out a new approach to the problem of defining the elements of happiness, taking as a basis a general survey of our major interests. This will, I hope, provide a confirmation of the results already obtained. In my book *Human Values* I ventured to classify our interests in accordance with a scheme, which I shall reproduce here with certain minor modifications. In the large, the scheme is, I believe, almost self-explanatory, but I shall subjoin a few paragraphs of elucidation.

There are two grand divisions of values—values of action and values of imagination. The former are fulfillments of desires which involve adjustment to the environment and interaction with it, the use of real things or persons as means or ends, accompanied by belief in the reality of such things or persons. Values of the imagination, on the other hand, are satisfactions which depend more on free creation than on adjustment to the environment; the use of imaginary or "substitute objects" rather than real objects, and an attitude of "make-believe" rather than belief. In the case of both kinds, there are active and passive forms, as one would expect from our analysis of value, where we showed that the objective of desire is either an activity or a passivity upon an object. For example, among the values of imagination are art and play, and in the former we can distinguish the satisfactions of the creator and the contemplator; in the latter, we can distinguish the satisfactions of the player and those of the spectator.

The values of action include the following:

comfort—a round of pleasure of the senses, passively received or actively sought;

health—the satisfaction in biologic equilibrium, and the readiness for activities of all kinds which that makes possible;

ambition—the desire for a place of security (passive) and responsibility (active) in the social order;

love—the satisfaction in union with the life of another person, built up in that person by oneself (active), or built up in oneself by him or her (passive), loving and being loved (interesting forms of love are love between the sexes, or love mixed with amorous pleasure; and love of a community, or love of individuals as members of a group giving support to a desired "way of life");

the desire for knowledge—which we shall not undertake to define here, but shall assume to be understood by the reader;

technological satisfactions—the satisfactions which arise through our interest in the making of means and end objects, and in the efficient using, servicing, preservation, and economical and just apportioning of them among our desires, according to their rank in our scheme of values.

The values of imagination include the following:

dreaming—of this there are two kinds, the daydream and the night dream;

play—of this there are three kinds: phantasy play or the use of "toys"; games or the use of "play objects" (bats, balls, and so forth); and conversation or the use of words;

art—satisfactions mediated by so-called "works of art";

religion—where also certain "things" are made use of in securing satisfactions of this kind: idols, icons, altars, churches, and so forth.

Now for some brief elucidations: Although I have distinguished values of action from values of imagination, there is no absolute distinction between them. As we have noted, there is an imaginative moment in all action, anticipation, more specifically, planning and the making of hypotheses; and there is a "real" moment in all forms of imagination except the dream. Thus in phantasy play, the toy, while created into a dream object —the wax image into a baby, the piece of tin into a soldier—is still a real, serviceable thing; and in religion, although neither the temple nor the idol is ever God Himself, He is believed to dwell somehow within it; it is a symbol or substitute for Him. So in art. The statue is, let us say, Aphrodite, an ideal object, yet she has her dwelling place in the marble image, which is also a thing. For the artist too, say the sculptor, creation is partly imaginative creation, and partly technical and manual—the chipping of the stone. Games have equally an ambivalent status; as imaginative or "substitute" forms of victory, they belong where we have placed them, yet as species of exercise, they belong among the values of action, under health and comfort. Religion, finally, has an equivocal status, depending on whether one regards it as a system of mere myths, with no epistemological foundation, a sort of spontaneous or group poetry (as held by Santayana in our day), or as possessed of a core of truth commanding our belief, when it belongs among the values of action, either of knowledge or of love, or both.

A quick survey of this list—momentarily confining our attention to the values of action—reveals that certain values can be grouped together in a significant fashion. Thus health, ambition, efficiency, and religion belong together as species of security and power: Health—biological; Ambition—social; Efficiency—physical and social; Religion—cosmical. Another easy grouping places love and religion together as forms of harmony or union, since the mystical element in the latter forbids us to conceive of it in terms of power alone, leaving only sensuous pleasure and knowledge unaccounted for. Yet both these can, I believe, be shown to be species of either harmony or power or both. For it is not difficult to believe that the pleasures of the senses are values of harmony, since in experiencing them we are in unison with the co- or subconscious desires of the organism: the tongue's pleasure in the sweet sugar, the nose's pleasure in the orchid's smell, the eye's pleasure in the color and structural unity of the rose, for example, being my pleasures also. As regards the value of knowledge, it is, on the one hand, a value of power in its instrumental capacity, as has been recognized since Bacon; and, on the other hand, a value of harmony or union—actual between self and object in knowledge by acquaintance, and vicarious union through the concept in the case of knowledge by description. Thus all the values of action appear to be specifications of the values either of power or of union.

That, directly or indirectly, they are also specifications of achievement is easily shown. Ambition is obviously so. But so also are the values of efficiency, as illustrated by the projects of the engineer or entrepreneur in seeking their goals of construction or manufacture or sale; or, on a humbler scale, as illustrated by the aim of any family to keep its home in repair and to balance its budget. That love contains values of achievement follows from the fact that, in its active form, as a striving to build up values in another, it is susceptible of success or failure. Sense pleasures, knowledge, and health, as *possessions,* are not values of achievement, but rather, as we have described them, of power and harmony, yet insofar as we seek after them—and who does not?—they have the quality of achievement when they arrive.

The possibility of applying the foregoing analysis to values of the imagination might be taken for granted in view of their

largely secondary character in relation to values of action. Even
a hasty consideration of them, however, will make our argument
more cogent. Little debate would be likely to arise with regard
to the values of the dream. The daydream is patently a satisfaction in the imagination of ambitions or erotic desires; and the
night dream differs only insofar as such desires are subconscious—"repressed" or disguised. The phantasy play of the child
is a lucid mimic of the activities of parents or other adults, during which the physical toy is transformed imaginatively into a
relevant means or end object. Thus the little girl takes pleasure
in rocking, dressing, undressing, and feeding the doll, imaginatively conceived as a baby, according to the pattern of activities
of her mother or neighbor concerning a real baby. In the imagination, therefore, they realize the values of union, achievement,
and power characteristic of the corresponding forms of action.

The analysis of the values of games yields the same results.
Insofar as they are competitive, they give momentary and inconsequential prestige paralleling the more enduring and fruitful
glory acquired in the ambitious undertakings of "real life." In
addition, games provide satisfactions in goal-directed, but also
relatively inconsequential activities, independent of the satisfactions in winning. For example, even if I lose the tennis game,
I find satisfaction in putting a well-directed ball over the net.
Both of these satisfactions are species of power and achievement.
Finally, if games require the teamwork of a group, as in football, they illustrate the values of harmony.

Some readers may be surprised to find conversation included
among the species of play. But, of course, I am meaning by conversation talk for the sake of talking, not talk as a means to an
end. Thus understood, I should say that its values are partly
imaginative in the narrower sense, being satisfactions in the
recall of the values of action or other values of imagination,
partly satisfactions in communication, and partly satisfactions
in the virtuosity of speech. The first clearly introduce no
novelty; for when, for example, a man tells his friend how he

bested a competitor, he is simply reliving a value of ambition, or if he describes a brilliant tackle in a game of football, he is reliving a similar value of imagination. In this aspect, conversation is not unlike the phantasy play of the child. The second sort of values in conversation, those of communication, belong among the values of union, for my desire to communicate through speech has as its end to make my interlocutor participate in the life which I am recalling. The third type of satisfaction through conversation is one of power as exhibited in the mastery of words as a medium for the expression of thought and feeling, and the mastery of persons as they may be dazzled by it, as when I tell a "taller" story than anyone else.

With the doubtful exception of religion, the most complex satisfactions in the list now under discussion are those of art. Yet in them also, I believe we find nothing generically or essentially new. Students of art have sought to discover some unique element; but in vain. For beauty can be analyzed into a complex (1) of satisfactions of the senses—colors, lines, tones, lights, and so forth, and their harmonies; (2) satisfactions from the imagination of objects and events "represented" or "imitated," such objects and events being accepted by us not as real but as if real; (3) satisfactions from what I call depth meanings or universals, prominent in all symbolic art, but also present in covert form in most, if not all, works of art; (4) satisfactions drawn from the harmony of all phases of the aesthetic experience one with another; and lastly (5), for those who are acquainted with the difficulties confronting the artist in the creation of his work, satisfaction in mastery over the medium—the difficulty overcome.

For example, in Cézanne's "La Montagne Sainte-Victoire au Grand Pin," the first layer of the aesthetic experience consists of lines, vertical contrasting with horizontal, diagonal, undulating; colors, yellow, green, blue, violet, orange, delicately contrasting or blending into one another; with tones or "values" harmoniously distributed over all; then, "lying behind" the

shapes which these lines and lights and colors compose, are the
imagined big pine, the mountain Saint-Victoire, with its foot-
hills, the aqueduct, the plain with its trees, houses, roads, and so
forth; and behind the sensuous surface and the imaginary objects there is the depth meaning, present in all Cézanne's works,
even in his still lifes, with their banal tables, apples, and table-
cloths, of a universal repose and equilibrium—all phases of the
entire work fitting into each other most marvelously, marvelously because of the difficulties which any painter, professional
or amateur, and even any mere art lover must feel inherent in
composing all these elements into an organic whole. Yet there
are no generically new values in this picture. In the first layer,
there are sensuous satisfactions and their harmonies; in the
second layer, there are the imaginative equivalents of what
would be the values of the pine and the mountain and the rest
were we to perceive them instead of merely imagining them;
in the third layer there is fulfilled momentarily and in miniature that desire which we all feel for rest and equilibrium; and
pervading all these layers of satisfaction there is a feeling of
harmony, perhaps the most characteristic type of feeling in any
aesthetic experience; and last, as already indicated, there is an
experience of power, no less strong because concentrated in so
small a space and with regard to such fragile things as pigments
and canvas and brushes, colors and lines and lights. Beauty is
sensuous, imaginative, and, let us not forget it, conceptual
happiness in miniature, in the mode of make-believe, not of
belief. Sometimes, as in life, the happiness is a tragic happiness,
but happiness it is nevertheless.

Since therefore there are no new values of imagination, and
since all the values of action are specifications of achievement,
of union, and of power, we can fairly conclude that all values
are of this sort.

To some readers, this result is sure to seem unsatisfactory,
even if they are convinced of its prima facie soundness. For they
will insist that there must be some single primary value of which

our three are but facets, and that our conclusion can be no more than a preliminary to a more searching analysis. Yet to this objection I would offer the following answers: first, that no one has so far succeeded in reducing any two of our triad to species of the remaining one, or in finding a fourth of which all three would be specifications; second, that even if we adopt the hypothesis of a psychic cell, comparable to a biological cell, out of which all the manifold kinds of activity may be supposed to have developed by fission and differentiation, in a fashion parallel to the development of the enormously complex organism from the single, simple cell from which each life starts, we should be compelled to admit the existence of an irreducible complexity within that psychic cell itself, comparable again to a complexity within the biological cell. Since the biological cell consists of activities conducing to self-preservation, and other activities leading to the creation of a new cell, either by division or by conjugation with another cell—forms of power and achievement, and of union—how could we expect anything fundamentally different of the psychic cell? And, apart from such a basic polarity, how could we hope to understand the conflict and tragedy of experience?

CHAPTER VI

THE EVALUATION OF VALUES

OF ALL living beings, it may fairly be said that man not only possesses values but evaluates values. Deciding how we shall eat or sleep, or dress or walk, as well as what high deeds we shall perform, involves the exercise of a selective process, which, in accordance with certain norms, rules out certain desires and their attendant satisfactions in favor of others. It is true that in man, as in the lower animals, selection is not wholly conscious. It has been proved that for each person there is an optimum and typical way of sleeping, walking, or standing, representing a selection, of which he is scarcely aware, from innumerable postures or positions, that determines in a measure just how he shall walk or sleep. Yet apart from such strictly bodily activities, man knows in general what his standards are. Many of his myths, such as that of Paradise or the lotus-eaters, and the fascination of far off South Sea isles—of Samoa or Tahiti—are symbols of a secret longing to be rid of standards with the pale cast of which his life is sicklied o'er. Yet really to be rid of standards would imply getting rid of oneself; for they are man's own most characteristic work. The standards he may relinquish constitute a top layer of himself, leaving the foundational layers untouched; and he soon finds that he has merely exchanged one set of standards for another.

The fact that desires are themselves subject to evaluation implies a double process of selection in human experience. For, as we have seen, desire itself implies selection from a set of possible objects that might satisfy; hence if desires are themselves selected, the process occurs twice over. What an exquisitely fashioned thing is a deed!

Yet it would be a mistake to view a standard as a sort of external judge or censor, impersonal and unrelated to the life of desire. A standard is an objective of desire, but of a desire of higher order, a desire regarding desires and satisfactions of a specific sort; and like all such objectives, more permanent than those of lower order. Hence, when any desire is satisfied in such a fashion as to come up to standard, there is an increment of satisfaction. We can, in fact, distinguish within any satisfaction two components: the satisfaction resulting from the assuagement of primary and relatively spontaneous desires, and the satisfaction that accrues from meeting the expectations constitutive of the objective of the higher order standard desire. It follows that if the standard is not met, the primary satisfactions will be qualified negatively, because, as long as they persist, they will be immersed in a background of higher-order frustration.

Suppose you are entertaining your friends at an evening party, enjoying the food, the drink, and the games, and experiencing the usual pleasure in seeing your friends and in conversing and playing with them. But suppose that, suddenly, you realize that the party is not "going off" the way you would like it to go, in accordance with your standard for such occasions; then all your satisfactions, although they may persist, will be diminished by reason of their new background of disappointment. If, on the contrary, the party does proceed according to the standard you have set, you will experience a special kind of satisfaction, and the primary satisfactions will be unaffected. And if, to consider a third possibility, the party is better than you had anticipated, surpassing your expectation, there will be a surplus of pleasure. Or, to take another example, suppose that you read or write a poem; then, if it is the kind of poem you admire, whatever pleasures of expression or imagination you may experience will be normal, whereas, if it does not measure up to your standard, they will be diminished in intensity. It may even happen that failure to meet a standard will make satisfaction impossible. I recall watching a young woman enter a small exhibition room, full of fine modern pictures, give each a momentary glance as she walked around the four sides of the gallery, and then depart. None of the works of art she had seen had meant anything to her since none was what she expected a picture to be.

Two types of standards may profitably be distinguished—internal and external. An internal standard is one set for a specific kind of activity, an ideal of perfection for it, to yield a maximum of satisfaction through its exercise. It is the standard of the chess player for chess, of the poet for poetry, of the military strategist for a campaign, of the baseball player or fan for baseball. But every activity has effects, beneficial or deleterious, upon other pursuits, and enters into competition with them if for no other reason than that a man can do no more than one thing well at a time. Moreover, whatever he does absorbs not only the available time and space, but also the energy that might be at the disposal of some other desire. Its value, no matter how great intrinsically, will therefore be judged from the point of view of competing desires; each, so to speak, will judge the other. Hence, even though my game of chess is excellent and provides all the pleasures to be expected from winning most of the time and from the exercise of my wits, it may be condemned if it interferes with my professional aims by keeping me from sleep so that I arrive tired at my office, or if it excites jealousy of a young wife whom I adore but am neglecting. Or the Battle of the Bulge may be a fine piece of strategy, long to be admired and studied in military academies, yet, as instigated by a ruthless dictator, may be condemned. Now the standard of the other interest, from the point of view of which a given interest may be judged because of its effects, being extrinsic to the given interest, may be called external.

Memory, comparison of satisfactions, and conflict of desires are all involved in the formation of standards. Any activity is undertaken against a background of a remembered previous activity of the same kind, which haunts it like a ghost. Such a memory is already a standard—the initial standard for any activity, to which it must measure up. The first poem we read sets the standard for all poems read; the little girl's first party, for all subsequent parties. Memory becomes expectation. If, however, the new experience surpasses the initial one, it will supplant the latter as standard maker. But since satisfactions are complex and may be forgotten, and since no one of a kind will surpass another of that same kind in all respects, the standard usually takes the shape of a general expectation or schema rather than of a particular memory. Satisfactions will then be evaluated in terms of this schema as good if they meet it, as better than ever or best if they surpass it, or as bad if they fall short of it. It should be noticed that in such cases "good" no longer means value in the generic sense, but in the specific sense of "standard value"; that is to say, in the sense of satisfaction which is had through the meeting of an expectation regarding satisfactions of that kind. In terms of the standard, satisfactions are placed in series according to the degree in which they conform to, surpass, or fall short of it. Since, however, meeting or surpassing the standard increases, and falling short of it decreases, satisfaction, the standard does not function in a purely intellectual way, judging, classifying, and ordering, but actually determines satisfaction itself. Moreover, as a generalized expectation, the standard does not necessarily supplant the standard of memory if some shining instance of satisfaction is remembered or preserved. The touchstone method of criticism of values, of which Matthew Arnold was a familiar exponent in the field of literature, may persist throughout the entire range of values. In this case, the standard desire may be described as a "desire for satisfactions equal to *this* (the touchstone)."

Since standards are the objectives of desires of higher order, they affect satisfactions of lower order not only by qualifying them insofar as these do or do not meet standards, but also by functioning as plans or models in accordance with which new satisfactions are created. The nature of the poem the poet writes is determined not only by his need for expression, but also by his conception of the kind of form in which expression should be cast. Similarly, the party the child gives is determined by his notion of what a good party is like. The use of standards inevitably embraces the means and end objects required to bring values into existence. To achieve the standard in playing baseball, I need a standard bat and ball; with an inferior article I must fall short. Without a racket of such a kind and weight, I cannot do my best at tennis. Therefore, even as all values become subject to standards, so all objects concerned with values become standardized. In our civilization, where means objects have become so largely multiplied, and their procurement and manufacture occupy the dominant place in the lives of most people, the very conception of standardization is becoming falsely limited to them. In terms of such standards, objects are accordingly judged as suitable or unsuitable, efficient or inefficient, good or bad. But I would again insist that judgments about means are not directly judgments on values, but on *valuables*. A value is a satisfaction, never a mere thing. Yet indirectly, as we have noted, appraisals of means do affect the existence and nature of satisfactions; for as the means are, so, very largely, are the satisfactions.

The account we have so far given of the way standards are built up is limited in two ways: it applies only to internal standards, and it has taken no explicit account of the social factor in standard making. With regard to the latter point, it is obvious that, just as values are social in the ways already described, so standards of values are social. The individual lives with the knowledge that his standards are known to others, and they live with the knowledge that theirs are known to him. Since standards and primary values are thus, for the most part, open to the view of all members of a communicating group, comparison of satisfactions is not confined to those within one person's experience, but extends to satisfactions of all members of the group. The little girl compares her party with those of other little girls; the poet, his poems with those of other poets. Insofar as theirs surpass his, they become a goal for him to attain to, if he can. He learns from them ways of varying and intensifying his satisfactions, and interested persons, such as parents and teachers, take the trouble to show him how perhaps he might bring his own values up to the intensity, volume, and height of their own. Thus, his standards not only grow spontaneously but their growth is fostered by people who love him or are otherwise interested in him. And, in order to overcome his loneliness and to escape ridicule or more serious penalties, he strives to conform his norms to those of other members of his group, particularly men of authority or power.

In a preceding paragraph, I showed that besides the standard internal to a given desire, there are others, relatively external, to which it is called upon to adapt itself, because it enters into competition with them for time, space, and energy and has effects upon them. All other interests will, I said, judge it as beneficial or harmful to themselves. Yet that way of expressing the matter is only half true. If it were the full truth, a center of experience would be a loose bundle of desires, independent in much the same fashion as two or more men who quarrel, and the judgment of one of them would be as "right" as another— that of my interest in chess as that of my interest in my wife, that of my desire for a brilliant military victory as that of my concern for the welfare of my people. But, on the contrary, as we have shown, there are no separate desires, since all are inter-woven in the matrix self, the desire of highest order. It is the matrix self, rather than any one of the competing propensities, taken separately, that passes final judgment. And, this being so, even the so-called external standard is not really external; for it, too, is a part of "me." Each interest has its "day in court" before the matrix self, and condemnation by the self is its very own condemnation. The ultimate evaluation of values is the work of the matrix self, which, however, as involved in all de-sires, must take the internal standard of each into account. Moreover, as we shall emphasize—developing philosophically what is indeed obvious—not all desires are on a level but com-pose a hierarchy within the life plan.

In the process of evaluating values, the matrix self can do no other than appraise in terms of its own ultimate values. A stand-ard external to it would have no validity for it. So-called super-natural standards may seem to be external, but they derive their authority from something within the self, which gives allegiance to them. They must win its will before they can win its obedi-ence. In the end, therefore, the problem relating to every desire is how it affects the achievement, the power, and the harmony of the matrix self. In this chapter we shall study the evaluation of values with special reference to achievement, inseparable from power, which is concerned with the means to achievement. In our next chapter, we shall be specially concerned with harmony.

The evaluation of values is, however, not without paradox. For the life plan is itself a pattern of high order desires which has grown up in time through a choice among impulses which, so to speak, have offered themselves as candidates for inclusion in it. That is to say, elements of the life plan which sit in judg-ment upon incoming impulses have themselves been subject to the same process of evaluation. We seem thus to be involved in a circle, which might appear to require that we step outside, to find some supernatural power of Kantian principle inde-

pendent of desire, in order to establish an ultimate standard—
a suggestion already rejected by us. Only desire can judge desire.
There is no way out of the circle of all desires.

And yet, although real, the circle is no "vicious circle." For
at any moment the existing pattern of desire (matrix self) judges
every new impulse, rejecting, encouraging, or perhaps even
adopting it as an element of itself, when something like a revolution may occur within it. The fact that the existing matrix was
established in the past by the same sort of process does not
diminish its reality or authority in the present. The process is
somewhat analogous to that which obtains in a self-perpetuating
group, like a club, where the existing members choose new ones,
who in turn have a voice in the selection of other candidates,
and may even expel those who will not conform to the rules.
And, after some years of growth, the matrix self becomes crystal-
lized and relatively fixed in its essential core, changing only at
its periphery. Moreover, at no time in the life of history of the
individual was there no matrix self, however humble and rudi-
mentary. What it was like in its earliest stages is a matter for
speculation, but that it was something definite when, with the
union of egg and sperm, the psyche began its somber career, is
certain.

The appraisal of a desire is, we have insisted, no mere intellectual judgment, but part of a process in which the desire, as
it arises, is either rejected or admitted into the scope of the life
plan, and, if admitted, given a definite place there. In this process certain principles may be said to operate in the sense that,
when one reflects on what actually occurs, one may describe it
in terms of them. In putting the matter so, it is not implied
that these principles for determining the place of an interest in
the life plan are used as rules of thumb, or that one is necessarily aware of them at all. They are the formulations of the
philosopher, yet such as anyone who reflects on his choices must
accede to. Different ways of expressing and grouping them are
perhaps possible. The following have recommended themselves

to me as convenient. Needless to say, they are in no sense a priori, but are empirical—the formulation of actual procedures. I name them the principles of attainment (perfection), beneficence, and rank, respectively. These are highest principles valid in all fields of value, but each field—aesthetic, moral, athletic, economic, or other—has its own special norms which it is not the purpose of the general theory of value to investigate.

By attainment I mean the realization by a desire of its own internal standard. In its competition with other interests, the degree to which a satisfaction measures up to its ideal counts. If it falls notably short, we tend to discontinue it, or limit it in favor of other desires. The emotion of discouragement is the sign of failure to reach perfection. Thus, if I take to writing verses and find that I am incapable, after many trials, of composing what I regard as good poetry, I will probably be so discouraged that I will abandon verse writing for, let me say, gardening, where perhaps I can reach an easier goal. If I do approximate the objective, I will encourage the interest. The final selection by some man of a profession in which he achieves success after trying several others in which he seems not to be able to "get anywhere" is another illustration of the principle.

Its validity follows from the ultimate aim set by the ego of maximum achievement. But despite its importance, there are certain limitations to this principle, which may even seem to invalidate it. The unremitting courtship by some men of some one woman who never says "Yes" is an illustration of its apparent inapplicability. So is man's eternal effort to establish a social order of justice and freedom, which never succeeds. Moreover, it has been long maintained that the best desires are precisely those whose goals are unattainable. These limitations must be carefully considered, but however one may view them, few, I believe, would deny the general validity of the principle. It remains the part of wisdom to do the things that one can do most excellently, and not to waste time and energy over those that one can do only indifferently well or not at all. Yet the significance of the failure of the principle in some cases must be assessed.

The failure may be due to sheer unadaptability like that of the carp which, when enclosed in a glass tank, never learns to avoid bumping its head against the walls of the container. This kind of failure is a simple case of evil. Sometimes fixation is the underlying cause, as in the case of the persistent wooer whose conduct may also be regarded as evil since, by reason of his fixation, he is continually frustrated, whereas, if he would court some other woman who might say "Yes," his impulse to love might be satisfied. On the other hand, it is rash always to assume that there is nothing but evil in such cases. For one cannot tell, apart from intimate knowledge, how large the imaginative rewards of the fixed impulse are. The mere sight of the unwilling beloved, or any little token of regard or affection she might give her suitor—a touch of the hand, or a kiss on the cheek—may be magnified by pleasure into a value which no outsider can judge. Who then dares to say that his passion is evil? Of liberty and justice as examples of unrealizable goals we have already said something, yet something more needs to be said now. Their case is not unlike that of the persistent lover. For liberty and justice are so important that any approach to realization is a major vlaue. Moreover, desires with unrealizable goals should not be confused with those such as love and curiosity which are insatiable and without terminating objectives, yet provide triumphs along the way in the shape of single acts of kindness or single discoveries. In a measure, liberty and justice are of this nature, since the unending development of cultures, introducing ever new conflicts, makes any once-for-all ideal social status impossible. And besides, there is usually an alternative to abandoning a desire—namely, to lower its goal to within reach of attainment.

So, failing, always failing to achieve the ideal in the large political field, one may be content with an approximation to it, or find happiness in a fuller realization in the smaller circles of the family and one's friends, and thereby be saved from despair. Perhaps the unrequited suitor does something analogous—he ceases to aim at possession and contents himself with *une bonne amitié*, which, so say the French, *vaut l'amour*. Or, to shift to a trivial illustration, failing to make the ideal score at golf, one sets it within one's reach. This lowering of the standard is, it must be admitted, a confession of defeat; but is not a rout, since it is like the strategic withdrawal of an army trying to shorten its lines. By saving the energy that would be expended on a fruitless endeavor to reach the ideal, the goal of maximum achievement on the part of the matrix self is more nearly attained. It is a well known fact of psychopathology that neuroses both in children and in adults are caused by the setting up of impossible goals, either by the persons themselves or by their leaders. Many a high-minded parent has almost ruined her son by putting before him unattainable ideals of purity of mind, unselfishness, or scholastic proficiency. The wisdom of life requires readjustment of standards to within the range of the possible, save only with regard to those that are so precious that the joys of striving and of partial success compensate for failure to attain the uttermost. But it hardly needs to be said that a goal may be set too low as well as too high; for in doing that one risks missing the chance of a signal success. Our principle demands maximum effort within the possible along with renunciation of the impossible. And what is possible and what impossible are individual truths to be discovered for the most part only by trial and sometimes also by error.

The principle of beneficence is based on the obvious fact that all desires are interrelated and therefore, from the point of view of any one of them, may be helpful, malign, or relatively indifferent. So, to make use of the illustration already employed in another connection, chess-playing is malign if it injures the happiness of a wife that I love, benign if, playing the game with her, it strengthens the tie between us, relatively indifferent if, played at the club infrequently, it does not affect our relationship. The principle demands that those desires be favored, other things being equal, which are most consistent with the realization of the cluster of goals which constitute the matrix self or may win its approval.

It is in terms of this principle that external standards are set up. In accordance with it, certain desires will always have a preferred status. The desire for food and drink is obviously one of these, for when it fails, all other desires fail too, since it sustains the body, whose existence and co-operation conditions the existence of all desires. Usually the native intensity of this desire guarantees its cultivation; but in illness, when it wanes, it requires coaxing. The desires that have to do with earning a living are similarly important for, together with the organic, they make all others possible. Obviously to be encouraged, also, are the interests which bring honors or rewards which aid in promoting the life plan. Finally the virtues, such as thrift, courage, temperance, and prudence, which protect values, are essential. On the other hand, such an interest as smoking among the young and healthy, which appears to have little effect upon other desires, may be counted as unimportant. Clearly malign, in accordance with this principle, are the interests, like that in strong drink, which, unless held in check are directly injurious to all other interests, or bring upon us the penalties of the law.

It is significant that a satisfaction which, by definition, is good in the generic sense, may be bad in terms of this principle, and that a frustration, by definition generically evil, may become good insofar as it promotes, as it may, our other desires. So, for one afflicted with heart disease, the frustration of the interest in tennis may be good, as also, on a higher plane, may be the renunciation of an "illicit" love that initiates poetic composition or saves one's reputation. It is essential for clearness in the theory of value that these two senses of good be distinguished— the generic sense, which applies to every satisfaction, and this new specific sense, which may be called moral, and does not apply to all satisfactions.

The principle which we are calling beneficence covers the principle of cost, to which Mr. Dewey has attached so much significance. For when we assess a satisfaction in terms of its cost, we are, in the end, judging it in terms of the damage it does to other desires. Even if we limit cost to time, energy, or money spent, this remains true, for when a desire consumes any of these, that much is withdrawn from possible use by others. In general—in terms of this principle—low cost desires are to be preferred to high cost ones, even as in general those which are less maleficent are to be preferred to those that are more so.

The question naturally arises as to whether and how far the principle of beneficence applies to the effects of a desire on the desires of other persons besides ourselves. The name which I have given it would seem to imply that it does. But it follows from the egocentricity of desires that it can apply for each person who is seeking to order his life only to such effects as touch either those persons with whom he can identify himself through love, whereby they count for him as he counts for himself, in proportion to his love, or to those persons who will help him through gratitude or hinder him through vengeance, or for other reasons may affect his life. And it is obvious that the circle of these persons includes all with whom he may come in contact.

That the principle of beneficence (or, in its specialized sense, of cost) is not sufficient is clear from the following reflections. For, when one desire damages another, how shall we know which to prefer? Why should we not prefer chess to the happiness of a wife? Why not the other way around? And are there not cases where we feel justified in sacrificing the most widely beneficent desires, such as the desire for health or for food (in the case of hunger strikers) to desires such as those which we call patriotic or religious? Or, in terms of cost, why should the lover pay twelve dollars for two dozen roses for his sweetheart, or why should Cézanne sacrifice a lucrative position in his father's bank in order to paint pictures which never paid him much in

his lifetime? If the principle of beneficence needs supplementa-
tion, so does that of attainment. We noticed that the latter had
to be supplemented by the former because, even when we can
go very far with a desire, we may decide to give it up because
of its injurious effects on other desires. But this supplementa-
tion is not enough, for again, why not prefer the desire which
brings us great enjoyment to those which it injures? And neither
one or both of these principles suffices in deciding between two
things, both of which are equally innocuous as, let us say, bridge
and chess; or when both are highly beneficent, as are law and
medicine, and we cannot tell which is the more so. We clearly
need some principle of choice that will express (or establish) an
order among desires within the life plan. We shall call this the
principle of rank.

We might think that this order (*ordre du coeur*) was determined entirely by the pressures of the social environment,
and would be a reflection of them. And there is no doubt that
economic exigencies and the mores of the group are efficacious,
largely through the penalties they impose on my desire in establishing a hierarchy of desires. In a measure, however, we have
already taken account of these in our discussion of beneficence,
where we saw that the importance of desires was related to their
consequences, favorable or unfavorable. Yet that the order cannot be established wholly on this basis has already been shown
by our illustration of why the principle of beneficence must be
supplemented. The rebel, the hero, the saint, and the artist
often withstand these pressures in favor of some preferred aim.
Among ordinary folk also, no one is clay in the hands of the
social potter; or if he is clay it is his choice to be clay. In the
end, the order of the heart is self-chosen. Should we leave the
matter thus, as the existentialists leave it? To a degree, in view
of the freedom and indeterminism of choice, they are right.
Yet not wholly so, I believe. Choice is not completely covered
with darkness; there is something we can say about it to illumine
it. For the rank of a desire is a function of the intrinsic charac-

ters or dimensions already studied by us, to wit, its primary intensity, duration, volume (area, number of subinterests), height, harmony, and a character which we have not yet mentioned, but which is very important, namely, symbolism. Quality is not included because it does not seem to determine choice except as it is correlated with the other characters. And it is noticeable, in this connection, that it has no degrees.

None of these attributes or characters, however, belongs to a desire as if it were isolated from a self, as there are no desires as such, but only desires of this self or that self. There is no love of country as such, but my love or your love, with a fixed intensity, volume, or duration; and whatever intensity, volume, or duration it has, belongs to it as mine or yours, and varies as such. Moreover, none of these attributes is sufficient by itself to determine rank, but must be balanced against all of the others in a fashion for which no rule exists or has been discovered. This balancing is the work of each individual self.

For reasons that will appear, we shall leave intensity to the end of our discussion and consider duration first. That the longer-lasting satisfactions should be preferred to shorter ones has been the almost unanimous opinion of moralists. This is true in regard to two of the meanings of duration specified—attachment to long-range desires and recurrence. The self is interested in its whole future because it is *there* in all its moments; hence not to promote or not to protect such desires is to create misery for itself. The headstrong or intemperate man acts as if he would not be present tomorrow. The satisfactions that last longest in these senses color most moments of our waking life. Such satisfactions as those taken in being loved or in reputation may be carried around by a man at all times, even when, in moments of relaxation and play, they pass into the background of his mind. On the other hand, a desire that flashes and never reappears, if neglected, will cause misery now, but never again. This does not imply that fleeting desires are of no importance—all desires are important since they are mine—

and their standing may be high owing to other factors, such as intensity, which may compensate for shortness of life. Duration has to be balanced up with the other determinants of rank. As Aristotle said, there are momentary joys that are worth years of dullness. Moreover, no satisfaction, however evanescent, is utterly transitory. Through its echoes it may endure forever; the memory of a brief high moment may have immeasurable worth.

That the greater the volume or scope of a desire the higher its rank—other things being equal—would be disputed by few. Volume depends, roughly, as we have seen, upon the number of subinterests under the control of a master system interest. These interests most nearly represent the self as a whole. It is not, however, the mere number of desires that counts but the desires as organized. Failure to cultivate, or injury to, unorganized miscellaneous desires, while significant, is not so significant. Moreover, by itself, number is no determinant of value. Desire a plus desire b is not as such of more worth than a or b alone. Worth, like value, is always *for* some matrix self. That this is true becomes especially evident when a belongs to one and b to another self. Then, viewed apart from a point of reference, it becomes meaningless to assert that a plus b is greater than a or b. It is true, of course, that when both a and b are satisfied, there are more satisfactions in the world than when only a or b is satisfied. Yet it does not follow that it is better so. It can be better so only for some self that makes both a and b its own, through the sympathetic imagination. The reason why, by contrast, the formula holds when both a and b are desires of the same self, is that, if a alone is satisfied and b frustrated, the satisfaction of a is qualified negatively through b's frustrations, and vice versa; whereas, if both a and b are satisfied, then the resulting satisfaction of the self is greater (other things being equal) than if only one of them were satisfied, for the satisfaction of either is enriched and intensified by the satisfaction of the other. When, on the other hand, the two desires are in separate selves, there is, without love, no *greater* satisfaction than either *a* or *b* alone, even when both are satisfied, although there are *more* satisfactions.

If height were nothing but rank, it would be trivial to recognize it as a factor determining rank. But when it is identified with self-transcendence, as we have tried to show that it should be, a problem arises. It is traditional to place the self-transcendent values of love, beauty, religion, and truth first in rank, but the philosopher cannot simply accept this tradition with natural piety; he must try to explain it. Moreover, selfish people, Philistines, and atheists do not appear to agree with the tradition. What, then, is the "pull" of these values? The answer has already been given in our discussions of the dimensions of value—insofar as a person unites his life with that of others, by an act of sympathetic imagination, he adds their satisfactions to his own, thus increasing the volume of his own. Moreover, through this union with the self of another, he escapes from the awfulness of his loneliness. The inference might be drawn that height would take first place as determinant of rank, since the union of self with the values of others theoretically is limitless. Yet this would be a rash (I do not say a false) conclusion, for height has to compete with other determinants of value such as primary intensity. In the case of those whom we call selfish people, the actual limitations of height are evident. And all of us, needless to say, are selfish in some degree (the saints alone excepted), which is another way of saying that the sympathetic imagination has actual limits in the lives of us all. But we cannot here pursue these reflections, which lead on to the problem of the conflict of values and the related problem of the possibility of a universally valid standard, topics of the following chapters.

Symbolism as a determinant of rank differs from height, volume, and duration, and also from intensity, in not being an "attribute" or "dimension" of value in the sense, already explained, of a variable character native to all values. For, by contrast, symbolism is obviously acquired and restricted. That this is true can be seen by reflecting on a simple example of symbolism, making the sign of the cross. To the unbeliever, this act is a mere pantomime, trivial and inconsequential, while to the believer, for whom alone it is symbolic, it is fraught with important consequences. And as symbolic it ranks high and may be preferred to many other acts in the scale of deeds to be performed. The significance of saluting the flag and of wearing an engagement or wedding ring are other familiar illustrations of value through symbolism. Recent studies in psychopathology have revealed a rich, unsuspected fund of examples of the power of symbolism. Apart from symbolism we could not understand the importance to the psychoneurotic of his compulsive acts, such as washing his hands twenty or so times a day.

Without attention to the peculiar nature of symbolism, one might be tempted to regard all complex values as symbolic. For besides their intrinsic value, most acts acquire further value through their connection with desires other than those which directly motivate them; and this acquired value might be classed as symbolic. So, for example, it could be held that eating is symbolic of health and good fellowship, because when we eat we promote health, and when we eat with friends, the satisfactions in eating are suffused with those of good company. Yet the satisfaction of more than one desire in a single act does not by itself make the act symbolic in the sense in which I am using that term. It gives that act depth of value, but does not by itself create symbolism in it. In order for symbolism to exist, there must be a certain structure in the value complex, of which the following characteristics are important: (1) either what we call the symbol or what we call the symbolized must be relatively in the foreground, when the other member of the pair will be in the background (one member of the pair, indeed, may be so far in the background as to be subconscious, as in psychopathic rituals and compulsions); (2) one of the pair will be relatively less important than the other; and (3) there must be fusion between the two. Language offers illustrations of all these points. For, generally in prose, the word as symbol is relatively in the background as compared with its meaning, which is in the foreground; while, in poetry, since the music of the word is of overwhelming importance there, the relations between word and meaning are often reversed, the word being in the foreground and the meaning in the background; and seldom does it happen that the two are of equal significance. In language there is also fusion of the two. For the meaning is carried in the word and seems almost to become its attribute, making the separation of the two very difficult. Thus the word "red" seems red; the flag, American; the genuflexion, religious. Besides the above elements of structure, there is another (4), which to my knowledge has not been accurately analyzed or described: what is symbolized "shines through" the symbol, more or less distinctly. A word illustrates this, where the meaning usually comes through clearly; in the psychopathic act, it comes through only remotely, and obscurely.

The symbolized content may be either desires or satisfactions, as in crossing oneself, or echoes of these; usually both are there. The laying of the wreath on the grave of the beloved is symbolic as expressive of present love, but also of memories of the beloved. It has been said that symbolism is vanishing from our culture. This is true of public symbols, but the importance of private and familiar symbols remains. The young married woman who resented dusting and sweeping in her parents' home, but performs such tasks with zest in her own little ménage, illustrates the persistence of private symbolism. For, even if she does not sweep the room "as for Thy law," making the action fine, she does sweep it as for her husband's love. And every means object is significant of the end it serves, and so impels its possessor to tend and conserve it when not in use—the tea cup, of drinking tea, the good sharp knife, of cutting. The reverence we feel for all aesthetic objects depends on symbolism. The musical pattern, the composition of pure colors and lines, are symbolic of abstract feelings and attitudes aroused by them, and appearing to shine through them; and, when "representation" is added, there is symbolism of objects and acts as well. Hence the high rank of the great symphony as expressing the triumph of each hearer over his fears and frustrations, and of the painting of the Madonna as radiant of worshipful love for the Divine Mother and Sweetheart.

Harmony in an experience as a ground of choice can be considered very briefly since, when embodied in the total self, it becomes one of the facets of the supreme value and, as such, will receive extended treatment presently. Other things being equal, that harmonious single experiences are higher in rank than inharmonious ones follows simply from our reflections in the chapter on the dimensions of value. For we saw there that inharmonious values imply frustration, and frustration—other things being equal again—is always to be avoided. Attention to any one of the illustrations of inharmonious values given will confirm this judgment immediately. Who would not rather have the harmonious satisfactions of the wife who is compatible with her husband than the inharmonious ones of the unhappy wife, or the pleasures of innocent love than those of a "guilty" love? Yet the preference for harmony is not absolute, as we have been careful to show. None of the factors determining preference so far studied is absolute. How, in particular, the preference for harmony is to be qualified is a matter for special investigation when we shall consider it in its most inclusive scope as an attribute of the matrix self.

In our study of the dimensions of value as determinants of rank, we come finally to intensity, which we left to the last because of its decisive, yet puzzling role in preference. The first step toward clearness with regard to it is to make a distinction, seldom made, between primary intensity, which every desire has when it first emerges into consciousness, and secondary intensity, the intensity of a desire after reflection on consequences and after competition with other desires. For the moment we shall be concerned with primary intensity.

Surely one good reason for preferring one thing to another is that initially we want the former more strongly than the latter. What other reason have we for many of our simple preferences, as for tea over coffee or the rose to the orchid? Superficially, indeed, it might seem as if there could be nothing else to weight the alternatives in such a way as to make us choose one. Yet exactly that may happen and in the following manner: the consequences of choosing a may be so disastrous that the initially less intensely wanted b may be preferred; or b may have such favorable consequences to the matrix self that again it will be chosen. Similarly if, in competition with a, b is higher than a, b may be selected. In either case, however, the choice of b is possible only after reflection, for only then does the imagination of the frustrations or joys caused by a create the pull that yields the choice of b.

In view of our use of height as a determinant of choice offsetting intensity, one might naturally raise the question whether scope, duration, and symbolism might not also function in the same way. Yet to put the matter thus would show a misunderstanding of the relations of these specifications of desire to intensity. For, in the first place, all these specifications, excepting perhaps symbolism, being dimensions, are present to a degree in every desire, since there is no desire or satisfaction without its scope, height, duration, and intensity; so that it can never be possible to offset intensity as such against volume or any other dimension as such. The only intelligible question would be whether, say, a of greater volume and less intensity could outweigh b of less volume but greater intensity. But even this way of stating the matter misrepresents the situation, for it seems to imply that all attributes are independent variables. Yet it is certain that they are not independent. Scope, height, and symbolism all tend to increase the intensity of a desire. In the case of scope and symbolism the intensity is a function of the intensities of the desires or satisfactions present in the foreground or in the background; just what function I do not know. The case of height is peculiar, since the increased intensity of the imagined satisfaction of another person increases one's own satisfaction. Something of the sort occurs also in duration, for it is the imagination of the recurrence of the satisfaction which gives to the more enduring desires their superior strength. Apart from imagination, the more enduring have no greater force than the less enduring; the impetuous man thinks only of the good of the present. When height, scope, and harmony of high degree are intertwined, as they are in love and beauty, intensity is increased in three ways. When symbolism involves both height and scope in its background of desires, the intensity of an impulse rises in a twofold fashion. On the other hand no one of the attributes can be reduced to the others, or exists in like degree in any two desires. Ambition has a scope almost as inclusive as the whole self, yet is lower than love in height; and however symbolism may be relative to volume and height in the desires involved, its special pattern, whereby the symbol becomes as it were lit up by the content symbolized, is irreducible to volume or height.

For all these subtleties of relationship, intensity has a unique status; in the end, what I most want to do, that I shall do. The preferred is what I most intensely desire. But, in order to appreciate the full truth of this statement, it is necessary to recur to our distinction between primary and secondary intensity. The primary intensity, it will be recalled, is that of the desire as it first emerges into a consciousness; the secondary intensity is that of the desire when it has competed with other desires, and its consequences upon them has been reckoned with. The victory of a desire is not decided by its intensity as compared with that of its antagonists, each in isolation from the others and independent of their consequences. On the contrary, the victory of the victorious is a function of its superior intensity after it has struggled with its opponents and all consequences have been reckoned with; only then is its intensity *my* intensity—in other words, not what it wants, but what I want, decides. Primary intensity is *its,* secondary intensity is *mine.* Nevertheless, despite the pre-eminent status of intensity, it would be a mistake to try to reduce the other dimensions to it; for that would be equivalent to maintaining that height, volume, symbolism, duration, and harmony did not matter. But they do matter; for whatever intensity belongs to the higher, the more voluminous, and so forth, is due in part to their height, volume, or the rest. And how in any given individual all these factors function to cause the decision which flowers in the final intensity of the desire that wins, no one can know on the basis of a knowledge of generalities such as these which we have been studying. In order to know what act will emerge, one must mix one's knowledge of principles with an imaginative insight into the present pattern of desires in the matrix self of the individual person, for these are the efficacious forces. And even so, one's prediction will be precarious, owing to the limits of the imagination and to the element of indeterminism in any decision. This holds of oneself also, though to a lesser degree, for self-knowledge, too, has its boundaries.

In his treatise, *The General Theory of Value,* Ralph B. Perry has offered three principles for the measurement of comparative value about which something may profitably be said, in relation to the foregoing discussion. His principles are *intensity, preference,* and *inclusiveness.* When employed together, they are held to establish what we have been calling the rank of an interest or object of interest. To illustrate in Perry's own words: "An object, wine, is better than an object, water: (1) if the interest in the wine is more intense than the interest in the water; (2) if the wine is preferred to the water; and (3) if the interest in the wine is more inclusive than the interest in the water." [1] Again,

---

[1] Ralph B. Perry, *The General Theory of Value* (New York: Longmans, 1926), p. 616.

"Any given interest, such as Robinson's thirst for water, may wax or wane or vary in degree of excitement. Let us speak of this variable magnitude as the intensity of the thirst. Now suppose Robinson, still governed by thirst, to be solicited by several alternatives, such as wine, cold water and tepid water, all of which are eligible, that is, promise the satisfaction of his thirst. Robinson then prefers wine to cold water, and cold to tepid water. He does not, strictly speaking, desire one *more* than another, but one *rather than* another. Preference expresses itself in the form, 'this is more to my taste than that,' rather than the form 'my taste for this is stronger than my taste for that.' " [2] Finally, "a supply of water desired both for drinking and for bathing is better than the same supply of water desired only for drinking, or only for bathing—not in the sense of being preferred, nor in the sense of being more intensely desired, but in the sense of being more inclusively desired." [3]

Now there are at least two severe criticisms which should be directed against these principles. First, they are not, as is alleged, independent; and second, the nature of what Mr. Perry calls "preference" is not clear. Let us begin with the former, and test both by his own illustrations. For example, it appears to me certain that if I prefer cold to tepid water, then, when I am thirsty, I shall want the cold more intensely than the tepid, and, if I am presented with both, my interest in the tepid will decline in intensity or vanish altogether. And why should I prefer the cold water to the tepid water? The answer is in terms of "inclusiveness" (volume): the cold water satisfies not only thirst, as does the tepid water, but also my desire for something to cool me off. If wine is substituted for water, this becomes obvious. If I prefer wine to water, that is because the wine not only satisfies my thirst, but also my desire for stimulation and for certain tangs. And surely, if I prefer wine to water, I shall want

[2] *Ibid.*, p. 616.
[3] *Ibid.*, p. 617.

wine more intensely than I shall want water, when you offer me both; and, as in the case of cold versus tepid water, the desire for the latter will sink to apathy.

If it is hard to disentangle preference from intensity, it is equally difficult to discover just what preference is. Is it the same as what we have been calling "height"? This seems some-times to be the case, as in the discussion of Bach versus Strauss,[4] where the issue appears to be between the finer and nobler and the less fine and noble. Sometimes, however, it appears to de-note something as inexplicable as the choice between one flavor and another, as of tea rather than coffee, or between one per-fume and another, as of orchid rather than rose.[5] But how does this differ from intensity? Mr. Perry's concept of preference is, I fear, an unanalyzed mélange of categories that should be, but are not, distinguished: primary and secondary intensity, inclu-siveness, height, and probably rank itself. Despite its faults, however, Mr. Perry's discussion of his three criteria remains one of the few valuable essays of its kind.

[4] *Ibid.*, pp. 640, 651.
[5] *Ibid.*, p. 616.

CHAPTER VII

HARMONY

HARMONY has already been shown to be one of the three facets of the supreme value. But, assuming that the reader would have a fairly accurate preliminary notion of what the word "harmony" means, we did not offer a careful definition or analysis of it. This we shall now undertake to do. We shall also describe, in a general way, the chief methods by means of which harmony may be achieved. The great importance of harmony follows, we saw, from the fact that if there is conflict between major interests, the life plan can with difficulty be realized; or, even when conflict exists between relatively minor desires, there is a loss to happiness through the effort to resolve it on their lower plane. Paradoxically, however, it must be recognized that conflict may be creative of values that could hardly exist without it; yet the paradox is resolved through the fact that such values can arise only through the effort to solve the conflict and achieve harmony. In this chapter we shall, so far as possible, limit the discussion to internal conflicts, reserving the study of conflicts between individuals to the following chapter. But internal and external conflicts cannot entirely be separated, and some of the methods of resolution are the same. Every external conflict has its inner side, and every internal conflict may have had its origin in some external conflict in the past. Thus, the conflict within the adolescent between his conscience and certain kinds of sexual expression had its origin in a conflict between himself and his parents who condemned such acts; on the other hand, the conflict between an employer and his men may turn inwards into one between his own desire to display his power through total victory over them (ending in rule or ruin) and a desire for a peaceful settlement through compromise. Nevertheless, the accent may be on one or the other side of a conflict, and, as has been said, we shall study the inner side now, making the necessary supplement in the next chapter.

Three conditions are necessary for the presence of harmony. The first is negative: that, in the end, the desires involved shall not conflict. This means that the fulfillment of one does not cause the frustration of the other. But even so, all the conditions are not complete. For if these were all, harmony would not be itself a value: the value would consist merely in the satisfaction of the one or more desires whose conflict had been resolved. On the contrary, however, harmony is a value on its own account, with its own specificity. This value arises in the following way. As soon as conflict begins to appear, each of the desires involved is either partly frustrated or frustration is anticipated. Hence there emerges a desire to end the conflict. The fulfillment of this desire is the specific moment in the value we call harmony. Harmony is thus obviously a desire of the second order—a desire regarding desires.

Certain methods for the solution of conflicts have been constantly in employ. Usually they are not known by name—although the name of at least one of them is in common use—yet they would be recognized as being of the kind and as answering to the description we propose by anyone who employs them and is informed concerning them. There is no pretense on our part that those we analyze are the sole methods available; all that is claimed for the list is that it is the best that we have been able to compile after a survey of human problems and the literature that concerns itself with them. The methods are renunciation, substitution, sublimation (a special case of substitution), compromise, and integration. We shall offer a description of each, some examples, and an appraisal of their relative advantages and disadvantages. It will become clear that they are not mutually exclusive, but, on the contrary, usually involve one another.

Renunciation. The conflict is resolved by the renunciation of one of the opposing desires. For example, a young man, eager to get on in the world, gives up his desire to marry his college sweetheart, fearing the burden on his ambition that would be entailed. Or, confronted with the choice between two careers, singing and politics, both of which attract him, he renounces the former. The conflict is resolved, but at an obvious cost, which, as in the cases cited, may be high. Sometimes renunciation occurs when there is no obvious conflict. A desired course of action is abandoned because of the unfortunate consequences that would ensue if one followed it. What is ordinarily called prudence is just this. But, as a matter of fact, there really is conflict, only it is concealed. The conflict is between the desire for the end abandoned and the desires whose fulfillment would otherwise be put in jeopardy.

On the other hand, if the conflicting desires are relatively unimportant, as when, presented with a bill of fare in a restaurant, we have the choice between spinach and carrots, and want both but have little appetite, the loss may be trivial. Life presents us constantly with such conflicts, and we bear the burden of renunciation easily. Even when the desires are not of small importance, the suppression of one of them may still cause no great sorrow if the other satisfies some dominant motive. If the chosen profession brings honor and prosperity, the one renounced may be almost forgotten. A governorship may induce one to forget singing. Or, when a man, in love with two girls, makes his choice, if he is happy with the one preferred, he may nearly forget her whom he has lost. Life with its new problems and interests bears us forward on its eager stream, and our backward glances may cause us little regret. In any case, renunciation seems better than the indecision which leaves us with neither desire appeased and deprives us of the peace which is a favorable condition for happiness. Few would deny, however, that renunciation is a hard method. What appears to be the greater good is indeed realized, but sometimes at a cost so great as to be almost unbearable. Yet oftentimes there is no other way out.

It might be thought that renunciation, being a voluntary process, could be sharply distinguished from frustration due to unfavorable circumstances. So we might try to distinguish the frustration caused by the death of a man's sweetheart from that caused by his renunciation of her due to the opposition of her parents; or the frustration caused by the imprisonment of a member of the political opposition in a totalitarian country, when there is no alternative, from the same fate when he voluntarily gives up his freedom rather than accept the alternative offered him of joining the party in power. Besides the presence or absence of choice and an alternative, there would seem to be another closely related difference—the presence or absence of conflict. These differences are real, but choice and fate are so closely intertwined that they cannot always be sharply distinguished. Thus it is "fate" which confines our choice between carrots and spinach, for if food were more abundant and our purse larger, we might have had both; and in a polygamous country we might not have had to choose between Kate and Jane; and in a democratic nation, no such alternative would have been presented as that between the renunciation of freedom and political integrity. So fate establishes our choices for us, and, while renunciation may be free, that renunciation is necessary at all is not our affair.

The presence or absence of conflict is also a genuine differentia—at first. There was no internal conflict that had to be resolved when the beloved died (we were happy together as only lovers can be). Yet a conflict soon develops. The matrix self, in its search for harmony and happiness, would have us forget her, so that the wound inflicted by her death may heal. Yet we cling to her, and in so doing cleave to our sorrow. On the other hand, the very impulse that tied us to her would cause us to forget her for a new love. The old conflict between the eyes and memory, celebrated by Dante, begins to appear. Every psychic wound engenders an internal conflict of this sort—between the will to psychic equilibrium and the will to nurse our wounds, between the creative advance of the wave of life and the undertow of the past.

Renunciation is a drastic method for the resolution of conflict. Sometimes, as we have noted, the frustration may be so slight as to disappear in time, or is partly compensated for in the satisfaction of the chosen desire. Yet oftentimes the frustrated impulse does not die, and the value created by the preferred alternative is an insufficient compensation. This is especially true of impulses of strong primary intensity, such as those which have their roots in the ambitious or sexual spheres of the mind. A hidden misery then persists. It follows, therefore, that some new method will be tried, in order that happiness may be achieved.

One of these methods is *substitution*. In order to resolve a conflict or alleviate a frustration, a new object is found for one of the conflicting or simply frustrated desires, of such a sort that there is no longer a conflict with the preferred desire, and at least partial satisfaction of the frustrated impulse is achieved. Substitution is either of one object of desire for another, or of one desire for another; the latter we shall discuss as a separate method, since it is involved in what is called sublimation. The possibilities included in substitution can best be understood by means of examples.

Suppose, for example, that a young Jew is in love with a Gentile girl and that his parents, whom he honors, object. He can resolve the conflict by marrying some desirable girl of his own race; this is clearly a case of substitution. Or consider the case of the unmarried woman or the barren wife who adopts a child or mothers her neighbor's children, or takes into the house stray cats or dogs. Or consider the widower who marries a second time, usually some woman ten to twenty years younger than himself. For another example, we might cite the middle-aged man who, for the sake of his health, substitutes golf for tennis. Finally, there are the men and women who, failing at one profession or business, try some other occupation instead. These are all cases of substitution.

Through substitution much value is created, but it would be sheer illusion to suppose that frustration is entirely eliminated. This can be shown by an analysis of the examples cited. The young man who transfers his affections from one girl to another, in order the better to please his parents, may in the end be happier (and so will prove himself to have been wise), but there is something he will miss, the peculiar rapture that accompanies first love and rebellion against authority. The "old maid" who mothers her neighbor's children may find a substitute for the active side of motherhood, but not for the passive side; she will fool herself if she thinks they will love her as they love their real mother. When the widower marries the young girl who has bewitched him, that is very sweet and joyful, but she cannot mean quite the same to him as the high-school sweetheart whose books he shyly offered to carry on the way home from school and who shared his early professional struggles. The adopted child may be loved as much as the real one but cannot be loved in quite the same way; for he is not the issue of his parents' passion and cannot perpetuate their physical selves. Golf, no less than tennis, may give equal opportunities for skill, victory, and companionship, but does not provide the latter's zestful, muscular pleasures. And while one profession may be as good, or better, than another from the point of view of ambition and income, it cannot offer the same type of activity as the other, and therefore not its specific pleasures. The substitute object can never quite cover the full value of the original. It is true that, oftentimes, it is better. The new wife may be a more congenial and helpful mate than the first, and the new profession better adapted to one's capacities and enduring interests, but even so, it will not *match* the original. And sometimes it will be less good. In order to picture these possibilities, we need two diagrams, as follows:

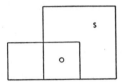 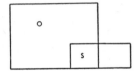

In neither case does *s,* the substitute value, quite cover *o,* the original value, even though in the former, *s* is greater than *o,* and in the latter, less.

Sublimation. This is a kind of substitution, but of activities rather than of objects, although, as we know, no absolute distinction can be drawn between the two, for the reason that activities depend upon their objects. More specifically, however, sublimation is the substitution of a "higher" for a "lower" form of activity. By means of this substitution, the misery of the frustration of the "lower" disappears in the happiness of the successful pursuit of the "higher." So, it is claimed, the activities of the muses may compensate for the frustrations of *eros* and, in general, all the pursuits of the imagination may perform that function in relation to activities concerned with "reality."

The general theory underlying this claim has been well expressed by Theodor Lipps by means of his concept of psychical storage (*psychische Stauung*). In the case of normal, successful activity concerned with real things, the energy of desire flows from the organism where it originates, around and through the object, and this free flow of directed energy is happiness. When, however, desire is frustrated through some defect of the object, or perhaps through the absence or loss of the object, the energy of desire cannot flow freely but is blocked and piles up within the organism or psyche. This damming up is misery. If, however, some new outlet can be found for this energy, happiness may take the place of the old misery. In the case of art, the current of desire finds a path, as it were, vertical to that of action, the pathway of imagination. If my friend dies, my habits of action toward him, of play or of conversation, cannot flow freely about him but are turned back into the organism; this is sorrow. If, however, I can write a poem about him, the energy of my interests will find a channel for their relief. The situation may be pictured as follows, using an arrow as the symbol of desire, and a box as the symbol of its object:

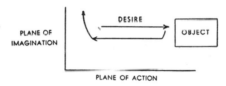

This we may call the generic theory of imaginative sublimation. Freud and his followers have given a more specific interpretation by identifying the energy of desire with *libido* or *eros;* and the followers of Nietzsche by interpreting this energy as "will to power." In accordance with either of these interpretations, the energy of any desire could be transformed into that of any other, in a fashion similar to the transformation of one kind of physical energy into another, as mechanical into thermal or chemical. Hence, theoretically at least, sublimation should provide a perfect substitution, without loss. William James in his essay "The Energies of Men" has provided an application of the theory in his concept of possible "moral equivalents" of war.

The theoretic foundation for the concept of sublimation has already been examined by us and rejected. We came to the conclusion that there was no evidence for the existence of a single primordial desire or energy of desire. We did, to be sure, discover that all desires are illustrations of power, harmony, and achievement, but that these three (three not one) are not the substance of desire, but rather facets or generic aspects of desire. Desires are not specifications of these, but the matter of which these are the generic aspects or forms, even as red and green are not made out of hue, but hue is an attribute of red and green. And it does not follow that because all desires have the common aspects of power, harmony, and achievement, that they are equivalent, any more than it follows from the fact that all specific colors are colors, that they are equivalent and capable of substitution for each other. No painter or decorator would dare to substitute red for blue in his design merely because they are both colors! The individuality of each, whether of color or desire, cannot be theorized away, as we discovered in our reflections on substitution, of which sublimation is a kind.

Yet for all the defects in the theoretical foundation for the concept of sublimation as a way to resolve conflicts, it retains a certain validity. Our interests are complex and overlap in their components and, so far as they do overlap, they may be substituted one for another. Pugnacity, courage, and opportunity for adventure exist in sports, mountain climbing, and high level flying, but also in war; hence they can be substituted for war. Aesthetic experience in its various forms in the arts can be substituted for "real" experience, since imagination contains something of all desires and objects. But it must not be forgotten that substitution as such is not sublimation. Sublimation is the substitution of the higher for the lower, and the higher appear to have a substitutional efficacy superior to that of the lower. Is this appearance a reality? Or is it an illusion fostered by our wish that others cultivate the higher interests for the sake of their advantages for us?

The answer to this question will be given in the extended analysis of the superior lure of the higher interests given in our next chapter. That this lure exists we shall show to be a fact, and we shall try to explain it. We shall show that the higher desires have certain advantages for the individual himself, and not merely for others, in their competition with the lower. The lives of saints and artists prove that this is true. On the level of their unique experiences they are the happiest of men. Yet sublimation, like substitution, can with difficulty be complete. With regard to this we have some testimony from artists. Consider, for example, what one of them has to say: "But I am unhappy in not being able to apply myself to anything but music. I know that I am feeding on an illusion and reality is the only thing worth having. My health is not good and my nerves are in a state of increasing weakness. My life lived entirely for the imagination and without sufficient action tires me so that I can only work with sufficient breaks and long intervals of rest; otherwise I pay the penalty with long and painful suffering. I am very lonely; I often wish for death. While I work I forget my troubles; but the moment I rest, they come flocking about me. What a splendid life is an artist's! How willingly would I part with it for a week of real life." [1] As for the saints, certain practices which they have recommended prove that, even for them also, sublimation is difficult: the mortification of the flesh is a form of renunciation verging on partial self-destruction, not itself sublimation, but an aid to sublimation.

Compromise. This may be described as a method for resolving conflict by providing some satisfaction to each of the conflicting desires. The principle illustrated is clearly stated in the adage, "Half a loaf is better than none"; and since the two desires belong to one self, as much at least is gained (since one-half plus one-half equals one) as would be gained by the complete assuagement of one desire at the expense of the other, in repression. Instead of all for one and none for the other, there is something, though not all, for each. Compromise appears to be the

[1] Quoted by R. Rolland, *Some Musicians of Former Days* (New York: H. Holt, 1915).

better way when neither desire can be fully appeased nor completely uprooted. The ideal formula for renunciation (that is to say, the formula when the preferred desire is completely satisfied and the other desire completely repressed) would be (a) "1 plus 0 equals 1"; but for the most probable circumstances the formula is (b) "$\frac{3}{4} - \frac{1}{2}$ equals $\frac{1}{4}$," because the preferred desire is not completely satisfied, and because we must subtract something for the adverse effect on the total value in the self caused by the continued frustration of the renounced interest. In comparison, the formula for compromise is something approximating "$\frac{1}{2}$ plus $\frac{1}{2}$ equals 1," which is clearly as good as (a) and better than (b).

These facts concerning compromise can be illustrated by the following examples. Suppose that I wish to buy a fine edition of a certain book, but also wish to buy an expensive suit of clothes. I cannot afford both, but I could purchase either one and forego the other. There is, however, an alternative. I can buy a cheaper edition of the book and also a less expensive suit. This is a compromise. Or suppose that I would like to take revenge on a man who has injured me by beating him; but, fearing the law and his reprisal, I merely insult him, in this way partly satisfying my hate and partly allaying my fears. This also is compromise. An example from a higher sphere would be the following. A man feels that he cannot ignore the evidence offered by the "higher criticism" of the Bible and by science against strict fundamentalism in religion, but at the same time cannot abandon his belief in God for atheism. Accordingly, he becomes an agnostic.

The advantages of compromise have been recorded by us; we must now record its disadvantages. We find an interesting difference between the esteem in which compromise is held in external disputes, compared with the dispraise of compromise in the inner, higher life. Few, I believe, would question the indispensability of compromise in dealing with the minor conflicts of life, such as illustrated by our example of the book. Whatever regret might persist because we could not have both of the things we wanted would not be serious, and in most of these cases is submerged by the ongoing wave of life. And if our desires persist and seek full satisfaction later, holding them in abeyance for a time does no great injury. Perhaps when we are richer, we may buy the fine edition of the coveted book, but meanwhile we shall enjoy, without much sorrow, the humbler edition we possess. The value of compromise depends upon our willingness to accept a part instead of the whole; but even if our willingness be most entire, if our desires are not very important, it matters not too much. When, on the other hand, the desires are intense, if renunciation of the whole of our demands is not genuine, there will be severe partial frustration, and a layer of misery will be laid down underneath the happiness of the surface of the mind. Every unhappy marriage that persists as a result of tacit or spoken compromises is an illustration.

To stern moralists and to those pure souls that will have all or nothing, compromises involving conscience and desires high in rank show a taint of shame. To some men and women it seems shameful to live in wedlock with an unloved partner, even though the unity of the family and the peace of mind of the children is preserved. To others, it is disgraceful for a public man to accept the support of a corrupt city boss, even though such deals are necessary for the election to high office of the best available candidate. On the other hand, to Chamberlain and Daladier, the Munich pact, which must have hurt their consciences, did not seem too high a price to pay for world peace, although we with our hindsight and freedom from responsibility may condemn them. Roosevelt, who signed the Atlantic Charter, was apparently willing to sacrifice Poland and China in order to make sure that the Russians would remain on our side and enter into the struggle in the Pacific. But it looks as if Jan Masaryk felt that only suicide could atone for the shame of his yielding to Gottwald, even though the internal peace of his country would have been the high price he would have paid by refusal. But now we are in touch with the specific problems of ideal morality which will concern us later. At this point, however, two reflections would appear to be pertinent. The first is that these examples seem to show the inadequacy of compromise as a method of achieving harmony. The second is that, to the writer of this book at least, they demonstrate how individual a matter conscience becomes when the issues involved are unique and tremendous, and therefore how arrogant it is for any one man to set himself up as a sovereign judge, in God's place, when he has had no decisive part to play in the matter at issue. To anyone who does assume that role I would say, "Would your decision have been different? Are you like God, Who, being omnipresent, can feel the relative weight of the values which tipped the scale in favor of compromise? Let him who is without guilt cast the first stone."

Integration. Two desires integrate when they co-operate in the service of some new interest, through which each finds a partial satisfaction and in assuaging which a new satisfaction emerges. Hence, when all three belong to one self we have the formula "1 plus $\frac{1}{2}$ plus $\frac{1}{2}$ equals 2." 1 represents the satisfaction derived from the new interest, and each $\frac{1}{2}$ represents the partial satisfaction of each of the original interests. It is to be noted that, as in compromise, each of the original desires renounces something. In fact, integration rests on compromise, but supplements it by means of co-operation, through which there is sheer gain. The end result is a greater satisfaction, as shown by comparing the formulas for the two methods.

A sharper picture of integration can be given through the analysis of an example. Let us consider again the conflict between the claims of science and those of faith. The adoption of agnosticism as a philosophy represents a good compromise, we saw; for there is renunciation of the claim of science to be a metaphysics and, on the other side, there is renunciation of the tendency of faith to invade the proper domain of science, including historical research; while at the same time science is left in possession of "phenomena" and faith of "things in them-selves" or "reality." In contrast, integration would be repre-sented by an idealistic philosophy, in terms of which religion would renounce, as in agnosticism, any attempt to do the work of science, but would conceive of the whole field of phenomena as manifestations or appearances of God. Science, in its turn, would forego all claims to a final interpretation of the world, but would remain master in its own house and would, besides, make its contribution to the new attitude by revealing the never-ending wonders of nature. Thus, instead of a division of territory as between science and religion, a union of the two is effected, by means of which a new mystical attitude toward the world emerges, with its unique satisfactions.

Or consider the case of the young scholar in Latin-American studies who has the opportunity to embark on a political career. The offer is flattering, and ambition is aroused. Yet he fears that, if he accepts, his work as a scholar will be ended. After much hesitation, he consents on condition that he become am-bassador to a South American state. At first glance this might seem to be a mere compromise with his scholarly interests, which would find some opportunity for satisfaction in the hours of leisure afforded by a not too busy diplomatic post. But when we consider how useful his knowledge of Hispanic American culture will be to him, and how much goodwill will come to him from the educated citizens of the state to which he is ac-credited because of his continuing studies in their history and way of life, it becomes plain that here is no compromise, but an integration of his scholarly interest with ambition.

As a final example of integration, let us consider the high order interest which we call a man's interest in his family, com-posed as it is of many minor interests, which at times will come into conflict with activities of a different sort. One conflict will be between his love of wife and children, which will demand much of his time and energy, and his desire to "get on in the world." When dominated by the latter, he may sometimes regret that he assumed the responsibilities of marriage, which may appear to require him to remain in a safe but unremunerative and unglamorous position, instead of seeking a new one more in accordance with his ambitious dreams. Or, by contrast, when in full enjoyment of the sweetness of his relations with wife and children, he may wish he were like some of his more easily contented friends. Now in this situation there are available the three optional methods for the resolution of conflicts already studied by us. One is renunciation. The young man may abandon ambition and settle down to being an ordinary, placid, family man. This is not a good solution, however, because it may involve denying his family many of the things they want, on account of his small income, and perhaps some loss of respect on the part of his wife and his children, who may have expected big things of him. As a second choice, he may make a compromise—and I suppose that this is what most men do—partly sacrificing his family life to ambition, and partly sacrificing ambition to family relationships.

But there is a third way, that of integration. To become effective, it requires the willing and entire co-operation in deed and in spirit of all members of the family. The wife must be prepared to forego her husband's attentions for long periods and put up with some irritation on his part when he is tired and absorbed in his problems, and she must be willing to take some of the responsibility for the care of the children that would ordinarily fall upon him. The children must be given to understand that father has important work to do, and that they cannot expect him, except rarely, to play with them and be their good pal as often as other children's fathers are. The man's work must thus become the central, co-ordinating fact in the life of the family. All must be willing to take certain risks involved in change of employment and make sacrifices for savings and investment. But in these circumstances, if the man is successful, most that was lost will eventually be returned to the family through the increased income and more honored position in the world of the father. And, in the rarer moments when husband and wife can come together in love and communication of feeling, the tie between them, instead of being loosened, will become tighter through mutual admiration and the sense of triumph in the common cause that has integrated their lives.

Positive Laws of Satisfaction. So far we have been concerned with methods specifically designed for resolving conflicts. But harmony has positive aspects and is not, as we have seen, a mere state of absence of dissonances. It is like a musical chord, which is harmonious not only because of an absence of beats, but because of a sameness, in spite of variety, of fundamental, underlying acoustic patterns. A harmonious life must, indeed, resolve conflicts through repression, sublimation, compromise, and integration, but it must also exemplify certain laws of satisfaction. When I say "must," I am not introducing a categorical imperative; I am saying that harmony is achieved only when experience possesses a certain form, and therefore that, if harmony is achieved, this form must either be purposely sought for or spontaneously exist there. These laws of feeling pertain to art as well as to life, to imaginative as well as to active experience; they can be discovered in either field. I personally first looked for them in art and then, having found them there, looked for them in life, where I saw them present also. No one of them is exclusive of the others; on the contrary most of them are present together, both in works of art and in lives felt to be good.

First, there is the *law of the theme*. This designation is obviously borrowed from music and has an extensive application to aesthetic values, with regard to which I would refer the reader to my *Analysis of Art*, Chapter II. The law is, however, pervasive in every realm of values, as I wish now to show. The principle means that when harmony is achieved, there is some one or there are several dominant desires, to the satisfaction of which other desires are subordinated, and in terms of which a life can be "understood," and events in that life predicted with some probability. The theme is the master passion or *idée mère* (to borrow a phrase from Taine) of a career. The existence of a matrix self depends on the embodiment of this principle to some degree at least, and every happy life exemplifies it. In the lives of great and masterful men it is vividly illustrated—in a Napoleon, a Caesar, a Newton, a Lenin, or a Balzac; but also in humbler lives where the desires centering around the family or earning a living are dominant. When there are no themes, a life is composed of distracted and scattered interests which, lacking discipline and centrality, interfere with and frustrate each other.

The *law of the variation of the theme,* sometimes called *identity in difference.* This principle, together with the third (contrast), is essential for maintaining the intensity of master passions and their resulting satisfactions. For without variations in their objects and opportunities, desires tend to become mere habits, and the satisfactions accompanying them sink to minimal intensity. The simplest kind of variation is repetition in space and time. If one views space and time abstractly, repetition becomes almost the negation of variation, since there is no quality which distinguishes one moment or one point from another; but viewed concretely, since each new moment of time and each new place in space introduces a fresh situation, there is variation even thus. In art repetition plays a great role, as exemplified by musical design and architectural ornament. The importance of repetition for value is derived from the fact that each new appearance of a desire brings with it echoes of past appearances, so that the satisfaction is big with its past and gains in importance continually. Moreover, a certain amount of repetition is necessary for the adjustment of a desire to its object, without which it may be clumsy and ignorant of the full possibilities of enjoyment that may be provided. On the other hand, mere repetition tends toward habituation and satiation, so that variation within the repetition is necessary to keep the satisfaction keen and alive. In music we find that repetition of a theme is accompanied by change in key or voice, by inversion, or by some other similar device; in ornamental design, if a shape is repeated, it is repeated with a change of color, or is given variety through the juxtaposition of a contrasting thematic shape, as when two themes alternate in the egg and dart motif in architectural ornament. Similarly, outside of art, while we demand the familiar, we require it in a new form or dress. We like our old familiar rooms, but we give them fresh paint and fresh curtains; we prefer our old companions, but we hope that they will meet us with fresh ideas and new stories of their own or other people's adventures.

Contrast. From one point of view, contrast is merely the extreme of variation, any large variation being a contrast. But when the variation becomes great enough, something new is introduced; instead of novelty being felt as variation *of* the theme, it is felt as departure *from* the theme—a competing theme is introduced. It is like the difference between gradual change and revolution. There are at least two reasons why contrast enhances satisfaction. In the first place, merely as a kind of variation, it prevents the habituation that tends toward dullness of feeling. By providing a radically new object for desire, it wakes up that desire and even the whole life of desire as sharing in that particular endeavor. But—and this is one of the most striking effects of contrast—it arouses desire for the very object with which the new object is set in contrast. So the new friend or the new member of a club enlivens the zest for conversation and conviviality, which was perhaps beginning to grow stale in oneself, but he also enlivens one's interest in the old friends or club members. In the aesthetic world this double effect is impressive. To put blue against gold, or dark against light, vivifies interest in both the contrasting areas. When the emergence of the Baroque style gave new zest to the architectural interest jaded by the hundreds of Gothic buildings, a closely following result was the revival of Gothic; even as functional architecture first supplanted the classic and then led to a classical renaissance. And a man turns from masculine to feminine companionship, then back again to the masculine; or goes from the city to the country for refreshment, only to return with new appreciation for the exciting opulence of the metropolis. The dialectic of Hegel, with its opposition of thesis and antithesis, has no more validity than is given to it by this reason for the value of contrast; and the well-known tendency in art and politics to go to extremes is an illustration.

The second reason for the efficacy of contrast is completeness. If we have only the blue, we have but half a color world; only the masculine, but half of the human; only the intellectual, we lack the sensual, and vice versa. The demand for balance in the arts, and in morals for a balanced life, is essentially the same as the demand for completeness through contrast. Balance seems, in addition, equality between the contrasting elements. This is certainly true of mechanical balance, where one weight in a scale pan is equal to another; it is true also of balance in the fine arts, in painting, sculpture, and architecture, where a sort of "humanized" mechanical balance is demanded, since we see things more or less in terms of the human body, with its contrast and balance of right and left. This sort of balance is symmetry, obvious or subtle. But, in general, value balance requires only so much equality between the contrasting elements as is required for completeness. A balanced diet does not require an exact equality between the amounts of proteins, carbohydrates, minerals, and vitamins to be consumed, but only so much of each as is necessary for the healthful nourishment of the body. A balance between the "bodily" and the "spiritual" values does not imply equality between them.

Conflict. At first glance, there is something paradoxical in setting down conflict as a positive law of value. For, if harmony is an aspect of the highest good, is not conflict sheer evil? Is not the theme of this chapter precisely ways of avoiding and resolving conflict? On the other hand, how can the following facts be overlooked? (1) The most magnificent works of art, especially

of tragic art, are representations of conflict, engaging the sympathetic participation of the audience. (2) Contrast is always on
the threshold of conflict, if it does not actually pass over into it,
for the interest that centers in the new in any temporal whole
(as in music) has to compete with the interest that centers in
whatever may be strikingly different in that part which is passing away, while in a spatial, contemporaneous whole of elements
(as in a picture) there is a conflict of interest between the lure
of any theme and its complementary opposite) as dark and light,
warm and cold, horizontal and vertical. (3) People sometimes
deliberately "pick a quarrel"—youngsters, bored spouses, even
grave and presumably responsible statesmen. Finally, (4) there
is an intensification of experience resulting from conflict, industrial, social, and political, as reflected in the individual's
experience.

These facts add up to a demonstration that without conflict
experience would be at a lower level; and that the good life
cannot be attained by avoiding them, but by meeting and overcoming them. (Although having stood the heat of the day, one
may welcome rest in some asylum for contemplation.) There is
implied the truth that any planned society or utopia designed to
exclude conflict would not be so good, other things being equal,
as one that included it. *Die Negativitael ist das Leben!* But the
paradox referred to must still be faced. The overcoming of it
depends on the insight that conflict is essentially a means, not
an end, and that the end itself is the satisfaction incidental to
the activities, always of maximum intensity, aroused for its
removal. Conflicts unresolved are evil, for they involve frustration; hence the practical maxim, not to run into or initiate a
conflict which you cannot resolve.

Evolution. By evolution in this connection I mean a type of
experience which moves forward in such a way that each moment contributes to the enrichment or intensity of later moments, all leading up to a novel point of consummation or
climax. It is obvious that such a form of experience is very

advantageous in comparison with one that does not have this character. Illustrations from the fine arts are: melody, beginning with the tonic and proceeding to new tones, each of which, in conserving the value echoes of all its predecessors, is enriched by them, and all of which lead on to the high point of return to the tonic or some other tone belonging to the tonic chord; a story or drama, where each scene or incident gathers interest from the preceding ones, and, by complicating a conflict established at the beginning, then increases the interest further either through its gradual resolution or its sudden termination in a "happy" or a "tragic" ending. In life, as opposed to art, a successful research project is an illustration; for, as data are gathered and a hypothesis is found, each stage in the process of verification of the hypothesis is cumulative of cognitive value, up to the climax, when the establishment of the theory is effected. Another illustration would be a campaign for political office, say the presidency, the climax of which would be, of course, election. The solving of any problem or the resolution of any conflict provides illustrations of evolutionary experience. It is noteworthy that the process may develop by easy transitions from one moment or stage to another (variation) or by sharply contrasting moments, through which an element of conflict may be introduced. Since, in a way, evolution is the form of all purposive experience, the realization of the objective of desire being its goal or climax, and all earlier moments having significance in relation to this, one might raise the question of the propriety of including it as a special law of value. But in ordinary purposive experience there is usually waste and distraction en route to the goal. What I am calling evolution is the purification and perfecting of this experience.

The special values of evolution may be focused by comparing it with rhythm. The significance of rhythm is an oft-told tale. It has even been thought to be the basic principle of the arts, and some readers may be surprised at our omission of it from our list of laws of value. Its significance for life in the large is also a trite observation. Its fundamental character is shown through the fact that as a form it is abundantly illustrated in those spheres of experience where dependence on organic conditions is most direct and easily discovered. The rhythmic emergence and recurrence of hunger and satiation, of muscular activity and repose, sexual desire and assuagement, are related to rhythms in the body, not so constant as those of respiration and heart beat, yet well established. The preservation of these rhythms, over long periods, seems to contribute to maximum intensity of satisfaction and appears to be connected with the ultimate rhythms of the Omega system.[2] Despite its importance, rhythm is not, I believe, as basic and important as theme and variation and contrast, since it can be analyzed into a combination of these. For let us look at any rhythm, such as that of respiration. It is a repetition of units or themes, each of which is a balance of two opposed, contrasting subthemes, inspiration and expiration, spaced at relatively equal intervals. Meter is a repetition of so-called feet, again at relatively equal intervals, each of which is a balanced contrast of accented and unaccented elements, constituting a theme of themes

The values of rhythm are, therefore, those of theme and variation, contrast and repetition. So far as we can relate them to organic rhythms, there is probably a further value, explicable through concordance with the rhythms of organic life, upon which all values partially depend. Without this concordance, there is conflict with the organic substructure, introducing into the value harmony a dissonant note, hard to resolve.

The difference between rhythm and evolution may now be stated. Although both are a succession of moments, there is no consummation or climax in the former, to match that of the latter. Inspiration, expiration, inspiration, expiration; diastole, systole, diastole, systole; hunger and repletion, hunger and re-

[2] On the Omega system, see the author's *Experience and Substance* (Ann Arbor: Univ. Michigan Press, 1941), Ch. XVI-XVII.

pletion, and so on; but no movement to a goal. In the organic field, the only end point seems to be death, and instead of an accumulation of value issuing in some beautiful finale, we seem to notice a gradual reduction of value in the wearing out of the body. There thus appears to be a certain sinister quality in rhythm, the merely rhythmic betokening fatigue or habituation, a degradation of value. In order to offset this, rhythm needs to be united with evolution, and irregularities must be introduced into its slumberous monotony. Exactly this we find to be true of the arts, as in poetry, where an evolution of thought accompanies the basic rhythm of sounds, itself enlivened with deftly placed eccentricities.

Hierarchy. The stratification of values in different orders, corresponding to interests of different orders; the existence of major interests composing the matrix self, topped by an interest of highest order which unites them all—these facts illustrate the principle. Normatively expressed, it is embodied in the familiar admonition, "Put first things first." The mere existence of the motto shows that the hierarchy of values, although based on fundamental grounds, is not always realized; for interests lower in rank may assume the place of those which are higher. The general may fail to subordinate strategic advantages at certain points to the over-all plan of campaign; the impressionable man may endanger the happiness of a well-loved wife because of the fascination of some pretty girl; the allurements of an avocation may lead to the neglect of a vocation. The failure of the principle is of the essence of evil, since, as a result, the life plan is put in jeopardy, perhaps brought to ruin.

The Importance of Initial, Central, and Final Elements. Elements of these sorts have unusual significance either in the course of experience or in the objects of experience. The first time of anything—the small boy's first long trousers, the youth's first love, the young man's first position, his first investment, his first book, are glamorous in a way that subsequent experiences cannot be. In art, the first chapter of a novel, the first scene of a play, the opening bars of a musical composition, have pre-eminence. Sharing this pre-eminence are also the final elements: the last act in a drama, the closing episode in a novel, the last line of a poem, the finale in music, the border of a formal design, the last course at a banquet, the last no less than the first play of a game, the last battle; farewell! no less than hail! Somewhere near the middle, too, is generally important in any career; and in aesthetic objects, in a picture or a rug, the center is where significant elements of the composition are likely to be placed; the central are "central."

From these facts one might be tempted to deduce that there is an aspect of sheer form in values, as has been maintained ever since the time of Plato. All our principles of evaluation of values might also be cited as evidence for this inference. And they are indeed evidences of the existence of form, and of a rather specialized kind of form, in experiences of value. It would be strange, in view of the pervasiveness of form throughout experience if this were not so. But they are not evidences of sheer form, of form as a necessary and sufficient condition of value. For throughout our discussion of the formal principles of value we have shown that not the form by itself but the satisfactions mediated by form are determinant of value. With regard to the principles of form now under discussion, no less, we can show reasons inhering in desire-satisfaction.

The reasons are as follows. Initial experiences of value have increased importance because, first, they are not subject to the law of habituation or diminishing value, hence have what we call "freshness"; and because the expectation aroused by desire is not diminished by comparison with other experiences of the same type, which, if lower in intensity, will lower the expectation (disillusion). The second component of satisfaction, the imaginative satisfaction in expectation, is therefore high in intensity in all initial experiences. A third factor may also play its part. Curiosity is aroused in connection with expectation, and its satisfaction is added as a new component to the original satisfaction. Final elements are important because they appear at the point of resolution of conflict, of solving of a problem, of consummation. It is, therefore, not so much because they are end points that they have peculiar significance, but because of what occurs at these end points. Yet in spatial aesthetic objects, the bordering elements, which are last as the eye travels from any point within, would appear to have importance because of mere position. There is, however, even here a reason: the border isolates the object from surrounding things, and because it fulfills this function, so important in the value of aesthetic objects, it deserves and gets special attention. Moreover, as the eye moves, it must stop there, for if it goes beyond, it enters, as it were, foreign country; the border is a sort of road block for the eye. The central elements might also appear at first to be significant because of mere form, but here too there are, as a matter of fact, reasons which are not purely formal. In spatial aesthetic manifolds, the center is the spot from which the whole can best be surveyed and appreciated at a single moment, and there also the eye tends to rest. It is fitting, therefore, that elements of consequence be placed there. In temporal value wholes, the point near the center is often the "turning point," the place where a crisis occurs on the way to the resolution of conflict or attainment of a goal; or, if there is a period of aftermath and taking account of results, the resolution itself occurs toward the middle of the whole course of value events. By middle or center is, however, meant no strict mathematical center. The signal importance of the third act in the Shakespearean drama will illustrate what I have been saying in regard to temporal wholes; and almost any painting by Raphael will serve as illustration for spatial wholes.

Uniqueness. The law of the special value of the unique seems to be in opposition to the principle of variation, especially in its lowest form, repetition. For the one demands that if there is a theme, it reappear with variation; the other, that it do not reappear. Yet there can be no doubt of the validity of the principle of uniqueness. "Fair as a star when only one is shining in the sky." What has well been called the "isolate" in decoration and other aesthetic wholes, for example, the portico in Renaissance architecture, the single rose window in the Gothic style, the Grave Diggers' Scene in *Hamlet,* the solitaire gem or other item in aesthetic jewelry, the "one and only" in the realm of affection: these are decisive illustrations of the special value attaching to uniqueness. There is a simple explanation of the principle: the unique object has no competitor in its sphere, hence the entire satisfaction can be attributed to (objectified upon) it. Conversely, there is no opportunity for the law of diminishing returns, which depends upon the existence of a series. The special value of first and final elements is, to some extent, an illustration of the principle of uniqueness. The first book published is a unique object; so is the victory parade or the winning of a highest honor.

But, although the value of uniqueness is thus established beyond peradventure, its opposition to the principle of variation and repetition raises this question: can the unique object provide complete satisfaction to the desire centered upon it? Desire may require many objects for its appeasement, as a man may need many friends. Hence the demand, in a unique object of affection, for the infinite variety that will not stale. Such an object is, in effect, many objects, for each of one's encounters with it is unique; and, through its different appearances in our lives, the principle of the variation of the theme is illustrated, and the reconciliation of this principle with that of uniqueness is achieved. Yet for some desires, even such a rich object is insufficient for satisfaction, and many objects, not just one varying object, are required. So we have here, as elsewhere in the world of values, a crossroads, an opportunity for free decision.

In addition to the foregoing laws of value, there are certain alleged laws often referred to in the literature of the subject, to which we must now, in conclusion, turn our attention. These are the law of diminishing returns, the law of marginal utility, and the law of complementary value.

The *law of diminishing returns* has applications in the theory of economic value which I shall not consider here, except incidentally.

In its more general aspects, however, it has applications throughout the entire realm of value. As such it is equivalent to the law of habituation: the law, namely, that values tend to lose in intensity if the objects and occasions of desire remain unvaried. As must have been noticed, most, if not all of our laws of value, may be regarded as ways of circumventing this principle. It is a principle which parallels the law of entropy in the physical world and may perhaps be identified with it metaphysically. It is a kind of fatigue of the psyche, a *tedium vitae,* that has to be compensated for in the ways indicated.

When applied to objects of desire, it means that our interest in later increments or examples of a kind diminishes, so that, to use the stock example, the later slices of bread that we eat when we are hungry are diminishingly interesting to us. Our hunger is pretty well satisfied by the earlier slices; hence the later ones add little to our total satisfaction. The variation of the objects, their arrangement in evolutionary series, the introduction of contrast and conflict—adding, say, a bit of jam to the later slices, promising special treat with the last slice, introducing dark instead of white bread now and then—these are well known devices, as already described, by means of which the law can be opposed and overcome.

The *law of complementary value* is the law that a thing having no or very little value by itself may acquire value or greater value by being part of a whole which without it would have no value and with it does have value; or which, having a little value, comes to have much value in similar circumstances. There are the familiar illustrations of the bolt and the nut, which have no value apart from some machine, which itself has no value without them, but with them does have value; or the musical tone or chord, which by itself may have small value, but which, in its place in a melody, has great beauty.

The ground of this principle is laid in one of the fundamental facts about value—its system character. There are, as we have claimed, no unit desires, at least there are none discoverable; every desire, as we know it, is a configuration of lesser desires. It has, therefore, what Mach called its *Gestalt-qualitaet* or form character, which depends on the relation of its constituents. Hence any one of these constituents, if lacking, makes the form character of the whole impossible, and, when present, has a special value as contributing to, or participating in, this character. The same considerations are valid for the complementary objects involved in satisfactions, and obviously for the means objects necessary for their existence. These latter, although not wanted for their own sake, will be wanted as means necessary for the existence of satisfactions and will therefore come to possess corresponding attributive value.

The law of marginal value. This principle asserts that wherever a series of like objects, or increments of like objects, are necessary for the satisfaction of a desire, the attributed value of each one of them is the same and is equal to that of the last object, the "marginal" object, at the margin where another object would have no value, since the desire will have been appeased. We cannot study here the application of this principle to economic value, and shall offer only some general reflections applicable to the entire field of values.

In the first place, the principle is valid for objects viewed as means, that is, to attributed value (as recognized in our statement of the principle), not to objects as ends or complements of desire. In other words, it is a principle of evaluation, not of primary value. For it is clear that, to use again the banal example, the various slices of bread that assuage hunger do not have equal primary value, but a relatively diminishing value, according to the law of diminishing value. It is only when we are contemplating supplying ourselves with a stock of such objects and notice that each is like the other, and that any one of them could serve to give us any satisfaction in the series of satisfactions, even the first and greatest, that we realize that the attributed value of each, measured by the cost to us in getting it, is the same as that of the last item, provided that we can get all that we need at this cost. That is what we are willing to "pay" (in the economic and in the general sense) for each. If we pay more, we are foolish; if we are not willing to pay as much, then we must be willing to forego the satisfaction entirely.

The limits to the application of the law are obvious and have often been pointed out. It is not applicable where the objects concerned are not alike, wherever an object has a uniqueness reflected in a unique satisfaction. Since, accurately considered, all things are unique, the law is only approximately true; it is true only so far as standardization of means objects is possible. To aesthetic objects and to objects of affection it does not apply, and in the field of endeavor where there is some unique terminal object to be coveted and striven for, it cannot hold. For all such objects we are willing to pay more than for any mere marginal one. But, on the other hand, in the economic field, where standardization of objects has come to be the rule, it plays a great role.

CHAPTER VIII

THE RELATIVITY OF VALUE AND ITS LIMITS

IF IT be true, as I believe has been shown, that expressions of value are lyrical or practical, then they are neither true nor false; hence, as wholes, are not in the logical sense propositions. Rather they are directed (vectorial) currents of feeling, forces tending toward goals, which overflow into expressive media and may spread, in new lateral directions, into neighboring centers of experience. So—to employ again an expression that has already served us well—if the lover says to the beloved, "I love you," he is not saying anything about his feelings, but communicating his feelings, and his expression is a deed, a vectorial current from himself to her. The lateral spread of feeling would be illustrated by the expression "I love her" uttered in the presence of other "neutral" persons. This, by itself, is not, as a whole, a proposition, since its truth is never in question, as would be the case if he had said, "It is true that I love her," but rather a diversion of the current to *us*, which, in the intimate situation, is concentrated toward *her*. For this current must first be felt by us before we can say "he loves her," when now at last and only now, among all three expressions, have we come upon a genuine whole proposition. Until now, the expressions used as illustrations are no more true or false than a thunderstorm or the sun emerging from the clouds.

These are typical of all expressions of value. And if they are neither true nor false, the problem with reference to them is not to confirm or to refute them but, as we shall see, something quite different. The primary reason why this is not understood is the confusion between the two types of expression distinguished by us, expressions *of* value and expressions *about* value. The latter are, indeed, propositions in the usual sense and, as such, are either true or false or probable. They have their importance, but it is a different importance from that of the former. How it is different, and how our problem with reference to each kind is different can be shown by means of two illustrations.

First, let us consider the case of an instructor in a class in music appreciation. His aim is to build up in his pupils an appreciation of what is called "good" music. Being an enthusiast, he wishes to give extra time and energy to promising students. This implies that he must be able to make predictions as to whether, as a result of his efforts, any given student will enjoy some test musical composition of fair intricacy, say Bach's Toccata and Fugue in B minor. These predictions would be in the form "A will enjoy Bach's Toccata," "B will enjoy Bach's Toccata," "C will enjoy Bach's Toccata," and so on. Since they are about so-called future events, these propositions will be only probable, yet, even so, they will be genuine propositions. Their importance will obviously be pragmatic; they will serve as guides to the instructor's efforts. If "A will enjoy Bach's Toccata" is probable, then the instructor will continue his special efforts with A; but if false, he will discontinue his efforts. Let us suppose that the proposition is probable, and that, as a result of the instructor's teaching, A does eventually enjoy Bach's work and exclaims "Oh, how beautiful Bach's Toccata is!" Now this utterance will not be a proposition about A's feeling, but an expression of his feeling, its overflow into words channeled into the experience of the instructor. And what will be the instructor's attitude? Not to consider this a proposition to be verified or refuted but as a *fact* confirming his prediction, and as something for rejoicing and sympathy. One does not sympathize with a proposition, but one sympathizes with a feeling and its expression.

Or consider a second illustration. The scene is a meeting of four ambassadors in London. Mr. Molotov, the representative of Russia, is speaking. He says, in effect, "I advocate a strong central government for Germany with its capital in Berlin." Is this a proposition? Hardly. For when, after translation, Mr. Marshall has understood the meaning of Molotov's words, he does not say to himself or to his colleagues, "Mr. Molotov is declaring that he advocates a strong central government by Germans with its capital in Berlin"; rather he says, "I am opposed to a strong central government." That is to say, he does not seek to refute Molotov's statement as a proposition about Molotov's feelings; he opposes those feelings. He sets up a current of feeling counter to Molotov's, a force against his force. His expression is not an attempted refutation of a proposition, but an incident in a cold war.

It might happen, to be sure, that after translation from Russian into English, Marshall would say, to the translator, "Does Mr. Molotov really advocate a strong central government in Germany?" In this case Molotov's statement could be re-expressed as, "It is true that Mr. Molotov does advocate a strong central German government." And that, indeed, would be a proposition, and Marshall would accept it as true; that is to say, he would believe it. But then that would be a different expression from the original one; and, instead of opposing it, Marshall would assent to it.

Yet, while the appropriate attitudes toward a volitional expression are not belief or disbelief, there are parallel attitudes, as indicated, which we may characterize as support and opposition. To these should be added a third, indifference, which corresponds to undecidability in logical propositions. Thus, in a town meeting or other democratic assembly, someone makes a motion or "moves." Now the "motion" is a typical volitional expression; for it says, in effect, "I wish that so and so," say "that a new civic center be established in Ann Arbor." This latter part of the "motion" is a proposition in the logical sense, as we have seen, but the statement as a whole is not. Yet it is a proposition in the practical sense—something not for belief but for action. Notice how appropriate is the language used. Somebody "moved" and the chairman "puts the motion." These words are literally correct, for motion metaphysically speaking is the expression of desire. Moreover, the appropriate attitude toward a volitional statement is well expressed when the chairman says, "All those in favor of the *motion* signify by saying 'Aye'; opposed, 'No.'" Instead of "in favor of," the term "support" is, of course, also in general use. In the one case, a force is added to the force of the "motion"; in the other, a counterforce is set up. But whoever gave support to or withheld it from a truth? The third possible attitude, however, should not be forgotten—indifference. Some in the town meeting will not vote either way—they will neither support nor oppose the motion.

When a volitional expression gives utterance to a satisfaction rather than to a desire, a different pair of terms is in use; yet it is noticeable that they constitute a polarity other than that of belief—disbelief, and essentially the same as support—opposition. The pair is sympathy—antipathy. These attitudes are appropriate toward expressions of satisfaction of all varieties, sensuous, aesthetic, or ethical. I sympathize with or am antipathetic toward an expression of pleasure in Bach's Toccata or a perfume, or toward some expression of ethical appreciation, as when someone says, "What a fine fellow George is!" Occasionally, sympathy and antipathy are interpreted as sameness or difference of feeling, as when we say, "I have the same feeling toward it as you have," or, "I have a quite different feeling in the matter"; and that is correct, for the feeling is the same or different in *kind*.

The view that expressions of value are neither true nor false has awakened not only the disagreement but also the antipathy of certain writers, sometimes amounting to moral censure. It is felt that the general acceptance of this view would result in moral anarchy and the ruin of our civilization. Those who combat it regard themselves as potential saviors of a lost world. For example, C. I. Lewis in his recent book, *An Analysis of Knowledge and Valuation,* has this to say: "But this is one of the strangest aberrations ever to visit the minds of men. The denial to value apprehensions in general of the character of truth or falsity and of knowledge would imply both practical and moral cynicism." [1] Yet we find Lewis himself wavering as to the truth or falsity of felt expressions of value, asserting both that they may be true or false and that they cannot be judgments or be classed as knowledge.[2] And his whole argument against the view I am supporting rests on the possibility of predictive judgments *about* values, which, so far as I know, no one ever denied.[3] Moreover, he specifically exempts moral judgments from the sphere of empirical value judgments,[4] thus, with regard to these at least, going over to the camp of the enemy.

Now I hope to show that the kind of theory I am expounding does not result in moral anarchy. And I conceive it to be of the greatest social importance to realize what manner of expression value expressions are, so that we may know how profitably to deal with them. To treat them as logical expressions about which we can dispute on purely rational grounds, or as scientific statements to be confirmed or refuted by the methods of science, is to waste one's time and to neglect the methods which are, in

[1] (La Salle, Ill.: Open Court Publishing Co., 1947), p. 366.
[2] *Ibid.,* p. 375.
[3] *Ibid.,* pp. 371-72.
[4] *Ibid.,* pp. 552-54.

fact, applicable. In crises, it may in fact be dangerous to mis-understand their nature, for, trusting to "reason," one may leave the military defenses of one's way of life weak. And, looking about the world with an unprejudiced eye, one does not get much encouragement for the theory that persuasion as to values is a wholly rational process, or that scientific method has been of much avail. That there are, nevertheless, other methods for resolving problems of value will be shown in the course of our argument.

First, however, it is necessary to make clear just what the opposing points of view regarding values are. Against us is the theory that values are not, as we hold, experiences of subjects, but objective facts of some sort, and that ethical expressions at least are expressions of those facts, and may be verified or re-futed with reference to them, in some fashion not too well de-fined in the theory. We have already rejected this view in our chapter on the definition of value. Against us also is the view that expressions of value, or at least some of them, such as the ethical, are rational and self-evidently true in a fashion similar to logical and arithmetical expressions. If this were so, a man could be persuaded that his conduct was right or wrong, start-ing from premises axiomatic and universally admitted, as he can be persuaded that 496 plus 387 equals 883 on the basis of the admittedly true premise that 1 plus 1 equals 2. On the contrary, we have shown that moral principles are either tautologies, and hence insufficient as premises in moral arguments, or else state-ments which are essentially volitional, not rational, in character. In all moral discourse, therefore, we must take for granted that our interlocutors are in substantial *sympathy with* our own volitions. Identity, not in truth or in reason, but in desire is where we have to begin, and without this, there can be no argument.

Moreover, although we know much that is true *about* values, what we know is general in character. For this reason, and be-cause of a certain contingency in events, we can never predict with certainty the values of another, but only with greater or less probability. This in itself would eliminate the old dogmatism from moral discourse, which was based largely on a deterministic theory of conduct. Finally, since values spring from volitions, which are always those of an individual, the conscience of one man, meaning by conscience his total sense of values, can never be wholly the same as that of another. Each person's hierarchy of values is a personal decision, to some extent free. In fine, there is a basic egocentricity or, to use a term previously much in use, a basic relativity in values.

Nevertheless, and this is too often forgotten, within any culture, valuations are for most participants, over a large and over the most important area, the same. For most practical purposes they are the same. This fact alone goes far toward mitigating whatever anarchic consequences might be carelessly drawn from the egocentricity of values. There are, to be sure, and there always will be, exceptional persons whose life plans will deviate widely from what is common in the mass. There will be the "hardened criminals," the psychopaths, the aggressors, the saints, and certain types of men of genius. Moreover, there is no identical normality or mental "health" for all men; there is only health and normality relative to individuals. Yet the fact remains, as we have said, that, by and large, what a man wants is what others in his group want, and what shall be his conscience will be the conscience of others. This follows from the social character of values.

Even between cultures there is a basic uniformity. Our major interests in comfort, health, ambition, and the rest, as we have distinguished and described them, are essentially the same. Only the forms of these, the ways in which they may be realized, are different. In a patriarchal, pastoral community, ambition will take the shape of accumulating holdings in land and cattle; in a modern capitalistic society, it may show itself in the accumulation of property in stocks and bonds. As Max Scheler has shown, even the values underlying what seem to be the strange and immoral customs of primitive peoples are seen to be the same on careful scrutiny. For example, human sacrifice seems to violate all our ethical sentiments, but would we condemn it if we believed that there existed cruel powers in whose hands rested our safety, demanding the flesh of our children? Is it so different from sacrifice of our golden lads in war? The beautiful and the brave were expendable then; are they not expendable now? In both cases the value set upon the preservation of the community is the same; different are only the beliefs as to what endangers it. Among certain primitive tribes there exists the seemingly cruel custom of putting to death the older people, with appropriate ceremonies. But the custom is shocking only because we neglect to look into the circumstances surrounding it. For when we inquire, we discover that the food supply of these tribes is so scant that the younger and the older members cannot live together for very long. Hence, for the older people the proper attitude is *nunc dimittis*—now let thy servant depart.

In general, a study of primitive customs discloses not so much a radically different sense of values as a lower plane of knowledge. The wide agreement within a culture, and between cultures, is largely responsible for the illusion of the objectivity of values. The individual member of a group, finding his own valuations reinforced by the agreement of others, forgets their essential egocentricity. Moreover, they do have a kind of objectivity. For that I prefer this to that, and that millions of my fellows do so likewise is, indeed, a fact as stubborn as any other fact, and something to be reckoned with by anyone who is not in sympathy with us. Yet what should not be forgotten is the kind of fact values are; facts of feeling, of desire, of satisfaction, and decision, with no lodgment in the universe outside of centers of experience.

We are now, I believe, in a position to consider what can be done when there is opposition between my values and the values of other persons.

One thing that can be done is to agree to disagree. This is the usual procedure with regard to trivial matters. Thus if you like to smoke Camel cigarettes and I prefer Marlboros, so long as there are plenty of both kinds obtainable, I shall do nothing. The same attitude would be maintained with regard to the choice of a vacation spot when you and I are not intimate friends or do not belong to the same family: you prefer the mountains, I the seaside. We may generalize and conclude that as regards purely sensuous pleasures and recreations, we tend to agree to disagree. It is noteworthy, however, that with reference to certain other types of values, our attitude is different. We do not tend to agree to disagree concerning aesthetic, ethical, scientific, ambitious, and, until recently, religious values. The reasons why we do in some cases and not in others are complex, and it will illumine the whole field of values if we discuss them.

One chief reason why we agree to disagree is indifference to the values of others. One might, indeed, be tempted to identify agreeing to disagree with indifference. But that would be a mistake, for sometimes we agree to disagree when we are initially or persistently interested. In any case, indifference is perhaps the major reason for agreeing to disagree. To all of the preferences of the majority of mankind we are indifferent, even if we know what they are, because we do not come into intimate contact with them, and because they do not have any discernible effect upon our lives. They have no reality for us. They can make an impact upon us only through the imagination, of which the capacities are limited, as we have had so many occasions to remark and shall have to insist often again. Only the missionaries—people of keen imagination in such matters—are without indifference to the manners and morals of the heathen. And even when we live in contact with other people we are apt, like the Pharisee in the parable, to pass over on the other side. In these circumstances, however, the limits of our imagination are not wholly involuntary. We *will* not to be aware of the desires, frustrations, and satisfactions of our neighbors, in order to maintain the established even tenor of our own moods and habits. If we did otherwise, we might have a new and difficult problem of harmonization on our hands. Our "conscience" would hurt, and we should have to deal with that. Like White-head's negative prehensions, we dismiss them into irrelevance and unconsciousness.

But even when we are not indifferent we may still agree to disagree. The matters concerning which we are opposed may be too trivial, as we have noted, to inspire in us the desire to take the pains to convert our opponent. This is true with regard to sensuous and recreational pleasures. To teach another person to enjoy the games, the perfumes, the food, the "smokes" that we like is a painstaking task. To be sure, it requires renuncia-tion on our part to agree to disagree even on such minor mat-ters, for the desire to share our pleasures extends throughout the whole range of our interests. This renunciation is especially great in the case of those whose company gives us keen delight. We would like to participate in our friend's relish in his coffee and cigars, and on our vacations we would like to enjoy mountain-climbing with him instead of lying idly in a ham-mock. Or at home we would give much to share his pleasure in a crossword puzzle or a detective story. Or perhaps we have tried to reach agreement with him and have failed, as so often happens when we discuss a play, a novel, or a picture. Then, as is always true when we argue about art, we agree to disagree as a second best, regretfully. Again renunciation is entailed, but of a deeper sort, because the satisfactions we have failed to share are profounder.

There are two types of situation where we cannot forego agreement without trying for it, and where in certain circum-stances agreement may be entirely out of the question. These circumstances are those where the dispute concerns values of high rank to ourselves or where power relations are involved. Since, however, most satisfactions depend upon the command of means, a sharp separation between the two cases is not always possible; yet sometimes considerations of rank are more important and, at other times, considerations of power.

The second way of dealing with opposition now becomes relevant; we may seek to educate our opponent. This method is relevant also with regard to those who are indifferent to our valuations. In my discussion, I am using the word education in a broadened sense to include all methods, other than force, which tend toward establishing in the mind of another person valuations similar to my own. So defined, education applies to adults as well as to children. Thus, the "Voice of America" is a means of education in this sense of the term.

Education may involve several activities which have important relevance for the theory of value. Most fundamentally, it requires providing another with experiences similar to one's own. Unless he has had experience of both Bach and jazz, it is meaningless to assert the superiority of the one over the other. Hence, if I wish to persuade you that Bach is better, I must expose you to Bach by arranging for you frequent and accurate performances of his music. And, of course, if you wish to persuade me of the superiority of jazz, you must induce me to listen to the finest jazz orchestra in the country. Confining our attention for the moment to aesthetic education, two other activities are also important. One of them consists in breaking down in the person to be educated the screen of prejudices that often separates him from possible enjoyment. Thus, people used to reject out of hand abstract painting because they expected representation. Now that they have become used to abstractions, this prejudice no longer exists. The habit of expectation has been broken simply by experience with a different kind of thing. It is more difficult, however, to destroy the moralistic prejudice which, for example, long prevented the British public from appreciating Goethe's *Faust*. Yet it can be overcome by suggesting that art may perform a function in life different from that of morals—the function not of regulating life but of increasing sensitiveness to all its multitudinous aspects. Another activity important in aesthetic education is calling attention, by any means available, to possibilities of enjoyment that may be overlooked. Thus it may be necessary to draw attention to the music of color and line in a picture, when only the satisfactions arising from the conceptual meanings (the representative aspects) are appreciated. Only so can the full possibilities of enjoyment be realized and a truly relevant preference emerge. Clearly, all these activities are interrelated.

In the sphere of moral education, the same principle is involved. To use a timely illustration: it is now well recognized that in order to re-educate the German people into a preference for democracy, they must be allowed to practice it. In vain will one discourse of the values of freedom, or of any other kind of value, to those who have no experience of them. Hence the futility of mere preaching and mere propaganda. To speak of love to the unloving or of courage to cowards is as futile as to talk to the deaf of the delights of music. Only by experiencing what it is like to love or to be courageous can one understand the intrinsic values of them. In writing these sentences I have the feeling of uttering the most frightfully commonplace thoughts; yet they have their point against all people who continue to speak as if values were somehow there, as a star is, to be known by looking for them, instead of recognizing that they can be known only by having them, for only by being had do they exist at all. And, once having been had, they can compete with other values, and a preference may arise.

The general process of education consists partly in enlarging the number of possible satisfactions, but also in stressing the higher as against the lower. We teach the child to swim and dive, but we put a special emphasis on acting courageously and loving the beautiful. In doing this, we assume that the higher have an advantage in competition with the lower. These advantages are of two sorts, extrinsic and intrinsic. Among the extrinsic advantages are the following, which have been widely asserted. (1) The higher are purer, in the sense of being unmixed with pain, while the lower are impure in the sense that we have to pay for them with frustration and agony of soul, either coexisting or subsequent. (2) The higher are independent: they are not contingent, as the others are, on the chances of fortune or the favor of other people, on wealth or social status. (3) They are less dependent on physical instrumentalities; hence less competitive and therefore more sharable with others. They are therefore reinforced with the satisfaction in union with other persons. (4) The values of love and of such qualities as intelligence, temperance, and courage, have special advantages. One advantage of loving is that it commonly inspires gratitude, through which we win the aid of other persons when we need it. This advantage is especially great in a complex civilization such as ours, where specialization of capacity makes the individual helpless by himself; yet since life has always been hazardous and powers limited, it has always been noted, even in simpler and ruder cultures. The advantage of courage is that it serves to protect all of our values when they are threatened; the advantage of intelligence is that it enables us to supply ourselves with better means for enjoyment, and that when it is combined with temperance, it enables us to make a more equable distribution of values between the present and the future.

No one would wish to question the soundness of this ancient wisdom, yet one does not have to be a cynic to recognize that it should be reappraised. (1) There is, in fact, a serenity belonging by right to aesthetic and intellectual pursuits, but especially in the case of the former, it appears as a contrast to and a relief from the frustrations of ordinary experience. This misery remains as a dark background of these values. Who does not feel it there while listening to great symphonic music? (2) The aesthetic and contemplative values require a measure of leisure, which most people have to buy and pay for; or, when not, as among the rich, other people have to pay for it. The Greeks, who made so much of this advantage, forgot the slave basis of their culture, which enabled even the relatively poor, in a warm climate, to enjoy the free play of mental faculty. (3) This point is an amalgam of two points. First, it means to assert that since, for example, in reading poetry I am not engaged in competition, I am not prevented from sympathizing with another's pleasure in the same activity; whereas I do find it difficult to participate with my competitor in the pleasure which he obtains in winning a prize which we have both sought. Second, it calls attention to the uniqueness of an object of competition, with the consequent impossibility of more than one possessing it; while, on the other hand, since such instruments of aesthetic enjoyments as books and musical scores may be multiplied indefinitely, the possession of one of these by one person does not deprive another person of the possession of its like. But these differences are not absolute. The very poor do not have the means to buy or even to rent books, to attend musical concerts, or to purchase instruments for the making of their own music. With my friends who belong to the upper two-thirds of the population I can share my aesthetic pleasures, but not with the underprivileged one-third. Moreover, the aesthetic pleasures are not the only ones that can be shared. As J. M. Guyau long ago remarked, we come together for tea or for dinner as well as for a concert; and my pleasure in tasting tea is probably more nearly like yours than is my pleasure in looking at a picture or hearing a sonata. All enjoyments that do not depend upon the possession or use of unique objects are sharable.

Only the extrinsic advantages of love and the virtues seem to be so firm as to be impossible to mitigate or to dispute. We must, to be sure, allow to the coward his momentary hold on physical safety, provided he can escape from social penalties; to the intemperate his intense secure pleasures of the moment, which must be reckoned as his no matter how great be the evils exacted as penalties for them in the future. To the selfish we must grant his undiminished, envied possessions, and to the unkind his satisfactions in aggressions and cruelties, even if they be followed by pains inflicted by vengeful victims and righteous judges. Let any man, if he will, reckon these satisfactions against those of love and the virtues.

Although it would be fanaticism to despise the external advantages of the higher values, no one who gives them superior rank would be willing to base their superiority on these alone. Such sayings as "Virtue is its own reward" and "It is better to love than to be loved" testify to the existence of the values resident in the activities of loving and being virtuous, taken by themselves. The case for the higher in competition with the lower cannot be fairly won unless these intrinsic values are taken into account. And the old conviction that man can be blessed only through them seems to imply that they are intrinsically better, higher in preference, as well as "higher" in the sense already explained. The very confusion between these two meanings of "higher" may express this conviction. Yet, unless our whole theory of value is mistaken, the claim for superiority in rank, for all persons, cannot be sustained. For rank is a personal affair, a decision of the individual, not a property of objective realities.

Nevertheless, a study of the higher values does reveal that, intrinsically as well as extrinsically, some of them at least have certain specific "lures." Both beauty and love in the warm sense (love mixed with sexual desire)—and perhaps there is no love without some warmth of this kind, since all love has a sexual root—are big values, values covering a large area or volume of the self, and so tend to have a greater final intensity than the thin, small values. They are whole-man rather than part-man values. Moreover, because they make use of the imagination, they expand the self by taking in the sentient beings of the environment. The only limits to this are the limits of the imagination. Both love and art have this power. As an illustration from art, we may quote Balzac: "On hearing the people of the street, I was able to wed myself to their life; I felt their rags on my back; I walked with my feet in their town shoes; their desires, their needs, everything passed into my soul, and my soul passed into theirs. . . . !" And with reference to love, let this passage from *The Mirror of Perfection* be a witness: "Blessed Francis, wholly wrapped up in the love of God, discerned perfectly the goodness of God . . . in every created thing. On account of which he had a singular and intimate love of creatures. . . . Above all birds he loved the lark. . . . Above all other creatures wanting reason he loved the sun and fire. . . . After fire, he most singularly loved water. . . ."

Moreover, it is characteristic of all the higher values, of knowledge and of courage, as well as of art and love, that they exteriorize us or, as the saying is, they take us outside of ourselves. The imaginative expansion of self entails this. And, as a result, that private misery which is part of the mind of every man—the totality of repressions in the deeper strata of the self—is extruded into the background and its intensity lowered in consequence. In addition, the higher values yield nonterminating satisfactions. Since, in our perilous world, we are never safe, courage cannot complete its task; nor, for the same reason, can intelligence; nor, for other reasons, as we know, can love or art. Hence, potentially, they are the most enduring values, giving their color to all moments of our lives and possessing that infinite variety because of which they cannot stale. Finally, through the expansion of the self, the metaphysical loneliness of each life is mitigated.

In view of the advantages of the higher values, one might perhaps wonder why they have not long ago triumphed over the lower. But there are two kinds of wonder: naïve wonder that ignores the facts which might offer some explanation, and sophisticated wonder which persists in the face of all the facts because, even when all is known, something remains unexplained. In this case, the facts ignored are the limitations of the imagination, upon which the higher values depend, by means of which the self expands into the lives of other persons or into the future of one's own life, and the competition of the higher values with the lower, whose primary intensity may ensure them a superior ranking in the case of some persons. The limitation of the imagination is the obverse of which the egocentricity of values is the reverse. How real this is can be brought home to anyone who asks himself what persons' deaths he would not rather contemplate than his own. The honest answer is, very few. Or consider how in panic, when the alarm of fire is given, the aim at mere physical safety is apt to outrank all chivalry and kindness. We give lip service to the higher, then act in favor of the lower without remorse. Only when remorse or regret follow do we know that we were acting in opposition to our own real valuations. To cultivate the higher values in others is obviously to the advantage of each one of us; to cultivate them in ourselves is advantageous also, for the reasons which we have been presenting, but in so doing we cannot ignore the lower, which are also our own. Our problem then becomes how to reconcile the higher and lower in ourselves—the problem of harmony, studied in the previous chapter.

A third method that can be used in the education of other persons in the values which we wish them to enjoy, whether in our own interest or in what we conceive to be their interest, is to reinforce them through allying them with other values. Thus, in aesthetic education, we can stimulate an interest in the intrinsic values of art through attaching that interest to an already established interest in history and biography by placing works of art in their cultural milieux, or in relation to the life of the artist. Of course, it is not easy to separate the aesthetic values from these other interests, but, given the close connection between them, we may be able to work to the aesthetic through the others. Another illustration is the attachment of success to service in most economic and political institutions where favoritism and corruption are kept at a minimum. Through service to the institution, the individual receives advancements in rank and increases in salary, with the result that whatever disinterested motivations to service may exist are encouraged,

through the support which they receive from the desire for rewards. This is not to the taste of utopian idealists, but it seems
to be the most effective way to secure maximum effort in the
public interest. Those who recommend offering loans and increased opportunities for trade to the Soviet Union as a means
of winning them to more friendly relations with us are advocating the use of this method. The administration to children
of rewards for good behavior and of punishments for bad behavior may serve as a final illustration.

Lastly, we may change the intentions of another person by
calling attention to their probable consequences. This is the
method of persuasion most in use when we argue with another
with regard to practical matters. It is obviously closely related
to the method just described, differing only in that, whereas
there we actually bring about certain consequences, here we
merely predict these consequences, trusting that the anticipation
of effects will do the same as the effects themselves. But, although such argumentation may take the form of reason, its
premises are passional, not rational. The premise of such an
argument is a preference for satisfaction A when reinforced by
satisfaction B, or a willingness to forego A when it has as consequence frustration B. Without this premise, the argument can
avail nothing.

When we argue, we usually know the other participant in the
argument well enough to be sure that this premise does exist,
but sometimes we are mistaken and waste our effort. So we may
argue with the alcoholic that if he continues to drink he will
lose his job and ruin his family, on the assumption that he
prefers his job and the prosperity of his wife and children to the
easing of feelings of guilt and insecurity that ensues on drunken-
ness, but this is often not true. The misery of guilt and insecurity may be so great that nothing matters more than assuaging
it. Alcohol is often a substitute for suicide. Or we may try to
deter a man from taking revenge by bringing to his mind that
if he kills his enemy he will be imprisoned for twenty years, and

occasionally that man, when behind bars, will some day say to us, "Revenge was so sweet it was worth even this." Moral arguments of this kind are cogent only when we know the dearest desires that constitute their major premises. In fine, we can never step out of the circle of a man's desires when we argue with him concerning matters of conduct. This is a universal predicament of the moral life, and one whose consequences we often lament, but we must remember that it is the basis of moral freedom. There is no external compulsion that can drive any-one to agree with us, not even a Kantian categorical imperative.

Should, however, all these methods fail, we are still not with-out resources. For one thing, we can again agree to disagree. With regard to art, sensuous pleasure, religion, yes, and morals, so long as our own values are not endangered, we can say, "I have failed to convince you that I am right and you have failed to convince me that you are right, so let us each go his own way." A defeat is admitted and a renunciation is involved, for we would have preferred to have the companionship of his mind, now lost; but renunciation may be better than the fruit-less renewal of what may have been a costly effort. So perhaps we may have to reconcile ourselves to the coarse manners and pragmatic philosophy of the multitude, because for the present at least we can do nothing about it, consoling ourselves with the thought that we have done our best, and that others, more skillful and fortunate than ourselves, may some day do better.

When, on the other hand, our own values are in danger through the opposition of others, we cannot simply agree to disagree. Danger may come from two interrelated sources, one, the limitation of means objects for which others are competing with us, and, two, their direct hostility to our purposes. Those who accept the Marxian interpretation of human affairs would probably explain opposition on the former ground alone. But it is difficult to see how such simple examples of hostility as that of the older toward the younger child in a rich family where toys are abundant, or the jealousies engendered by affection or, in the larger world, the enmities caused by contrasts of religious beliefs or by differences of race, class, and manners can be wholly explained in that way.

The simplest method of dealing with such oppositions, from whatever cause, a method in use throughout human history,[5] is to destroy them through killing the volitions that are their ground. Simple murder, assassination, warfare, however one may evaluate them morally, are all examples. The impulse to kill when opposition arises appears to be a part of our inherited psychic endowment and lingers on when repressed by love and fear in murderous day and night dreams from childhood into maturity. But there are good and obvious reasons why this method may not be tried. Love may forbid it; fear of failure when attempting it and of the reprisals that might follow failure; fear of the injuries that might be inflicted upon oneself by the enemy even if one did succeed; and finally the conviction that in one way or another the enemy, despite his temporary opposition to us, may be useful to us later; all may counsel against it. Thus, the appeasement of Hitler was due to doubt that he could be destroyed, fear of the consequences to ourselves resulting from war even should we win, and belief that his aid might be useful in a conflict with Russia.

Nevertheless for those who were unrestrained by any considerations of humanity, killing has appeared advantageous in relation to helpless opponents, such as backward colonial peoples. Yet even in this situation, it was never employed without danger and at a cost. For these people were not absolutely helpless, and the hate engendered in the survivors sometimes led to a cruel revenge, as witness the Black Hole of Calcutta and the reprisals taken by the American Indians. Moreover, the indigenes were often needed to develop the resources of the land they inhabited; hence a minimum of killing paid better in the end. In aggressive warfare between civilized peoples also it

[5] As an example we may cite the destruction of Melos by the Athenians, reported by Thucydides.

cannot be questioned that the conquerors, or at least those of them who survived, sometimes profited; and there was always the hope of being the survivors. But unless they exterminated their enemies, they too always incurred the risk of revenge, and paid a high price for victory in the loss of their brave compatriots, and at the expense of their own treasure. When final reckoning is made, the feud between Germany and France, for example, will be seen to have profited neither. At first the French were aggressors, then the Germans, partly out of revenge. The Germans now lie in the dust of defeat; but what, in the end, have the French gained? Security? But a new danger threatens, against which the Germans may prove to have been the sole bulwark. During World War II it was suggested by ordinarily kind persons that the only solution of the "German problem" was to exterminate the German people, or so to restrict their opportunities for earning a living that half of them would starve, as proposed by a certain one-time secretary of the treasury. But so to do would have left the whole Western world at the mercy of the aggressor that would move into the vast cemetery of men, women, and children lying in the graves dug by their Christian enemies after squads of trained asphyxiators had done their work between the Elbe and the Rhine. And what an example to set the nation that may one day defeat us!

The explanation of why, in general, men prefer peaceful to warlike methods of dealing with hostility given by Hobbes in the *Leviathan* and by Plato in the first part of Book II of the *Republic* is not flattering but remains in great measure true. The will to peace and the regime of law and justice do, as Plato said, offer a mean between the advantages of inflicting, and the disadvantages of suffering, injury. How and how far this statement of the case is true will appear in the pages following. One error common to both Plato and Hobbes was, of course, the complete neglect of the influence of love in initiating and sustaining peaceful procedures. We shall, in the right place in our reflections, try to show *how important this factor is,* all considerations to the contrary notwithstanding.

When, for whatever reasons, the will to peace exists, four well-known ways of protecting one's own values, or of securing the best possible issue out of a conflict, are available. Some of them have already been studied in the chapter on harmony; and it will not be necessary to restate these here. But it will be necessary to consider them anew from the present perspective. In that chapter, the perspective was that of the person seeking maximum satisfaction by reconciling conflicting impulses within himself, and compromise and integration were studied as means to that end; now, however, compromise and integration will be viewed as methods of meeting oppositions originating outside of one's self. But since external conflicts have their inner aspects, the inner and the outer cannot be separated, as we have already noticed. Yet the difference in emphasis on one or the other aspect is important. The methods available are compromise, a special kind of compromise, the division of spheres of control (balance of power), integration, and submission. Let us study compromise, first.

Compromise. The advantages of compromise with an opponent can be briefly summarized as follows, rephrasing and making use of the old adage, "Half a loaf with peace is better than a whole loaf with conflict and victory, or than no loaf with conflict and defeat." For those who like mathematical formulations, as a rough expression of the advantage of compromise however inadequate to the full truth, we may write: "1 plus $\frac{1}{2}$ is greater than 0" or "1 plus $\frac{1}{2}$ is greater than 1," where in the first formula 0 on the right is the case of defeat and, in the second, 1 on the right is the case of victory, while on the left 1 is the good of peace in each, and the $\frac{1}{2}$ is the partial good of the aim sought, so far as realized in the situation of compromise. The formula is inadequate for one reason because we may actually get more than one-half of what we sought, and on the other hand, we may get less; and instead of 1 we might need to write some fraction that would better represent what could be gained by victory discounted by what victory would cost to ourselves. On the side of compromise, moreover, are all the possibilities for the flowering of values which war withers or destroys, better represented by 2 than 1. The advantages of compromise must, of course, be appreciated and willed by both sides in order for it to come into effect.

Let us cite some simple illustrations. Suppose that I am a labor leader and desire a 20 cent an hour increase in wages. I have two choices of method: to strike for the whole amount, which is, in effect, a kind of war; or to negotiate, which implies compromise. I decide to settle for 10 cents an hour, thus avoiding the loss of wages that would follow from the strike and the possible forfeiture of the good will of the community—always a valuable asset. Or suppose I am a middle-aged man, married to a much-loved young bride. Before marriage I had played chess with "the boys" at the club and continue to do so now. My wife becomes lonely and jealous during my absence on those evenings. Noticing this, I agree to play once a month only and to invite some one or another of my wife's friends to come in and stay with her while I am away. Again, suppose that I am a representative of the U.S.A. and claim that the boundary between us and Canada should be the 54th parallel part of the way and the 49th for the rest of the way. Ignoring the outcry "54-40 or fight" because I deplore the possibility of conflict with a good neighbor, whose friendship will some day be invaluable to us, I agree to the present boundary. Or finally, imagine that I am a student veteran, with a wife and little child living in a small suite, consisting of a bedroom, living room, and bathroom. I wish to use the living room as a study. My wife wishes to use it as a playroom for the child. I compromise by using it for only part of the day, leaving it to the child the rest of the day.

A significant complication that may occur in cases of compromise is the settlement of the dispute by third parties, of which allegedly impartial commissions, such as the War Labor Board and the Interstate Commerce Commission, are examples. Yet for the parties to the dispute no new principle is involved when recourse is had to these third parties voluntarily, in cases of an actual or threatened deadlock. The will to peace growing out of a distaste for the consequences of a feared conflict is still the motive. One prefers to accept an award that may be disappointing; and there is always the hope that it may be better than could be obtained by one's own efforts. The third party that makes the award has, of course, its point of view, which is different from that of either contestant. Yet it, too, is motivated by the will to peace and makes its own compromise. That it is motivated by the will to peace is obvious in a labor dispute, when the public, represented by the commission, may suffer severely, especially if some vital commodity such as coal is involved. That it makes a compromise is perhaps not immediately clear, yet can be made evident by the examination of one or two examples. In a labor dispute, the compromise consists in the fact that it would be better for the public that labor receive no increase at all, since the public pays for it in increased prices, yet an increase is granted; or, if the sympathy of the public is aroused for one side, it cannot give to that side all that it would wish and maintain peace. Even when a commission of neutral states is called upon to settle a boundary dispute (or when only the odd member of such a commission is neutral, whose point of view is the one we are considering)—for example, the Silesian question between Poland and Germany after World War I—there will be compromise. For the entire commission, or the deciding neutral member, if genuinely neutral, will side with both contestants, in the sense of "seeing both sides," and then, for the sake of peace, will make a decision that will be the best adjustment possible, yet will hurt the national pride of each a little.

This kind of case, as also that of the chess-playing husband and the family dispute over the playroom, illustrates how an "external" dispute may become "internal"; for insofar as the neutral commissioner sympathizes with both sides, there will arise a conflict within himself of the type studied in our last chapter. In the situation of the chess-playing husband the conflict becomes internal because of his love of his wife, being in effect a conflict between that and his devotion to chess; in the case of the playroom, the conflict is between the man's professional aims and his love of both wife and child.

An interesting question regarding compromise is, what determines the point between the rival claims at which the compromise is fixed? In very general terms, the answer is that it depends on the relative strength of the parties, as measured by their ability to sustain or perhaps win in the event of a trial of forces; and also, on the closely related desire for peace of the respective contestants. If the desire for peace is strong, or if for any reason a contestant is weak, he will obviously settle for less. When the dispute is referred to a neutral board, other considerations, touching the public interest, will be influential; for example, in the case of an industrial dispute, the ability of the company to pay higher wages without raising the price of the commodity to a point where it hurts the public too much, the cost of living as it affects the ability of the men to lead a decent life, and the like. What is called a "just" decision is one which, while it protects the public interest, gives some recognition to the claims and needs of the rival parties, with which the members of the board sympathize. No rational formula can ever express this.

The defect of compromise when the conflict is between persons or groups is much the same as when it is within an individual—it is likely to be temporary. The party with whom I make the compromise may use the interval of peace to build up its forces and then renew its claim with a better chance of complete success. In other words, there may be no real renunciation of the entire claim, no genuine acceptance of the compromise agreed upon. It is accepted only with a tongue in the cheek.

Suspecting this, I may have to devote the energies that I had hoped to use for peaceful purposes to prepare to meet force with force. This situation often prevails in industrial disputes and in international affairs. The Peace of Versailles was a compromise with Germany, yet was never accepted as such by the signers of the Treaty or by the upper classes. In particular, the status of Danzig and the Corridor, which clearly represented a compromise between the demands of Germany and Poland, was not accepted by the Germans (or the Poles?). In order to make a compromise "stick," force is often necessary—the so-called force of public opinion, which is really the power of third parties to the dispute who have a continuing will to peace—or else integration, following a compromise, by means of which new bonds between me and my opponent are forged, leading us both to forget the old dispute. Even when no special integration occurs, the current of life flows on, and new problems may cause us to forget the old ones, and perhaps forgive.

An important and special type of compromise is self-limitation of spheres of power. Of this the marking out among the great powers of spheres of influence in colonial or other undeveloped areas is a familiar illustration. The "two-world" theory of Walter Lippmann and others as a solution of our problem with Russia is a timely example. The motive for this, as of other types of compromise, is the will to peace. Again the maxim applies: half a loaf is better than none, or better even than a whole loaf bought at the cost of war. The self-limitation of spheres of power is exemplified within a society no less than between rival societies. Individualistic social theory has always accepted a doctrine of many worlds within a community. The recognition of property rights, combined with the accepted desirability of peace and of the rule of law as valid in disputes between citizens, is an instance of the self-limitation of powers within a community. And however this may be mingled with communistic or socialistic doctrines, it is likely to survive, in some form and over some areas of experience, as being best suited to the basic egocentricity of values. In present-day Russia the peasant retains as his own a small plot of land, the produce of which he can use either to sustain his family or for sale on the free market, and he can own his personal belongings and government bonds. Divisions of markets and price agreements between corporations in capitalistic societies are other examples.

Yet however natural and desirable such compromises between the rival power trends of individuals or of groups may be, they have the defects of all compromises, and unless supplemented with some form of integration, or some threat or application of force, are likely to be in the end temporary and unsatisfactory. Very aggressive persons or societies do not accept the conventions regarding the limitations of power as anything more than short-term expedients, to be abandoned when opportunities for the expansion of power present themselves. Fixed boundaries are incompatible with the native propulsiveness of life. Long eras of peace in international affairs such as the Pax Romana or the Pax Britannica have been due to the possession of overwhelming force by certain nations interested in keeping the peace and, within a society, either to such force in the hands of governing groups or to integrative tendencies.

Pure compromise unaffected by any process of integration is probably a rare thing in human affairs. For, as a rule, each side to a dispute not only needs its opponent but feels that need as a fact. It is recognized that one's opponent and oneself are members of a whole. So management in industry realizes the need of workmen, and workmen realize the need for skilled direction. A new interest thus grows up in the fostering of the whole which both may serve, and the hostility bred by the opposition of interests within the whole is softened. The need for compromise remains, for the opposition of interests is not completely eliminated, but it is rendered more lasting through the desire to maintain intact the solidarity between oneself and one's opponent. In industry a feeling of loyalty to the institution or organization is more likely to grow up among the older men, who have become attached through habituation to their jobs, than among those who have been taken on recently, in whom such a sentiment has not had time to develop. Any arrangements such as profit-sharing or old age pensions which tend to make for the identification of the interest of the workman with that of management increase the will to peace and co-operation.

In international relations the chief integrating force has been commerce. But little is accomplished unless the nations that trade with each other depend for their existence, or at least for the maintenance of what is regarded as a decent standard of living, upon the exchange of goods. If any nation is or can become self-sufficient, integration by commerce is weakened. Autarchy is the foe of co-operation. Cultural relations, common language, religion, or tradition are a help, as among the British dominions, and formerly among the various German states, but have proved disappointing in their efficacy unless supported by vital common interests. So far there has not appeared a loyalty to "humanity" or feeling for one world, or even a sense of being a "good European," strong enough to restrain the aggressiveness of men in power. On the other hand, these influences may be stronger than we know. It may well be true that without them wars would be much more frequent than they are. And history furnishes us with notable examples of integration between peoples who at one time were constantly at war with each other, as the Scots and the English, the French and the Burgundians, the Boers and the British.

It is within the political community and the family, however, that integration plays its greatest role, for there the dependence of each upon all—solidarity—is the greatest. The citizen's pride in his town or country and his loyalty to its interests add strength to the compromises and covenants defining the status and spheres of power of each, and aggressiveness is restrained in consequence. Such is the ideal of civil government. Naturally, pride and loyalty operate most effectively in times of danger and crisis, when the greatest of sacrifices, even life itself, will be offered to the community. In times of peace pride inspires good works and honest efforts to foster the welfare of all members of the group. The family is a tiny community, and there the motivations among the children and the parents causing integration are the same as in the larger world. But now integration passes into love.

The case of our chess-playing husband may be used to illustrate integration within the family. Suppose that, instead of making a compromise with her by playing the royal game with "the boys" only once a month, he teaches her to play with him. Then the interests of both are assuaged; the man has his game and the woman her husband's company, while a new interest, playing the game with each other, arises as a compensation for the sacrifice of the man, who might still miss his friends and the pitting of his own skill against theirs. This, of course, is but a simple illustration of the development of the so-called "we" form of living, characteristic of marriage and its great integrator, giving support to the compromises that must occur if the union is to be happy and providing satisfactions of a new sort, partly in the elimination of loneliness, partly in loving sexual relations.

The mere playing of a game, even when the players are not intimates, is an excellent example of integration. I wish, of course, to win, for the game would not be a "good" game—that is, it would not yield the satisfactions I expect from a game—if I did not. But I cannot have the fun of playing, let alone that of winning, without my opponent, and without giving him an opportunity to display his skill as a test of mine. Although we are rivals, there is yet complete solidarity between us. And, realizing this, I cannot fail to have an interest in "fair play," which at once limits my aggressiveness in the game and offers a new satisfaction—the satisfaction in being a "good sport," which will compensate for defeat, should I lose.

But the greatest integrator is love. For if, through the imagination, the desires of other persons become as if my own, and I seek to assuage them as if they were mine, this externality is destroyed; they become as it were parts of myself. I am not now pursuing my ends against theirs, but my own with theirs. Loving sexual relations afford a perfect example. For when love permeates sexual desire, I seek not only my own satisfaction in the sexual act, but that of my partner as well; hence I cannot be fully satisfied myself apart from my partner's pleasures. Moreover, the union of the two bodies parallels a union of minds, so that the loneliness of each is lost for a moment at least in an ecstasy of enjoyment, that is at once mental and physical.

How love may serve as an integrator was brought home to me as I traveled through Bolzano in 1936. I found that the German-speaking population was uniformly hostile to the Italians who had "annexed" the territory that had been theirs for a thousand years. But there was one notable exception, that of a man who had married a pretty young Italian girl. I asked him how he felt about the annexation, and he said that, of course, being German he opposed it, but that his marriage had made a difference in his attitude. The "fraternization" between the German women and the American soldiers in our "zone" is having a similar effect—to the great distress of those among us who would keep alive the flames of hatred and resentment.

In cooler forms, love may permeate all our relationships, acting there also as integrator. Among citizens, the integration springing from a realization of solidarity and growing into loyalty to a community may be strengthened through friendship, which, like love in its warmest sense, implies an imaginative absorption of the desires of others and the will to assuage them. Even in business, the executive sometimes feels genuine friendship for his "men," desiring their welfare not only because it increases the income of the firm through their greater efficiency, but for their own sakes as well. When love does exist, it compensates for the sacrifice entailed by every compromise. A more far-reaching love is that of the statesman who, feeling the needs of different and usually rival groups, seeks, by reconciling them to each other, to promote the happiness of them all. The widest reach of love is that of the saint, in our day represented by Gandhi, whose love embraced all mankind.

Yet by itself love does not solve any problem—a truth forgotten too often by loving souls. Long-established needs and rivalries still subsist even when love is present to make them all its own. Methods of assuagement and reconciliation must still be found. However, love does provide favorable conditions, as it were an atmosphere, for their solution. In the first place, it gives a new impetus to effort, for, as we have noted, by solving the problems of others, perhaps even of one's opponents, there is an opportunity to win a satisfaction which may provide a partial compensation for failure to overcome one's own difficulties. Second, by vivifying the imagination, love enables one to see the point of view of another—even that of one's enemy—with the result that more effective and lasting compromises and integrations can be arranged. This claim to superior insight must, however, be somewhat discounted by the well-known blindness of love, its tendency to idealize the thing it loves. Sometimes hate sees more clearly than love. And, in general, what love can do is not unlimited, for reasons already given. The range of the imagination is bounded, and love has to compete with egotism. Love leaves us with a problem within ourselves, even when we have found a way to solve the problems of others.

One solution always at hand is renunciation on our part and submission to the will of the one we love. Love supplies the motivation to submission, and its satisfaction supplies its reward. But when submission entails the renunciation of all the rest of oneself, either what remains is not very strong, or the love that inspires the renunciation so expands the self that the remainder is in the end greater than before love entered into one's life. In the former case, the outsider is likely to call love slavery; in the latter, it is called heroism. Apart from these extremes, the solution of the internal problem posed by love is to be found through the methods for attaining internal harmony already discussed.

Submission is a method that may be employed apart from love in meeting the opposition of another person. Instead of opposing his aims, one may give way to them. But to do so for no reason whatever is impossible, since to be is to desire, and utter renunciation would be equivalent to not being at all. Submission can, therefore, be no more than partial and for the sake of certain desires that do not submit. The hero renounces his life that his self-transcendent aims may be realized, and even the lover in his abasement reserves his love. If one submits, as every prudent man does, it must be with regard to aims that matter so little that it is not worth the cost to fight for them; or, if they are important, because one saves something precious which one fears one would lose in defeat if one fought (the justification of Pétain); or because one hopes to renew the conflict under more advantageous circumstances. When the slave submits, he saves at least his life, with certain pleasures that mere living may offer. The suicide does not submit; he fights hard and loses all. Even to death or to the will of God one does not submit without reason; for, knowing that the battle would be lost if one waged it, one submits in order to save oneself from the agony of inevitable defeat.

The gain to each side in integration is threefold: (1) there is the satisfaction arising from the fulfillment of the integrating interest; (2) the loss through the underlying compromises is lessened, because the willing co-operation of each tends to a furtherance of the aims of each; and (3) since peace is longer and more assured because the opposition of the two parties is moderated, the opportunities for the realization of all the aims of each are increased. If a mathematical formula is desired, one may write "(1 plus $\frac{2}{3}$ plus 1) equals 2 and $\frac{2}{3}$." Compare this with the formula suggested for compromise, "(1 plus $\frac{1}{2}$ plus $\frac{1}{2}$) equals 2." Yet it must not be forgotten that, as in compromise, there is an inevitable sacrifice somewhere. Even if, at long last, a

United States of Europe should emerge, each nation would have to give up something of its national sovereignty. Likewise in marriage, the old freedom of bachelor days is lost in the development of the we form of existence. But "when half-gods go, the gods arrive."

A sham form of integration must be distinguished from the genuine thing. It may have outward marks of the real one, and hence be confused with it—apparent service of a common end through a synthesis of activities, seeming stability and peace—but lacks one essential characteristic of real integration, freedom. Napoleon's and Hitler's empires, and the union of North and South immediately following our Civil War, were sham integrations. Because the synthesis is forced, co-operation is grudging, and service of the common end largely a pretense. For this reason the stability of the synthesis is likely to be deceptive. The old antagonisms await their opportunity to come into the open, and disintegration follows. Yet it does often happen that some of these forced integrations last for a long time, as witness the Austrian empire; and if they last long enough a true union may follow, such as occurred between the North and the South, the Scots and the English, and, most impressive of all, within the Roman Empire. When this does occur, there must be strong advantages in union that show in time; for example, commercial benefits arising from a customs union, especially when the integrated units are complementary to one another, as in the Austrian Empire. Out of a realization of these benefits, a genuine loyalty to the whole and a willing co-operation among its constituents may develop. Even within the small unit of the family it cannot be denied that in former times the force of the law and of public opinion which held a married pair together favored the growth of married love, which needs time to ripen, and when full grown may weather many a domestic storm and much incompatibility. It is doubtful whether certain integrations would have taken place at all without some initial application of force. The British Commonwealth of

Nations, now a free integration of states, was in the beginning, let us remember, an empire. And without the threat from Russia, would the quarrelsome states of Western Europe ever unite?

Aside from sham integrations, we have often confronted the problem of the role of force in human affairs. We have seen how, apart from the influence of love, it is a factor in fixing the point at which a compromise is determined. We have also considered the advantages of such methods as compromise and integration over the use of force. We have seen how sham integrations, resting on force, may nevertheless sometimes grow into genuine integrations. There still remains for our consideration the question of when force is more advantageous than any other method of overcoming opposition.

It would seem to justify itself, clearly, when persuasion, compromise, and integration fail, and the interests to be protected are so important that they are worth the cost of the use of force. Few would dispute its advantages when it is the sole method available for the protection of life and liberty against criminals and tyrants within the community, and against "aggressive" nations in international affairs. In the latter sphere, however, most everyone would admit that, in view of the contemporary cost of war, every effort should be made to reach a settlement compatible with the preservation of one's dearest possession— one's chosen way of life. The only alternative would then appear to be a submission equivalent to enslavement. Those alone—the preachers of nonviolence—who believe that love can conquer all will dissent. Perhaps, as they claim, this faith has never been put to the test on a wide scale, but a few years ago, there occurred an event that seems to refute them—the murder of Gandhi. To kill, even in the defense of life and liberty, is contrary to the impulse of love, especially in war where the people killed are rather helpless and sometimes innocent victims of a national policy which they have little or no part in shaping. But what else can be done?

Finally, few would dispute that force has a certain minor, preliminary role to play in the education of the young, while they are too immature to reason with; that is to say, when they are incapable of knowing the unfortunate consequences to themselves of certain of their acts or the advantages of obeying their parents. Force may then take the shape either of restraint or of punishment. Probably in either case there is a certain psychic cost in resentment built up in the child, but when exercised by loving parents, this becomes minimal, and in the course of time may disappear. Sometimes, however, it must be admitted that punishment does more good to the parents, by protecting them from continual, if small, annoyances, than to the children. It also provides the parents a relatively harmless means of "working off" an irritation not entirely incompatible with great love.

It will be objected to the views set forth in this chapter that they are of the philosophic brand called relativism. That is true, if by relativism be meant that the good and the better have no "absolute" meaning, but have meaning only with relation to an individual's life plan or matrix self. Even the higher values are not necessarily higher in rank for everyone. Whether they are or not depends upon how they fare in competition with intense lower desires. To say that the higher would be better for a certain person if he could once appreciate them to the full assumes that he could do so; but it may be true that he cannot and, if he cannot, the sentence would be as meaningful as to say, "If a stone were a bird, it could fly." For a man *is* his hierarchical pattern of desires. I know that it will always seem strange to those who prefer kindness to cruelty that other people do not. This strangeness makes us feel that somehow kindness *is* better. But so far no one has been able to give an intelligible account of what "is" means in this sentence. And there are other situations where the same strangeness appears. Does not the lover feel it strange if other people do not find his sweetheart desirable? And if he knows that she is still desirable for him, though others do not find her so for them, why should he be less confident in his own feeling about aesthetic beauty and charity even though others dissent?

Moreover, this feeling does have a certain justification, and it would be odd if it did not, for a feeling of this kind is an inarticulate judgment, and no judgments are wholly wrong. The justification consists in the advantages which we have shown to belong to the higher values in their competition with the lower. These advantages are not, however, absolute but relative—the very term "advantage" is relative; they are relative to competing desires, and it is not predetermined that they shall win. But the reality of these advantages for all who are capable of them provides, nevertheless, a secure ground for cultivating them in ourselves and in other persons. One wonders what more could be claimed for them as against the lower.

Finally, although the view here propounded is a relativism in the sense indicated, we have shown that a war of each against all is not its logical consequence. What follows is pretty much what we find in human affairs. For when A and B disagree over X, A liking and preferring X, and B disliking or failing to prefer X, we have shown that the following possibilities are offered: (1) either may try to build up in the other a liking for or preference for X; (2) either may bring to the mind of the other favorable consequences resulting from liking or preferring X, and unfavorable consequences from not doing so; (3) A and B, both wishing peace, may find some way of effecting a compromise between, or integration of, their opposing wishes; (4) they may reconcile their differences through love.

If some think that the theory of this chapter is a qualified rather than an unqualified relativism, well, these, in summary, are the qualifications. However that be, the philosophy of this book is an ethics of freedom. There is no value prison confining man, no categorical imperatives. There is, rather, an open perspective of choices and decisions. In the end, each man makes for himself what is for him categorical. "The service of the Lord is perfect freedom."

CHAPTER IX

MORAL VALUES

OF ALL types of values men have been most preoccupied with the moral. Is this to be explained by the greater importance of moral values, by a certain mysteriousness which they possess, or perhaps by a kind of rebellious ambivalence in man's own attitude toward them? Our answer would be that all three reasons have operated. For, because of the sanctions attached, duty has often been a matter of life or death to the individual; because of the intimate connection of morality with religion, duty has shared in the strangeness of the holy; and because morality has demanded the sacrifice of some of man's dearest wishes, he has hated it all the time that he has revered it. Morality is as important as our daily bread, as mysterious as God, as paradoxical as love.

The paradoxical character of morality has engaged the attention of philosophers since the time of Plato. It has many facets, but all stem from a single fact: in the case of morality, man is pursuing a goal that cannot be identified with his own satisfaction. In fulfilling my duty to my wife by ensuring her support after my death, I am not seeking my own welfare, I am seeking hers. In doing my duty to my children by providing them an education, my aim is not to give myself the joy of knowledge and skill, but to give it to *them*. The truth of these assertions becomes dramatically clear if it is my duty to offer my life for my country in time of war, in which case I make further satisfactions of my own impossible. And although we are not always called on to renounce all satisfactions, since we are expected to forego many of them, it would seem that the objective of duty is not only not the same as our own satisfaction but oftentimes opposed to it.

Many ways may be tried in order to nullify this self-transcendence of ethical objectives. (1) It may be asserted that the primary objectives of all desires are "disinterested," as Bishop Butler claimed, and therefore that the uniqueness of moral values is removed. By "disinterestedness" is meant that the objective of desire does not refer directly to one's own satisfaction but to an activity, which may be one's own or another's. When, wanting bread, I formulate my desire as "I want to eat bread," I do not refer to my satisfaction in the activity of eating, I refer only to the activity; or when I issue a command, "Open the window," which says, as we have seen, "I want that you will open the window," the objective of desire is not even my own activity but that of another. However, while these are significant facts, they do not nullify the peculiarity of moral values. For, in the case of the illustrations used (and they are typical), we can as readily restate the objective in such a way as to make *my* satisfaction the goal. I do not mean that we are always aware of its being the goal, but that it can always become the goal without any alteration of my desire. Thus, instead of "I want to eat bread," I can say "I want the pleasure of eating bread"; and instead of " I want that you will open the door," I can say "I want the satisfaction of your opening the window" or "I want you to open the window in order that I may get the satisfaction of breathing fresh air." But when duty is involved such a restatement of the objective is impossible. When, answering the call of charity, I wish that *you* will eat bread, I cannot define my objective as "I wish for myself the pleasure of your having the pleasure of eating bread"; for I should want you to have that pleasure even though I were struck dead before you got it.

In similar fashion (2), it could be argued that my aim in doing my duty is to satisfy my conscience, to achieve my own inner peace. Now there is no doubt that, in fulfilling my duty, I do, as a fact, achieve this aim, which may become an additional goal for me as at once a dutiful and a reflective person. But still that is not all that I am seeking when I do my duty. If I try to assist a friend by persuading him to renounce some troublesome passion, I am not primarily aiming at my own peace of mind but at his, even though in so doing I win the same for myself and make that a part of my purpose. Finally, (3) I might suppose that what I want is the knowledge that the persons who are the recipients of the benefits of my good deeds shall be happy. Now again, there can be no doubt that I may wish for such knowledge when, for example, I save money in order to provide for my wife's support or my children's education after my death. But the question obstinately presents itself, is that my primary and total objective? And again the answer is in the negative. It is true that if I know that something is so, it is so, but it is not true that if something is true then I know that it is true; the two statements are not equivalent. What I desire is primarily that it shall be so; incidentally, of course, I could wish that I may know that it is so or at least that it probably is so. That wish may take the shape of pleasant anticipatory imaginations, but, once more, although these are values that accompany the desire for the happiness of others, they are not the original objective of the desire. All such values of my own are incidental, but they are not what I am desiring in doing my duty. Thus, the peculiar self-transcendence of the objective of morality remains intact.

Certain conclusions might easily be drawn from this apparently unique status of moral values. It might be inferred that since the values sought in morality are the satisfactions of other persons, which are never empirically verified in the direct way in which one's own values are verified by experiencing them, moral values cannot, strictly speaking, be a species of values in general; and that the impulse to morality, since it cannot find assuagement in satisfactions had by the moral individual himself, cannot be identified with any empirical desire, but must be peculiar—an affair of faith, arbitrary decision, or the like. Such conclusions are not mere possibilities, since they have been drawn by some contemporary thinkers. One recent volume affirms the separation of ethics from value theory; a recent article is entitled "The Arbitrary as the Basis of Ethics"; and a whole school of British thinkers, using somewhat novel arguments or at least arguments expressed in novel language, follows the Kantian tradition in founding morality on a nonempirical, "a priori" principle. Although, as I have indicated, there are apparent grounds for such conclusions present in the facts, the conclusions themselves can be shown to be unwarranted.

Let us consider first the alleged nonempirical, unverifiable character of ethical values. Before, however, discussing the crucial point at issue, we should remind ourselves that what I have referred to as the values incidental to morality remain as empirical as any. To cite examples from the moral field not already harvested: the man who acts courageously in battle to defend a point under attack or goes out into "no man's land" in order to rescue wounded men in danger of death or capture possesses in his own experience the values of power and achievement, all the greater because of the dangers and obstacles involved. Values of mastery are also possessed by the man who exercises the virtue of temperance—self-mastery. Similarly, there are incidental, immediately experienced values in maternal care or in kindness to friends, satisfactions accruing to oneself from the assuagement of a loving impulse. There is undoubtedly an ecstasy accompanying the immolation of oneself in the supreme sacrifice, as there may be in suicide, in ridding oneself of the burden of life and adventurously returning to "broad-bosomed Earth," the parent of us all. Moralists have too often been sour-minded creatures to whom the joys of the virtues have been unknown or unacknowledged, because I suspect they wished to parade their own disinterestedness. Then, besides, there are the rewards that are heaped upon the good man, the very tangible medals, the honors and the praise, in addition to the grateful aid rendered by those whom he has befriended. Now it hardly needs to be said that I am not identifying moral values with these values; but it would be as one-sided to forget them as to base morality on them, as egoistic moral theories do.

But let us return to the study of the matter in hand: the primary values constituting the objective of morality. These we have insisted, against all arguments to the contrary, are largely transcendent in the sense that they are not values of myself, but of other selves. And from this fact certain conclusions as to the nature of morality were drawn: that its values are unverifiable, not empirical, and that morality itself is a matter of faith, arbitrary decision, or a priori intuition.

Let us, however, not accept either the premises or the conclusions embodied in this argument too uncritically. When we look carefully we can see that there are certain reasons for mitigating the force of both. There is some evidence for believing that the values of other persons are not utterly unverifiable, and there is the strongest kind of reason for believing that they are confirmable. Who that sees the smiling face of a child upon whom one has bestowed some little kindness, does not believe that he confronts the happiness there expressed, even as he confronts and can verify directly his own happiness in being kind? The skeptical arguments against what seems so evident are, of course, familiar, and it will repay us to examine them.

There is first the argument that my mind is in my brain and the child's in his; hence no matter how near we are to each other, there is an intervening gap separating the one from the other. And although currents of communication span the gap in space (rays of light and nervous impulses from retina to brain, with reverberations to many parts of the organism) a gap in time remains: the happiness of the child occurs before my own. Yet neither of these arguments is decisive. We cannot infer from the physical principle that two bodies cannot occupy the same place at the same time that two minds cannot; and the time gap is so short that even if the happiness of the child did begin before my perception of it, the two events, if both had some duration, as they clearly have, might still overlap and occur in unison. But the skeptic may present another argument; namely, that we are sometimes mistaken in our beliefs concerning other people's feelings, including their happiness or unhappiness. The actor on the stage can feign the indecision of Hamlet so cleverly that we spectators on the front row may have the illusion that we are copresent with that state of mind; and how often in real life we are deceived by those who can control the facial and verbal media of expression of feeling for dishonest purposes! Such considerations do, I admit, carry much weight, but not enough, I believe, to be decisive for a skeptical conclusion. The argument from the experience of the theatergoer is not decisive because it overlooks the fact that we never really believe that the indecision we feel is Hamlet's or belongs to the actor playing Hamlet's role. At most, we feign that it is his: it is *as if* it were his. The cases where we falsely believe that we are intuiting the feelings in another mind have more weight, for it may be argued that if our two minds overlap with reference to them, we should be as incapable of error concerning them as we would be if they were just our own. As Plato noted, there is no possibility of error with respect to the given, and our own feelings are always given; they are in contact with any judgments we may make about them. Yet there is an answer to this objection which, if subtle, is very simple and cogent. If the feelings of another are in my mind as well as in his I cannot be in error regarding *them*, but I can be in error as to their location; I know that they are in me, but I may be mistaken as to whether

they are in you also. Since this possibility of error as to location
does exist, certainty as to union with another's mind cannot be
obtained in all cases; yet the possibility of error does not destroy
the possibility of truth. Moreover, all the reasons usually cited
for belief in the existence of the other selves, including the
argument from analogy, have application here. Even if our
belief in the happiness of another when caused by our own kind
deeds cannot be verified in the strict sense of confrontation with
its object, it can be confirmed.

The values wrought by dutiful actions following upon our
good intentions are, therefore, not matters of mere irrational
faith. The desire to be good and to do good is justified by know-
able fruits, even as any other desire is justified. Nor is the decision to be moral wholly arbitrary. For there is an answer to
the question, "Why be moral?"—namely, that the desire to do
good can be fulfilled. If morality is arbitrary, so is all desire,
and so are all values; for the only reason why any desire should
be cultivated is that it can attain its end. There is, to be sure,
as we have shown, something arbitrary about any decision, and
in this arbitrariness morality shares; yet what must be brought
to clearness is that it is not wholly arbitrary, and not uniquely
arbitrary.

Yet the self-transcendent character of morality, if mitigated,
remains. The coalescence of minds is a relatively rare occurrence; and the fruits of moral action, especially when, as so
often, we have to do with the happiness of persons unknown
to us, or even unborn, are beyond our own experience. Fre-
quently they are beyond our knowledge. There are obvious examples of this in the field of international relations. Did the
Frenchmen who voted for an armistice with Hitler do good or
harm to their compatriots? For the affirmative, one may argue
that they bought time, preserved the fair old towns of France
from destruction, preserved North Africa as a base for Allied action, and that resistance was hopeless. On the other side people
argue that if the decision had been made to fight on, an example

of courage would have been given to all the world, and resistance would have weakened the Nazi war effort. Clearly, no one could have *known* the good or evil here. Even when the objects of moral effort are persons in our own town, or in our intimate circle, we are aware how difficult it is to be sure that our actions are not doing more harm than good, so hard it is to verify their effects.

The close kinship between duty and love has always been recognized by Christian philosophers, but not so consistently by secular thinkers. In this matter, the former are wiser than the latter, for in a genuine sense, duty is a kind of love; I have myself called it "group love," love of individuals as members of a group. The peculiar motive to duty, when abstraction is made from external rewards or punishments attached to it, is the same as love—the self-transcendent interest in promoting the interest of others with whom one identifies one's self. Both illustrate the profound sociality of the mind. This fact has great philosophical importance, since, by uncovering a "natural" motive to duty, we cut the ground from under "a prioristic" or supernaturalistic theories of duty. Yet the difference between duty and love in its usual connotation should not be overlooked. The love involved in duty is more impersonal and incorporeal. While remaining a form of Eros, it is not so obviously connected with the organs of physical passion as in the case of sexual love, and it is not confined to persons few and selected as in friendship, where also the glow of sex is dampened. The love that inspires dutiful action may be directed to any member of one's group, and the group may be as large as humanity. Its objects may be individuals personally unknown to us, as when we give money to the destitute in foreign lands, who have an existence for us that is purely one of thought or imagination. And finally, love in the usual meaning is more spontaneous in the sense that it is not a response to demands that we shall feel it. The beloved does not ask for our love, neither does the sick child; they inspire it.

With the self-transcendence of duty and its kinship with love in the mind, let us try to analyze and define it. In making this attempt we shall proceed athwart the view of certain contemporary writers that duty is indefinable. What in general it means for a concept to be indefinable, we have already discussed with particular reference to "the good." We have also discussed in a tentative way the alleged indefinability of duty (see Chapter I). It was there noticed that the theory of the absoluteness of duty should be traced to Kant's distinction between categorical and conditional imperatives: the one affirming that one should do or not do something unconditionally, as in the admonition, "Love thy neighbor as thyself" or in the commandment, "Thou shalt not kill"; the other affirming that one ought or ought not to do something *on the condition that* a certain end or purpose is adopted, as when one says to the invalid, "If you want to get well, you ought to take this medicine." In childhood and in the army we are taught the absoluteness of imperatives: "Don't ask why, just do it," our parents say, and "A command is a command," we are told by our superior officers. Duty and self-interest not only appear to be different, but even opposed. How often we say, "I want to do so and so, but it is my duty to do otherwise." How desperately the lonely sentinel on the night watch wants to go to sleep, but duty forbids it. Perhaps if our duty were always unequivocal, we should never be led to analyze it, but the well-known fact of the conflict of duties forces us into it. And, as we shall see, this conflict is not resolvable into mere ignorance of what our single duty is; we are on the contrary actually presented with opposing duties. Robert E. Lee, locked in his room in the Shoreham Hotel in Washington, trying in anguish to decide whether to accept the call of the Union or the South, knew this to be so. And as for the unanalyzability of duty, the only way to discover whether or not it is unanalyzable is to attempt an analysis. In this way also we shall discover whether the categorical can be reduced to the hypothetical imperative.

We shall begin with a description of what I shall call "the duty situation." On what we may describe as the first level of analysis, this consists of demands and responses to demands. The demands are initially made by certain persons in a more or less like-minded group upon some member of the group. They are usually demands of many members of the group. They therefore take the form, "We want you to do so and so." These demands, as a first approximation, are equivalent to "You ought." There is then a response, positive or negative: if positive, "We want you to" is transformed into "I want to," which is the equivalent of "I ought," and may be called the transformation of "You ought." And remembering that all desires (demands are desires) are dynamic, we can understand the transformation (the response) as due to three factors. (1) Owing to the social nature of the mind, "We want you to" tends almost automatically to become "I want to." The mere apprehension of the desire of another person involves its activity as a force in my mind pointed to its goal. His desire echoes in my mind or, to use another metaphor, attunes my mind to its vibration. (2) I imagine the dire consequences that may result from not doing what is demanded of me, or the favorable consequences that will result from my doing so. Their range is wide, extending all the way, on the side of penalties, from years of imprisonment for the young man who fails to register for the draft to mild disapproval for the person who fails to live up to some small point of etiquette; and, on the side of rewards, from honors and medals to a smile. (3) I may be impelled to make the transformation from "You ought" to "I ought" through imaginative identification with the persons who make the demands upon me, feeling the benefits or the harm to them from my action or neglect of action, as if they were my own. The first and the last, although closely related, are not identical. If (2) alone is effective, the act is not moral, but it is moral when (2) plays a part with the others.

It may be objected to this analysis that the moral demand

comes to us as impersonal, as for example, "Stealing is wrong," rather than as, "We demand of you that you shall not steal." But as a matter of fact in childhood, demands were definitely made by certain persons, our parents and teachers, and even in maturity we all feel imaginatively the pressure upon us of people in our social environment to do or not to do certain things. We imagine what "people would say" or "what people would do," if we did or did not perform our duties. This same example will serve to illustrate the impelling motives which constitute a sense of duty. For the mere demand upon us not to steal, being a force against stealing, is transformed into a desire on our part not to steal; the well-known consequences to ourselves of stealing—the years in prison following detection and conviction—so far as we can imagine them, and the imagined inconvenience to the person from whom we steal, as we put ourselves in his place, act as deterrents. The impersonal sentence "Stealing is wrong" hides the intensity of personal factors in the situation—the demands of those from whom we might steal and the demand of one's self upon one's self as one feels their desire as if it were one's own; the "you ought not to" transformed into the "I ought not to."

Although the demands are made by definite members of a group upon members of that same group, they are not made solely in the interest of those who make the demands. When I say to the child, "You should not steal," I am not interested solely in his not stealing from me, but also in his not stealing from other persons with whom I can imaginatively identify myself. The objective of morality may best be described as the preservation and fostering of a desired way of life for all the members of the group with whom identification is possible. Hence the demand as well as the response, the *you ought* as well as the *I ought,* implies identification. When this way of life depends on security of life and property, the injunction against murder and stealing will be valid. The relation of morality to the kind of life desired by members of a group is illustrated by the absence of any injunction against adultery among the Eskimos, where the quaint, and to strangers sometimes embarrassing, custom of lending wives to guests prevails.

Although, as in the family, the demands commonly originate from people in authority in a group, this is not necessarily true. We find, for example, that among groups of young people codes of behavior grow up in almost complete independence of parents, and unknown to them. And among adults themselves, although the authority of parents and priests and elders continues to operate, there may develop an indifference to or even rebellion against it, a more democratic method of establishing the code by compromise and integration prevailing instead. This is one avenue by means of which departures from the traditional morality occur. Most impressive are the changes wrought by great moral reformers, such as the Hebrew prophets. Many of such changes happen, as has often been noticed, by generalizing an attitude. Thus, if it is wrong to steal from one of my own tribe, or to kill him, it may become wrong to steal from a man of another tribe, or to kill that man. The extension of imaginative sympathy involved seems like an easy step to take, yet there is no way to explain it fully; when it happens, a leap occurs in the moral realm comparable to the emergence of novelties in the realm of art, or to the discontinuities in atomic radiation or the saltations in the origin of biological species. We are impelled to appeal to a principle of spontaneity or creativity, even though we must recognize that the original act, be it of morality, of love, of art, or of invention, does not happen without due preparation in a favorable environment, but like a plant can blossom only in a certain soil and under a certain sky.

Unless the transformation of "We want you to or not to" into "I want to or not to" is possible—unless demand can be transformed into response—the concept of duty is meaningless and inapplicable. One might as well speak of the duty of a stone to roll itself uphill or of a cat to play the piano. Duty, as we have analyzed it, is a configuration of demand and response, of desire answering to desire. When I say that the response must be possible, I mean that there must be some motive in the person upon whom the demand is made in favor of the response, either already there, or created by the demand itself. It is, of course, not necessary that the response should be positive; it may be negative: I may decide that what is demanded of me is not what I want to do. But however the decision may fall, it will represent my wish. It will not occur as the result of mere external pressure, as it were, mechanically applied, but will be my own free act and deed.

What is usually called conscience consists in the first instance of the demands of parents or other elders interiorized, that is to say, the transformation of "We wish you to" into "I wish to." These demands thus become part of the early life plan of the individual. But owing to conflicts among them and the attempt of the individual to reconcile them with his more private wishes and, in the case of original minds, owing to new views as to what is a desired way of life for the community, a private conscience develops. In the end this is nothing else than that part of the life plan which has to do with the general schema of our relations with our fellow men, insofar as we identify ourselves with them. Our sense of the rightness of an act is our feeling that it is expressive of kindness; our sense of guilt is our feeling of it as a frustration of kindness, so far as kindness is adopted into the life plan. Only conscience can decide what is right or wrong for us. Of course the demands of others may be *called* duty; those who make them will call it so, hoping to move us; but only the response of my heart will make it so. There are thus two senses of duty, often confused: duty so called (the demand as such), and duty accepted and willed by me.

Some time ago it was suggested by Bertrand Russell that morality is a matter of commands and imperatives, and our own analysis is in line with his view. It must not be overlooked, however, that the law also takes the form of an imperative, and that there are imperatives that are not ordinarily regarded as belonging either to the law or to morality. We must therefore make clear the distinction between (a) "Do not kill" as a legal command, (b) "You ought not to kill" as a moral demand, and (c) such an imperative as "Please open the window." As for the first two, it is I think certain that law and morality overlap. On the other hand, much that is immoral is not illegal, and there are always laws (such as the Fugitive Slave Law or the Prohibition Act) that are not felt to be moral, although the general observance of law has always been regarded as morally mandatory, since the security of the desired way of life depends on it.

The distinction between law and morality is covered by three points. First, the law concerns itself, in general, with what we might call the skeletal structure of a desired way of life, while morality includes all manner of details; second, the imposition of definite penalities is distinctive of criminal law so that there is no law where there is no penalty, whereas much that is felt to be immoral has no definite external sanction; and third, the law is not so much concerned with the motive to an act as with the act itself, being in general satisfied with obedience alone, while morality is definitely concerned with motive. We may express this last distinction by saying that the law says "I want you not to do so and so," whereas the moralist says "I want you not to want to do so and so." The parent is always concerned that the child shall wholeheartedly wish to do right for its own sake, and not merely that he shall do right in order to escape punishment. This distinction is not absolute, however, since the penalty for murder, for example, depends somewhat on the motive, as is shown by the recognition of "degrees" of murder.

To illustrate these differences consider the case of a man who forecloses a mortgage on a house where a poor widow is living. This is legal, but may be immoral if it causes great harm to the widow, a circumstance not foreseen by the law. Or consider an act of discourtesy such as a slighting remark to a hostess, which in the moral sense is unethical because it is unkind, yet is not illegal, since no artificial penalties are attached to it and since it is not important enough to be defined in a code of law.

We turn next to the consideration of imperatives occurring in daily life to which we do not ordinarily ascribe an ethical character. Why is a request such as "Please open the window," which is equivalent to "I want that you shall open the window" and elicits the response "All right, I will," not ethical, although it seems to follow the pattern of demand transformed into response characteristic of the moral situation? The first part of my reply would be to query whether there is not, after all, an ethical element in the situation. Unless a request for aid or co-operation interferes with some well-recognized duty or with some pressing business of my own, having high rank in my life plan, it is felt to have some ethical quality. This cannot fail to be so, since it is an appeal to my kindness (notice the etymological sense of this term), which, as we know, is one of the bases of ethical response. Even when we resent the demand, viewing it as an imposition, the very heat of our resentment shows that we have responded in some measure. I am, of course, not condemning the resentment (for there is nothing more important for the realization of one's life plan and for the performance of one's important duties than to protect one's self from the importunities of one's own good nature); I am only citing it as evidence for the semiethical character of every demand that anyone may make upon us. The other part of the answer would be to draw attention to the fact that what are ordinarily called duties are the demands that have to do with the more fundamental elements of the established way of life: demands connected with the family, citizenship, and one's profession. Of course demands which are inconsistent with the preferred way of life are not moral, as when a thug says to me, "Your money or your life," or when some Potiphar's wife tempts some Joseph.

In characterizing duty as a configuration of desires, however, it must be admitted that we have, in a measure, gone counter to a common way of speaking about duty. For do we not often

say, "I want to do so and so, but I ought not to," as if duty were
something that I do not want to do? Or again we say, "This is to
my own interest but it is not in accordance with what is right."
Instead of duty being itself a desire, it is spoken of as if it were
opposed to desire. Yet nowhere else in philosophy is there a
greater need for clarification of the meaning of words, or a
greater tendency to be misled by them. For it is evident that
"want" and "interest" are used in such circumstances, not in
a general inclusive sense, but in the restricted sense of selfish
wants and self-interest, where self-interest is equivalent to selfish
interest. But when we use "want," "desire," and "interest" in
an inclusive philosophical sense, it is evident that I simply cannot do my duty, unless I wish to—I *cannot* do anything otherwise. There is no exaggeration, and little paradox, in declaring
that there is nothing which I so much want to do as my duty.
The opposition is not between duty and desire, but between one
desire and another desire.

Yet to these last statements, two objections may be raised.
One would be that they fail to differentiate spontaneous action
from action under duress. The partisan who betrays his com-
rade under threats and torture is, to be sure, doing what he
wants to do *under the circumstances,* but not what he would
want to do if duress were removed. Sometimes free action is
itself defined as spontaneous in contrast to constrained action.
I wish, however, to point out that in a quite literal sense all
action is under constraint. It is always action in a set of circumstances and under the pressure of demands and dangers. These
dangers may not involve jeopardy of life and limb, but they are
never wholly absent. And even when a man is under duress, his
decision is still his own: there have been those whose lips re-
mained sealed under the rack.

The second objection would be that if dutiful actions express
desire, no indication has been given as to why one desire represents duty and another does not. If desire *A* is supposed to be

on the side of duty and desire B is opposed to duty, why is it not the other way round?

One answer to this question would be to say that *by definition* desires of a certain sort are dutiful (moral), in contrast to others which are not. Unless the concept "duty by definition" is itself further explicated, however, this answer would have the appearance of arbitrariness, as if such desires become dutiful by being given the name of duty. But even a name has connotation whereby its applicability becomes subject to test. The question is not what we shall call such desires, but what characteristics they possess which distinguish them from others. They have a unique feeling quality which we may provisionally call "dutifulness," reflected in the connotation of the name "dutiful." This quality, I should hold, is not unconditional or a priori but is based on elements of what I have called the "duty situation," already described. In the light of this description we can easily discern its nature, reading off the characteristics—it is self-transcendent, that is to say, an interest in the basic welfare of others, which, although genuine may be marked by a certain "externality" because it arises, not wholly spontaneously from within, but in response to a demand from without; and it is often in conflict with more self-centered desires. An interest of this kind *is* a dutiful interest.

The familiar distinction between "the right" and "the good," and between the "is" and the "ought," is preserved in the theory of this chapter. The pairs correspond to the two basic emphases in the fact of value—desire and satisfaction. What we have been calling "demand" is the right, and what we have been calling "response," is the morally good, the fulfillment of the demand. So, in a more general sense, what is wanted is what ought to be, and the fulfillment of this want is the good. The two remain distinct except in those rare circumstances where all that was desired has been realized, as in certain experiences of art or moments of love. But in these examples the coincidence of the "is" and the "ought" depends on their isolation, for if the scope of desire is extended to the whole universe, we see clearly that what we want the world to be like and what it is like can never be identical.

Because of this fundamental disparity between desire and its fulfillment, it is never possible to deduce with completeness any standards or norms from what is actual: the standards of art from extant works of art; the standards of morality from existing moral practices. The *Kinsey Report* may expose the sexual behavior of the American male, but it cannot dictate what you or I may wish that behavior to be. This contrast is, nevertheless, somewhat mitigated by the fact that, since the good is the fulfillment of desire, the actual will disclose our ideals, so far as desire is fulfilled there; moreover, owing to the social nature of the mind, whatever others desire *tends* to become what we desire. Whenever, therefore, an experience seems to give us all that we wanted, we shall be able to deduce from it some of the traits of the ideal. Its formal structure at least can be deduced, since that will be the same in all such experiences. Another reason why we cannot deduce more stems, not from the impossibility of realizing our desires, but from the fact that our desires themselves change. The various utopias from Plato's to Lenin's, and the various styles of architecture from the Greek to the functional modern, show how impossible it is to picture our ideals once and for all.

In explaining the ideal in terms of desire, in recognizing the obvious fact that desires change, in reducing duty to a situation where there is demand and response, we appear to be denying the absoluteness of duty. And this is true. For it is absurd to say that a man should have done so and so when there was no demand either from others or from within himself that he do it. We cannot, for example, maintain that it was wrong for a fifth-century Athenian to hold barbarians as slaves, when no one, neither the master and his contemporaries nor the slaves themselves felt that it was wrong or made demands that they should be freed. And, if still not content, one should ask, "Would not the Greek slaveholder have been a better man if he had condemned slavery," the answer would be, "Yes, better in our eyes, more in accord with our ideals." But admitting this, how can you lay those ideals as a charge upon him when he had no knowledge of them? Relevant though they are to us, they were not relevant to him.

It is true that a century later the Athenians began to question the righteousness of slavery, and one might maintain that, had Aristotle been consistent with his own philosophy, he could not have defended the institution as he did; for must he not have granted that even a barbarian slave was a man, a rational animal, and as such deserving of that life in accordance with reason which the philosopher himself had declared to be the sole kind of life appropriate to a human being? Was not the slave his *alter ego* and therefore, according to Aristotle's own notion, a potential friend? To this, however, I am confident Aristotle would have replied somewhat as follows: "Since your God, who seems to be more powerful than any of our deities, and therefore must be what I used to call the Prime Mover (although it the material universe is expanding indefinitely, as some of your wise men say, I find it hard to know his exact location); since God, I say, has graciously permitted me to live in Limbo, where news of what passes on Earth sometimes reaches me, I have heard that you have all sorts of curious and wonderfully wrought inanimate tools, which make the services of slaves, whom I called animate tools, unnecessary. And by the employment of these devices, many of you, as I learn, are enabled to pursue philosophy or spend your time in war against the barbarians. But with us it was not so. We needed slaves so that some could be free to enjoy leisure, and in order that the galleys should be manned and the mines worked to provide funds for the arming of our soldiers. Had we not made use of them, science would have perished and our city states would have been overwhelmed by the barbarians. In that case, since the tradition of science began with us, there would perhaps have been no wise men in America and no free institutions. And besides, the laws permitted the holding of slaves, and whatever the laws permit is right."

Against our entire analysis it may be objected that we have entirely neglected the contrast, so often noted, between customary or topical morality and ideal morality. That the former has at least a certain relativity to the mores, manners, customs, and circumstances of the group would be admitted. It would be granted that our account of morality in terms of demands and responses would apply to it. On the other hand, it would be asserted that ideal morality is absolute and universal, above the claims and counterclaims of various groups. If Aristotle had been able to generalize his notion of friendship and had been true to his vision of the life of reason in all men, he would have reached the plane of ideal morality. And whatever compromises one may feel called upon to make with it, it remains the standard, it is said, by which topical moralities must be judged and toward which as a goal we should like to believe they are evolving. This ideal morality has, moreover, been recognized throughout the history of civilized man, in India and China by their wise men and in the Western world by Stoics, Hebrews, and Christians.

Ideal morality may well be summarized by means of the three slogans of the French Revolution—liberty, equality, fraternity. In the East, fraternity has been emphasized rather than equality and liberty; in the West, liberty and equality rather than fraternity, although the Christian doctrine of the kinship of all men through the one God-Father qualifies the truth of this contrast. We who have found conflict rampant everywhere in the realm of values will not, however, be surprised to discover it here, even in the ideal.

Fraternity is the central member of the triad. For the term "fraternity" we may substitute the warmer Germanic term "love" or the Latin term *caritas,* not to be translated "charity" without caution. This has currently been redefined as "respect for the individual or respect for personality." The term "respect" is, however, too cold to carry the full implications of fraternity; for as the word "fraternity" indicates, there is implied the idea of the kinship of each with all: the imaginative identification of oneself with the life of another, so that the other ceases to be entirely other but becomes one's other self, *alter ego*. And, having appropriated unto oneself what is unique and, apart from the act of imaginative sympathy, inaccessible in one's fellow man, one strives to promote his dream as if it were one's own. To the process of identification there are no *theoretical* limits. The ideal of fraternity means the removal of all limits to it. Begun with our friends, relatives, and fellow citizens, it may embrace people of alien race, culture, and nationality. It may even, as with St. Francis, embrace the birds, the flowers, and the sun. Since, moreover, the capacity for identification is present in various degrees in all men, ideal morality has a basis and a claim that is universal. And that it is not arbitrary we have already shown by pointing to the advantages of self-transcendence.

Yet even on the plane of ideal morality, fraternity has its practical limitations. These arise because of the claims of liberty. In the Western world, the ideal of liberty has usually been defined in terms of civil liberty, exemplified in certain "rights"— the right to think for oneself, to assemble freely, to petition the government, to choose one's own representatives in government, to marry according to one's choice, to worship God after one's own faith, to select one's profession, to employ one's leisure time as one desires, to own and dispose of property. In order to ensure the possession and exercise of these rights, certain others have been added, such as the right to collective bargaining, to education according to one's abilities, and to at least a minimum of economic security in times of sickness, unemployment, and old age. Most of these rights may be summed up as self-direction.

They imply an "open society," with much decentralization of economic power, making it possible for a man to earn his living in another place if for any reason he is shut out from a given place, a "democratic" form of government with at least a two-party system of election, and rigid limitations upon government such as are embodied in the Bill of Rights. The ideal of liberty is obviously opposed to the various types of totalitarianism. As metaphysical freedom depends on the possibility of real alternatives, moral liberty rests on an absence of force in weighing one such alternative against another. If the ideal of fraternity demands that we help one another, the ideal of liberty requires that we do not interfere with one another. And there is no greater gift that we can bestow on a friend than to allow him the direction of his own life.

The conflict between liberty and fraternity stems from the fact that liberty means more than mere self-direction; it includes self-realization, the fullest possible implementation of one's own life plan—in familiar words, the opportunity for the pursuit of happiness. But in building the life of another, as fraternity requires, it may well happen that one damages that part of one's life plan that is not concerned with this self-transcendent activity. The woman who sacrifices the opportunity for marriage or a career in order to care for an invalid parent is a familiar example. Within each self, therefore, there is a conflict between these two demands. You cannot abolish this conflict by asserting that liberty must be subordinated to fraternity, for even when subordination is achieved, the pull toward self-realization persists. Like any other frustrated desire of high order it remains active in the self, taking its revenge in daydreams of power or unlawful achievement. And without liberty, fraternity becomes self-stultifying; for while wishing to give all to one's friend, one has nothing of one's own, no unique self, to give. It becomes a form of subjection, even of suicide. Only when freely given because of love and only when the life that is given is richly colored like the rose, is the supreme sacrifice worth while.

If liberty is thus revealed as based on two of the three ingredients of happiness—power and achievement—and fraternity as based on the third—harmony—the ideal of equality may be conceived properly as an attempt to reconcile liberty with fraternity, and so to solve the paradox of fraternity. For if fraternity becomes absolute, the situation results that if A has something to give to B, then B will give it back to A, when both will remain as they were to start with! The old problem of the two men on the raft that will hold only one for long is an illustration: if each insists on jumping off for the sake of the other, both will drown and neither will accomplish his purpose. The solution is the one often resorted to: to draw lots, giving each an opportunity to express his willingness to sacrifice his life, and at the same time making it certain that one shall survive, in order to make the sacrifice of either purposeful. So, in less pathetic situations, if each treats the other as his equal, not demanding more of him than of himself ("doing unto others as you would they should do unto you") each will have the opportunity to forego advantages for the sake of others, so giving love expression; yet at the same time, in keeping some private happiness, each will have preserved his liberty. Any relation less than equality would obviously be a one-sided solution of the problem. For if the other self has more than I, I may be jealous of him, even as he would be jealous of me. The multiple facets of the ideal of equality are disclosed when I say to another, "I am as good as you," and get the reply, "Yes, but you are no better than I am"; or when I say, "You are as good as I," and the other person comes back with "Yes, I am, but not a bit better than you." What are ordinarily called "duties" express the aspect of fraternity in the ideal of equality, and what are called "rights," the correlative and balancing claims of liberty.

It will not have escaped the notice of the reader that the moral ideal of equality, viewed as a way of reconciling liberty and fraternity, is analogous to the "spheres of influence" solution of the problems of conflict of power. And it will be evident that just as that solution in that field requires sacrifice on the part of each party, so equality demands sacrifice from the side of both liberty and fraternity. That this ideal is not based on "pure reason," but has its foundation in the life of passion, has already been shown in the analysis of moral statements in Chapter III and is evident, I hope, in view of the account just offered.

The difficulties involved in finding precise and accurate definitions of liberty, equality, and fraternity, and especially of equality, do not invalidate these ideals. A man knows in a general way what it means to be another's equal even if he does not have the capacity to express his meaning in adequate language. This inability will be a disadvantage to him in all sorts of ways (and incidentally will prove his inequality with jurists and philosophers) but will not invalidate his basic, or somewhat dumb, feeling in the matter. He will even be willing to grant that he was not "born free and equal" in a literal sense, yet if, being a Burmese, he finds that he can be struck by a white man but cannot claim legal redress or retaliate by striking a blow in return; if, brought into court, others can call witnesses but he cannot; or if, being a Negro or a woman, he finds the polls closed to him while white men are voting—in all such circumstances he knows that he is not the equal of others. He may acknowledge that in all sorts of ways he is unequal to them—in aesthetic sensibility, intellectual endowment, or muscular development, or in polish of language and manners; and he may admit that unfortunate consequences to himself follow from these disadvantages, which nevertheless he will not resent; yet he will demand for himself opportunities for self-realization equal with those of all other men, in those fields of expression and development for which he is capable. He will demand that privileges granted to his superiors rebound in the long run to his own good or to the good of those whom he loves, and he will resent any denial of them to himself or his kind based on such superficialities as color or racial origin. Our well-worn phrase "equality of opportunity" covers more accurately than any other formula just what is involved in the ideal of equality.

For example, economic equality in the literal sense of equal

income for all would seem at first sight to represent the ideal of
equality in that field, and in socialistically minded communities
like Great Britain there is a definite tendency in that direction,
as also in America in those trades and occupations where unions
are strong. Yet an enlightened socialist or trade unionist might
see that it would be to his advantage to permit very high pay
to his own labor leader or to business executives if such unequal
benefits resulted in stimulating or in cultivating unusual abilities or performances upon which his own material welfare depends. Or, so long as his own basic needs were provided for, he
might approve of economic inequality on the chance that his
children might enjoy a more abundant material existence. And
it may well be true that men generally prefer the *opportunity*
for affluence, so long as the opportunity is equal, even if they
themselves never achieve it. Equality of opportunity thus shows
itself again to be a way of reconciling liberty with fraternity
for, in the larger sense, as we have noted, liberty is more than
mere civil liberty and includes the will to complete self-
realization.

In calling the morality expressed in the ideals of liberty,
equality, and fraternity "ideal," I do not wish to imply that it
possesses a generically different kind of authority than is possessed by ordinary social morality. It is essentially the ideal of
love, tempered by that of self-realization, but love itself is one
of man's passions that has to compete with his other passions.
Its rewards are those of love, which, to be sure, are peculiar to
love but the rewards of any desire are peculiar to it. And only
by being felt can their lure and their authority be established
for anyone, in comparison with the lure and the authority of
competing values. Whoever does not know the joy of loving and
being loved can never be aware of allegiance to the ideal of
fraternity, or any superiority of love over hate and selfishness.
Even though God be on the side of love, as we believe, his parti-
sanship could not by itself establish the authority of love. Unless
one *feels* the values expressed in those wonderful lines of the

Apostle in the thirteenth chapter of First Corinthians, it is futile to argue for them.

Moreover, ideal morality conforms to the demand-response pattern characteristic of ordinary morality. For example, the ideal of equality in its various forms has grown up and is maintained through pressures put upon the individual by other members of his nearer groups, and then by members of wider groups to which also he belongs, and through his response to these demands. Equality before the law and equal suffrage for all citizens are easy examples of this truth: they would never have been recognized as "right" had not pressure been brought to bear on the privileged classes to grant them. The demand itself was the expression of the will to power of these groups in opposition to the will to power of the ruling classes. The demand for equal power by women and by the colored peoples illustrates the extension of this demand to wider circles. The granting of equality is the response to the demand, a response which expresses, first, an equilibrium between the will to power of those making the demand and those granting it (each of whom might wish all power for himself); and, second, the appreciation through the sympathetic imagination of the desires of other persons, as if they were one's own. The importance of the latter is proved by the large part which sensitive persons, themselves members of the privileged groups, have played in promoting equality for the underprivileged. And only when these forces operate does the ideal of equality abide and hold its authority in a community.

Like other men of good will, philosophers who have discoursed of morality have taken its side against our more selfish and impulsive desires. Yet at all times the established morality of a community has been subject to attack. This has been partly in the interest of its reformation without touching the *idea* of morality as such, but partly also it has been directed against the latter. The former does not particularly concern us now. As for the latter, all the special points have been made, I believe, in Plato's *Dialogues,* especially in the *Gorgias* and *Republic I* and *II,* by Callicles, Thrasymachus, Adeimantus, and Glaucon. The moderns, to be sure, have added their special nuances.

We may sum up the indictment under three principal counts: the relativity, the partiality, and the impurity of morality.

By the relativity of morality two items, obviously interrelated, are usually intended: first, that the mores of different groups are never the same and second, that their authority is not independent of the consciences of the members of each group, hence never universal and absolute. That the mores of groups are different has been demonstrated many times by anthropologists and is a fact obvious to any observant traveler. Even within groups, especially the urban groups of our large cities, whose inhabitants differ widely in tradition, divergencies are striking. It has often been shown, however, that many of these rest not so much on contrasts in valuations as on oppositions in belief. For example, the practice of human sacrifice to the gods, so revolting to us, does not indicate a low valuation set on human life; for we also, if we believed that the welfare of the community depended upon placating a jealous god, would probably offer such sacrifices, even as we now offer our youth for its defense in war. Similarly, the practice of Negro slavery, or the subjection of women and their exclusion from many privileges in the community, such as suffrage and the right to hold property, were based on or justified by false beliefs concerning the abilities of Negroes and women. Yet when all allowance has been made for the impact of belief upon valuation, there remains a residue of genuine opposition or contrast in valuation. For example, many differences in sexual morality depend upon the degree of jealousy in the male or female of the species, or on differences in people's aversion to brawling or fighting. In the Old Icelandic sagas we have the record of the morality of a people who seemed to be lacking in our aversion to both. In our time there are profound differences with regard to the relative evaluation of security versus initiative and the opportunity for the free expression of ideas, which have already caused differences in law and morals.

The ultimate relativity of all values, including moral values, has been conceded by us, with the qualifications noted. This relativity is, however, nothing *against* morality. Indeed, what could be better for a group than a code that fits its own special needs, like a suit made to order by a good tailor? The demand for uniformity in morals has no more justification than would the demand that everyone wear ready-made clothes or hats of the same size. So far as there are identical elements in human nature, codes will, of course, approximate uniformity; but so far as men and groups differ, they will and should be different. Such variations do not, however, undermine the authority of a code for the group whose code it is; for the authority of any code depends upon its ability to express the dominant desires of its members. It is true that differences present difficulties of adaptation for persons who must pass from one group to another, as is the case with all immigrants, and they may lead to conflicts; but these disadvantages are inevitable and unavoidable. In an earlier chapter I have tried to show how, under the supposition that both groups desire peace, they may be avoided or mitigated. That even within a single group there are conflicting codes, for the reason that each contains smaller groups and each of these is constituted of unique individuals, is a commonplace of observation already noted by us. Anyone who has lived in a large American city or known intimately some rural town is aware of the contrast between the "official" morality and the various class and private moralities.

That there usually (perhaps always) is an "official morality" is a witness to the second count that one might draw up against morality—its partiality. For it has been said that morality, as it stands, represents the wishes and the consciences of the powerful members of a group, rather than the wishes and the consciences of all its members, and is therefore essentially biased. The bias has commonly been in favor of those in power as against those not in power, of the majority as against the minority, of the rich as against the poor, of the old as against the young.

Few, I believe, who know any part of the record of history will deny the truth of this allegation. It gives color to the claim of the Marxists that morality is always class morality. And when this partiality becomes extreme, morality passes into immorality. For the motivation of morality is, as we have held, a kind of love for all the members of one's group. Nevertheless, morality may subsist when this love is unevenly distributed, as it inevitably must be, man being what he is. And to discard morality because it is defective would be analogous to abandoning a tool because it is not perfect, a knife because it is not of finest edge, a car because it is in need of some repairs, as if one could argue from imperfection to total disability.

Moreover, except in the extreme case where morality passes into immorality (which we obviously need not consider), some service has been rendered by the class in power to the class not in power, if only that of maintaining order. However inconsiderate of the rights of women, men have given their hearts to them and pledged them support; parents have nurtured their children; and those in power, from the feudal lords to the absolute monarchs of the eighteenth century, have provided their subjects some protection from "aggressor" nations and internal peace. While in the past, law and morality have sanctioned a measure of the so-called "exploitation of labor," some of its basic rights have always been secure, and exploitation itself has been mitigated by the benefits redounding to all members of the community through the directive functions of owner and manager. In general, the truth of the notion of class morality is limited by the essential services that one class performs for another, enjoined by law and public opinion. And in the course of time many of the defects have been measurably remedied, until, in some parts of the earth, something approaching equality between the two sets of classes has been attained, with the danger ahead that the scales may be tipped in reverse. To follow out in detail how this has come about and is still proceeding would be to write the history of the reform movements of the nineteenth and twentieth centuries.

The final count against morality is impurity of motive. This one is clearly connected with the last, for if morality is biased in favor of certain powerful classes, its motive cannot be the undivided love for all members of the group. And it must be admitted, I think—indeed, it has been admitted—that what are called "selfish" or "impure" motives have been effective in the establishment of a morality. For the demands which are the core of morality express the kind of life that I want for *myself,* as well as for others. I want *my* life and property as well as that of my fellow men. Historically, the achievement of justice in a group has been largely due to the continued pressure on the part of the underprivileged for the rights that have been assured to the privileged classes. Even envy, which contains a spark of hate, has helped to kindle the flame of justice. And no one who views human nature objectively would deny the element of conscious or subconscious cruelty in retribution and punishment or the support given to self-sacrifice by praise and material rewards. One might question whether, without the support of these impure motives, the so-called pure motives would be able to hold their own in the struggle for power between rival individuals and groups, or between rival impulses within an individual. If we look candidly into our own hearts, we will seldom find that purity which we are told enables us to see God.

Nevertheless, granting all this and even more that might be alleged, the alliance of impure motives with love is nothing against morality. I would, on the contrary, argue that it stands in its favor, as providing the widest possible base for morality, making it more nearly the expression of the whole man than merely part of the man. On the other hand, when the motive of love disappears entirely, leaving envy, cruelty, and selfishness supreme as incentives, morality is in a precarious state. Its defence is now in the hands of its enemies; the exploited become themselves the exploiters, and the new morality is little more than the old tyranny in a new disguise.

The weakness of morality when unsupported by selfish motives is shown by the attachment to it of external rewards and punishments. It has to be admitted that morality sometimes gives the impression of being concerned chiefly with bribes and threats. This might appear to be a refutation of our theory that morality depends, in the last analysis, upon love. In what is generally thought of as love, these are absent, it would be said. The friend and lover do not force their ways upon us; they woo us to them. Yet these facts do not prove the absence of love from morality, but only its relative weakness. The parent still loves the child while punishing it; and the child returns that love despite punishment. When love is entirely absent from the treatment of the criminal, or when there is no love for those whom the judge and jailer protect, then morality turns into immorality, and the majesty of the law is but a veil for private vengeance.[1] Moreover, rewards and punishments are not attached to the conduct of others only, but to one's own also. The lawgiver is himself subject to the laws which he imposes; he fears his own wildness as well as the recalcitrance of his fellows. And when one looks closer into it, one discovers that even in what is ordinarily called love, rewards and punishments are not utterly absent. The lover brings gifts to his beloved and sometimes adds a little force to his persuasion, and the friend is a "very present help in time of trouble," yet who would say that love was absent then?

Other defects of morality have often been urged against it: that it is static, that it cannot foresee new and unique situations, that it cannot offer a formula by means of which conflicts of

[1] A careful study of Isaiah, in which the prophet now threatens cruelly, now promises rewards to his people in order to bring them to righteousness, and yet obviously loves them all the time, is very revealing of the mixture of impulses in the moral consciousness.

duties can be resolved. These defects also must be admitted, but not as fatal or absolute. No one who has lived fifty years in America can have overlooked the changes that have occurred in morality with regard to sex, divorce, and business. And to expect that the established mores should provide in advance for the novel and unique would be equivalent to claiming exemption from the element of indeterminism which is present in the universal frame of nature. There is, indeed, no simple rule by means of which conflicts of duties can be resolved (although the methods of renunciation, compromise, and integration are available here); yet the private conscience of each individual can cope with them, not by rule of thumb, but in accordance with its own intimate sense of values. This intimate sense of values *is,* as we have shown, conscience itself. It can be as sensitive and exacting as the traditional mores, and violation of it may bring the same feeling of guilt, and conformity with it the same feeling of rectitude. A private conscience may be, as Hegel claimed, a public nuisance—that is to say, a nuisance from the standpoint of those who represent the official morality—yet its development was inevitable, as we have noted, in view of the mixture of traditions and rapidity of change characteristic of our age. It will always have a hard time, being itself the product of hard times, since conflicts with the established mores and with other private consciences are unavoidable; but nothing can save it from that fate. Yet conflicts are not as a rule unto death, for the individual usually finds his own values better served by conforming or compromising than by rebelling, adjusting himself to public opinion even more easily than he would to the weather (public opinion is a kind of social weather), since being born and bred into them, the mores are not so much without as within himself. Sometimes, to be sure, the conflict is unto death, but then it is of one's own choosing (since one can always submit if one wishes), and therefore gives no ground for complaint against the world.

A NOTE ON THE VIRTUES

The virtues are habits which tend toward the fulfillment of the life plan. Since the life plan includes our relationships to other persons, it is hard to draw a sharp line between self-regarding and other-regarding virtues, and what has been said about the mixture of motives is in line with this. Yet the distinction has some validity, according as a preponderance of motivation, selfish or altruistic, is discriminated, in which case *all* the virtues may be of either kind. Temperance is *moral* if there is great concern for the future happiness of individuals who may be affected by what we do with our appetites, otherwise it is mere prudence; courage too may be a readiness to face dangers for merely self-preservative or ambitious aims, or for the good of our fellows; wisdom may or may not include a sensitive knowledge of their possible good; and even justice, which appears to be necessarily altruistic, may be cultivated as a policy that "pays best" in the end. It may easily be discerned that the Christian virtues of faith, hope, and charity may also be given the same sort of ambiguous interpretation. For hope may be restricted to one's own private good; faith may look to rewards in Heaven; and so may charity also, unless it have the meaning assigned in First Corinthians, which is the meaning it always has in the pages of this book.

The praise of the virtues is the iterated theme of the moralist. Sometimes it is based on their extrinsic, sometimes on their intrinsic values. Both exist to justify them. The temperate man, who sacrifices a momentary good for a good that will occupy many moments in the future, makes a clear gain in value. If, giving way to impetuous impulse, he fails to do so, he is acting as if his life were to end today; he forgets that he will be there in the future to experience this greater good or to incur the perils that attend impetuosity. He acts, in effect, as if he took seriously Hume and other philosophers who deny personal identity—in which case the future would not concern him, since he would end in a moment. The courageous man may be regarded as a shrewd gambler, who risks life and limb for the sake of values that need protection; whereas the coward would be a poor gambler. Of course, these values may be his selfish ones or the values of other persons with whom he sympathizes. But in either case, he acts for what he conceives to be his greater good. The extrinsic fruits of justice are like those of love, which have often been described: the good will and promise of aid when needed, which like the bread cast upon the waters returns to the good man. The extrinsic values of wisdom are coextensive with those of all the other virtues, since wisdom is the indispensable means to them, as Socrates taught, being a prescience or a shrewd calculation of the probable greater good to oneself or to one's friends in the future.

The extrinsic values of the virtues would suffice to justify them; yet it remains eternally true that "virtue is its own reward." Both temperance and courage are vivid examples of the will to power, not over others but over a part of oneself, as who that has experienced the elation of self-mastery does not know at firsthand? And when Aristotle wrote that it is better to love than to be loved, he was proclaiming love's intrinsic value, the union of self with the life of another, and therewith the unburdening of private sorrow.